Canadians at Table

FOOD, FELLOWSHIP, AND FOLKLORE

Canadians at Table

A CULINARY HISTORY OF CANADA

DOROTHY DUNCAN

DUNDURN PRESS
TORONTO

Editor: Michael Carroll
Copy-editor: Patricia Kennedy
Design: Jennifer Scott
Printer: Tri-Graphic Printing Limited

Library and Archives Canada Cataloguing in Publication

Duncan, Dorothy
    Canadians at table : food, fellowship, and folklore : a culinary history
of Canada / Dorothy Duncan.

Includes bibliographical references.
ISBN-10: 1-55002-647-X (bound)
ISBN-13: 978-1-55002-647-4

    1. Food habits--Canada--History. 2. Cookery--Canada--History. I. Title.

GT2853.C3D85 2006   394.1'20971   C2006-903853-8

1 2 3 4 5   10 09 08 07 06

Conseil des Arts du Canada   Canada Council for the Arts   Canadä

ONTARIO ARTS COUNCIL
CONSEIL DES ARTS DE L'ONTARIO

We acknowledge the support of the **Canada Council for the Arts** and the **Ontario Arts Council** for our publishing program. We also acknowledge the financial support of the **Government of Canada** through the **Book Publishing Industry Development Program** and **The Association for the Export of Canadian Books**, and the **Government of Ontario** through the **Ontario Book Publishers Tax Credit program**, and the **Ontario Media Development Corporation**.

Printed and bound in Canada.
Printed on recycled paper.

www.dundurn.com

Dundurn Press	Gazelle Book Services Limited	Dundurn Press
3 Church Street, Suite 500	White Cross Mills	2250 Military Road
Toronto, Ontario, Canada	High Town, Lancaster, England	Tonawanda, NY
M5E 1M2	LA1 4XS	U.S.A. 14150

For Colin, Adam, and Glenn,
masters of good food, good fellowship,
and fascinating folklore

Contents

ACKNOWLEDGEMENTS

I WOULD LIKE TO EXPRESS MY APPRECIATION to all those who have contributed to this book and the stories it has to tell. Family, friends, neighbours, colleagues, and often total strangers have generously shared information, research, and clues for further investigation, comments, and criticism that have proven to be invaluable as I struggled to complete the manuscript.

First of all, a very special thanks to those dedicated individuals who actually made the publication happen: Barbara Truax for her constant support and attention to detail as the manuscript unfolded; and the staff of The Dundurn Group for their expertise, knowledge, and patience — Kirk Howard, Beth Bruder, Michael Carroll, Jennifer Scott, Ali Pennels, and freelance copy-editor Pat Kennedy.

Among those who made contributions were Carol Agnew, Colin Agnew, Julian Armstrong, Anne van Arragon Hutten, Jeanine Avigdor, Jane Beecroft, Dr. Carl Benn, Marty Brent, Bryan Brooks, Kenneth Brooks, Michael Brooks, William Brown, Jr., Christine Caroppo, Dr. John Carter, Dennis Carter-Edwards, David Clark, Janet Cobban, Derek Cooke, Nettie Cronish, Loretta Decker, Paul Denter UE, Dr. Victoria Dickinson, Naomi Duiguid, Judith and John Fitzhenry, Lawrence Fleece, James Fortin, Mary Lou Fox, Lillian Groves, Pamela and Peter Handley, Tom Henighan, Jeanne Hopkins, Robin Inglis, A. Isaacs, Ruth Keene, Rosemary Kovacs, John Laraway, Elizabeth Lavender, Louis Le Bouthillier, Marion Leithead, Joyce Lewis, Reverend John Linton, Michael Liposki, Dr. Glenn J Lockwood, Allen Maitland, Micheline Mongrain-Dontigny, Evan Morton, Harold Nichol,

Robin Ormerod, Michele Pacheo, Joyce Pettigrew, Dennis Pollock, Robert Robinson, Nancy Scott, Jacqueline Stuart, Ross Wallace, Catherine Watts, Ian Wheal, and Marion Wilson.

I must also acknowledge the courtesy, assistance, and support I have received while doing my research from the staff of the museums, archives, institutions, and repositories of collections of artifacts and documents, including the Anderson Farm Museum, Lively, Ontario; Anglican Diocese of Ottawa Archives; Archives of Manitoba, Winnipeg; Archives of Ontario, Toronto; Black Creek Pioneer Village, Toronto; Estate of William Kurelek and the Isaacs-Inuit Gallery, Toronto; Fort William Historical Park, Thunder Bay, Ontario; L'Anse aux Meadows National Historic Site, Newfoundland; Library and Archives Canada, Ottawa; Musée McCord Museum, Montreal; Museum of Northern History at Sir Harry Oakes Chateau, Kirkland Lake, Ontario; National Gallery of Canada, Ottawa; North York Central Library, Willowdale, Ontario; Ontario Archaeological Society; Parks Canada; Sears Canada Inc.; Smiths Falls Public Library; Toronto Reference Library; Tweed Museum and Heritage Centre, Tweed, Ontario; Village Historique Acadien, Caraquet, New Brunswick; and the Women's Culinary Network.

PREFACE

CANADIANS AT TABLE: FOOD, FELLOWSHIP, AND FOLKLORE is an introduction to the incredibly diverse culinary history of this vast land we call Canada. As we move along a historical path from First Nations to newcomers, we learn how skilled our ancestors were at surviving and prospering, despite the challenges of climate, geography, and environment.

Every topic touched on here deserves to be explored and recorded in greater detail. Every topic deserves its own publication or series of publications to understand and appreciate its true significance.

The sheer size of this nation, stretching from sea to sea to sea, and its dramatically differing regions, have spawned a bountiful legacy of food and beverages. In many regions of Canada, dedicated historians, cooks, chefs, authors, and other interested individuals have recorded their own rich local histories of food, beverages, and medicines. I hope their work and this brief overview will inspire others to tell their personal stories, to research local culinary traditions, to read local handwritten and published cookbooks, diaries, and other historical records, and to discuss with their neighbours, friends, and family how their food and beverage traditions have remained constant or changed over time.

How did our ancestors constantly adapt and invent recipes with a surplus of some ingredients or a scarcity of others, while trying to feed their family, their crew, or their customers? A great deal of experience and ingenuity has never been recognized nor recorded. I hope, by turning readers into reporters and scribes, to help preserve a more complete record of everyday Canadians and their everyday meals for future generations. I also hope

Canadians at Table will be the catalyst for new research, recording, and experimenting. We must treasure this, one of the greatest culinary histories in the world, one of which every Canadian should be proud.

Dorothy Duncan
Willowdale, Ontario
June 2006

CHAPTER ONE

In the Beginning

WERE THEY HUNGRY? WERE THEY LOST? Or were they simply following game across the land bridge that once connected Siberia and Alaska?

We may never know the elusive details about those first arrivals, or even when they arrived — the men, women, children, small families, or tiny groups of hunters and gatherers who were lured to this land mass. Historians and archaeologists believe that human hunters did not reach the western edge of northeastern Siberia (western Beringia) until perhaps thirty-five thousand years ago.[1] When they actually made the crossing is still hotly debated, but we do know that those first daring hunters lived by the spear and the snare as they tracked and attacked the woolly mammoths and mastodons that roamed the continent in prehistoric times. They lived a nomadic life, foraging and trapping small game in addition to hunting the herds of large animals they relied on for meat, and for life itself.

The established theory is that these hunters arrived in this new environment either on foot across the land bridge that once connected the two continents, or by coasting in watercraft. However, we must not overlook the traditions of Canada's First Nations, who believe their ancestors, those first people on this continent, were "from the land" or "from the soil," children of the Great Creator, who have been here from the beginning of time.

Whatever their origins and despite their limited technological resources — fire, spears, *atlatls* (throwing spears), snares, and nets — those first peoples must have been adept at surviving, for not only did they find themselves in a new environment, but some dramatic climate changes were also taking place around them. As the great glaciers of ice that had gripped the land melted, the climate warmed, and this development affected the vegetation the mammoths and mastodons depended on to survive, eventually driving them to extinction. The bands of hunters, therefore, were forced to diversify and turned to smaller game such as bison, deer, caribou, bear, fox, hare, and beaver. Fish, wild fruits, vegetables, and medicinal herbs became more important to their diet, as well. To ensure that everyday life was not just a feast or a famine depending on the success of the hunters, those early people became skilled at preserving some of their food by air- or sun-drying it or smoking it. They could then carry it with them more easily, or they could store it in stone-lined caches on well-travelled routes and return to it when it was needed.

In 6000 BC, the human population of North America was still sparse and was scattered in a myriad of isolated hunter-gatherer bands. If we judge from sites in many areas, people spent most of the year living in small family groups, exploring large hunting territories. They might have come together with their neighbours for a few weeks during the summer months at favoured locations near rivers or nut groves. The bands would have held ceremonies, arranged marriages, and traded fine-grained rocks suitable for tool-making and other commodities. Then they would have gone their separate ways, following migrating game, trapping small animals, and foraging for wild food.[2]

Although these were usually nomadic people, they followed a "seasonal round" that was influenced by the changing seasons and their knowledge of the grazing herds. They often had seasonal or semi-permanent camps to which they returned for harvests and hunts. A few bands appear to have settled in extended family groups or tribes in different geographical areas and survived by adapting in different ways to the food that could be found there. For example, the archaeological record tells us that among the oldest sites on the West Coast of Canada was one that occurred in the Queen Charlotte Islands (Haidi Gwaii) of present-day British Columbia between 10,000 BC and 8000 BC. There a combination of rich marine resources, bird flocks, and animal herds would have eased the challenge of survival.[3] Archaeologists believe there are many other early sites on Canada's coastlines. However, they are probably now underwater.

Abundant coastal vegetation provided both food and medicines. Blackberries and thimbleberries were flavourful additions to the diet and, in combination, were often used to cure nausea and vomiting. Roots of wild ginger were employed not only as a seasoning, but were also boiled to produce tea that was taken to cure indigestion and colic.

Like the early settlers on the Pacific Coast, other bands and nations eventually chose specific locations — on the dry, short grass of the prairies, for instance, some grew adept at hunting bison, one of the few big-game species to survive the Ice Age. These animals were found in large numbers after the glaciers retreated; in fact, it is believed that at one point six million roamed the prairies. Incredible patience was needed to pursue bison on foot, for it took days of slow stalking and an intimate knowledge of the animal's habits. Perhaps several bands would co-operate in a game drive. They would encircle a few beasts or, more often, stampede a herd into a swamp or a narrow defile. In some cases, they would drive the frightened creatures over a cliff or into dune areas.[4] After the slaughter, every part of the animal was utilized to survive — for food, medicine, clothing, and shelter. A large animal like the bison could provide meat for weeks, even months, if it was properly preserved by drying or smoking.

Farther to the east the woodlands and lakes teemed with smaller game, fish, and birds, and this plenitude attracted other bands. Communities developed at strategic locations on rivers and creeks to take advantage of caribou crossings, fish runs, and places where passenger pigeons nested. The men hunted while the women tended the nets and gathered wild plant foods, berries, and nuts. Ancient hearths have been discovered where meat and fish were cooked slowly on hot rocks.[5] Here, too, in the Great Lakes region, stretching from today's Manitoba through Ontario and into Quebec, was clay suitable for forming bowls and pots for food storage and preparation, and some pottery shards have been found that resemble cooking vessels from Siberia.[6]

In this area, the rich soil was cleared and crops were planted using pointed digging sticks, then was tended with crude wooden hoes, fertilized with whole fish, and harvested. Those tribes that realized the benefits of staying in one location and nurturing certain plants and crops were transformed from hunters and gatherers into farmers. Such tribes learned that maize (corn), beans, and squash assured them an annual and adequate food supply that was easily stored and traded to non-farming people as needed. These three foods took on a symbolic role. Native peoples considered maize to be their Sacred Mother, one of the Three Sisters, along with beans and squash, that should be planted together in hills and eaten in tandem.

In this region, too, were sugar maple trees with the gift of sweet sap, proving that the Great Creator was again providing both food and a strengthening medicine for their needs. When the "sugar moon" appeared in the spring, it was the signal that the people should move to the sugar maple groves and prepare for the ceremony of thanksgiving, in which they feasted, told stories and legends surrounding other harvests, and then began the harvest of the sap. The sap was placed in wooden or birchbark containers, then hot rocks were dropped into them until eventually the sap thickened into syrup to be used in cooking soups, puddings, fish, fowl, or game. Quantities of the thick syrup were also poured into cooling troughs and kneaded by hand or with a paddle until they were thick and creamy. This soft sugar was poured into moulds and stored to be used later by the harvesting families, or to barter with other tribes.

In the cool, rich virgin soil of the hardwood forests lurked a plant that became known as ginseng (*Panax quinquefolium*). This traditional Native medicine was called *ginens* and was used as a stimulant and to ease stomach pains and bronchial disorders, as well as to alleviate headaches, fever, asthma, and nausea. Long before European explorers ventured onto the North American continent, Dr. Stanley Holling tells us that medicine men in the Lake of the Woods area were using local plants to heal the sick.

Sarsaparilla was employed for coughs, while small spruce cones were eaten to cure sore throats. Blueberry flowers were dried and placed on hot rocks, and the fumes were inhaled to cure "craziness." Common chickweed leaves, steeped in hot water, were applied to sore eyes. The root of the lady's slipper was chopped up and moistened to form a poultice to be applied to relieve a toothache. Nettle roots were steeped to cure urinary-system difficulties and dysentery. Sumac blossoms, cut when the white bloom was on and boiled down in water, cured dysentery. Chewing the sumac root cured a sore mouth or aided a youngster who was teething.[7]

In the north, the evergreen forests were dotted with rivers and lakes and provided wildlife in abundance — moose, deer, and bear, as well as small game. In marshy areas, wild rice grew freely, another gift of the Great Creator. In the fall, when the "rice moon" appeared, the people would move out to camps near the rice fields in preparation for the ceremony of the first rice and for the harvest, which was carried out by the women.[8] The men then processed the rice in preparation for storing it for the long winter ahead, either as food or as another valuable barter item.

Farther east still, in the St. Lawrence River region and the land bordering the Atlantic Ocean, other bands and tribes harvested the riches of the land, rivers, and sea. The discovery of artifacts at several sites on the Atlantic seaboard has established a human presence dating back at least ten thousand years, when the land that later became Prince Edward Island was still joined to the mainland. Here nomadic bands are believed to have hunted caribou, seal and walrus, fish and birds.[9] They combined hunting with foraging, turning to the pursuit of the white-tailed deer and other smaller mammals as many of the large Ice Age animals vanished. By 8000 BC, a widespread shift to more generalized hunting and gathering was underway. The peoples of the eastern woodlands exploited a broad variety of foods and forest resources, consuming such foods as grey squirrels, nuts from the annual harvests, and seed-bearing grasses. It is believed that small game, fish, mollusks, and vegetable foods assumed greater importance in Native diets.[10]

In eastern Canada, the First Nations used local plants such as fiddleheads and blueberries for food, dyes, and medicine. Seed-bearing grasses, bark, and other natural materials were utilized for weaving baskets to hold and store food and other possessions. These, too, were valu-

able barter items among their own tribes and nations, and later proved to be appealing to the newcomers as barter or sale items.

On the island that became known as Newfoundland and the area known as Labrador, the First

For centuries First Nations and newcomers have treasured fiddleheads, the small green curled fronds of the ostrich fern that appear in low-lying wooded areas along streams in March and April.

Nations had a rich diet of salmon, flounder, smelt, geese, cormorants, seabird eggs, beaver, moose, wolves, lynx, hare, porcupine, and bear. They would hunt caribou during the animal's annual fall migration, not only for food but for the skins, which would be sewn together (fur inward for warmth) for cloaks and moccasins. Tools made of four-thousand-year-old walrus ivory and others made of bone, ivory, antler, and stone, dating to periods over the past eleven thousand years and including some artifacts produced by the now-extinct Beothuk people, have survived. Expert knowledge of fish behaviour and seasonal spawning patterns was key to the survival of Native communities who valued the hide, ivory, and oil of the walrus, and the oil of the porpoise.[11]

In the spring, many First Nations would move to the shores of the waterways and oceans to dig clams, mussels, and oysters, while others would spear shad, bass, salmon, and gaspereau (alewives). In mid-April, the suckers (a relative of the carp) began to run, and traps were set for them. The fish were filleted, tied in bales, and carried from camp to camp. During the summer, the First Nations speared pickerel, sturgeon, trout, and whitefish, which were either dried or eaten fresh, wrapped in bark or leaves, and roasted in a pit of coals. In the winter, they speared fish through the ice as they were needed. When the chiefs of the tribes met, or later when newcomers began to arrive, there was always a ceremonial exchange of gifts, with fish a symbolic mark of respect.

There may have been many waves of newcomers moving across the land, but it is now believed the final migration could have been that of those people who braved the ice of Arctic Canada as they followed herds of caribou and musk ox into this unknown territory. They built winter homes of snow and summer homes framed with whalebones and covered with skins. They travelled in hide-covered watercraft called umiaks and kayaks, or by foot and eventually by dogsled as they moved across the frozen tundra in search of food.

Fish, seals, whales, caribou, bears, and waterfowl were their quarry; harpoons and spears were their weapons. They, too, used their ingenuity to settle into the harsh environment of northern Canada and become self-sufficient, exploiting everything available to them to survive.

Despite their diversity of cultures, lifestyles, traditions, languages, and beliefs, and the rivalries that sometimes led them to war, these first peoples developed well-organized barter systems that spanned the continent from Hudson Bay to the Gulf of Mexico and beyond. This feat may have been accomplished through a multitude of hand-to-hand transactions. Thus, diverse items such as tobacco, feathers, seashells, furs, copper, mica, and chert were moved into new regions of the country to supplement what may originally have been found there.

Just as important were the food items that could have been exchanged on that barter system, long before European contact. Consider plums, maize (corn), wild rice, beans, squash, hazelnuts, black walnuts, butternuts, sunflower seeds, maple syrup, maple sugar, and more!

Hence, long before contact with the rest of the world, the First Nations had learned how to use the indigenous plants, trees, animals, marine life, and other resources that surrounded them, not only for food but for medicines, insecticides, clothing, tools, construction materials, and firewood. Eventually, food for their dogs (probably European stock that had interbred with North American wolves) came from the same source.

Was life for those First Nations just an endless round of hunting, fishing, foraging, farming, and making weapons, tools, and equipment so there was food for the next meal? Until the fifteenth century, when newcomers began their quest for the precious spices of the Indies, the history of the First Nations is, for the most part, an oral one, as their traditions, beliefs, and legends have been recounted through the centuries by their elders and storytellers. In addition to this oral history, we have some artifacts and images created by the First Nations. They range from spectacular crest (totem) poles to tiny bone carvings and delicate moose-hair or porcupine-quill embroidery that have endured. We also have the description by Sarain Stump, a First Nations artist who in the following excerpt from *Two Forms of Art* published in Saskatchewan in 1973, identifies her people by the names given to them when newcomers from Europe arrived:

> Although it is generally accepted that no proper writing was invented and used by North American Indians before historic times, it is certain that our ancestors supplied their need for a graphic recording system by using ideograms. These were usually codified symbols ... the Ojibwa Indians and related Algonkians of the Great Lakes region fixed on

birch bark rolls instructions for the proceedings of their complicated ceremonies. The Plateau people engraved, by burning, on chips of wood. Petroglyphs (messages concerning a particular location) are found in many areas of the continent.... The Wanapum (Wampum) belts of the Iroquois, capes and collars worn by Wabnaki dignitaries, quilled and bead embroidery created in the Plains and McKenzie Delta region and many of the ornamental designs on the baskets, pottery and textiles are informative symbols combined in artistic compositions. The creator is also trying to transfer, as faithfully as possible, the physical beauty of the natural world and all its creatures.[12]

Elizabeth Simcoe, the wife of Upper Canada's first lieutenant-governor, illustrated the food traditions of the First Nations in pictures, as in this sketch, and in words.

Little did the First Nations know that their natural world would one day be turned upside down. Life would never be the same again after people they had not even known to exist began to brave the northern Atlantic Ocean in search of the exotic and elusive foods and other resources they either needed or desired at home. Two worlds were about to collide, and when they did, the newcomers realized they had stumbled on a land of incredible harshness, beauty, and bounty. That bounty was at times destined to appear not only on Canadian tables but on the tables of the hungry around the world.

CHAPTER TWO

They Had Never Known Anything to Taste So Sweet

WERE THEY SETTLERS OR SOJOURNERS? Or were they simply searching for wood, so desperately needed at home in Greenland to build and repair their vessels, dwellings, and farm and household items? The "Men from the North," also known as Norsemen and Vikings, were reputed to be pirates, raiders, traders, and at times colonists. They were feared and respected from Russia to the Mediterranean Sea for their bravery and exploits. Many aspects of their life were simply a continuation of the ancient customs and traditions they had practised in their home countries — such as their long sea voyages, their construction of houses from stones and turf, their clearing of rocks and stones from patches of meadow, their hunting of whales, seals, and wild reindeer, and of course fishing. They lived by raising livestock as well as by hunting and fishing. In their native lands it was not possible to grow grain, but the sparse vegetation was nutritious and enabled them to keep many cows, sheep, and horses. They also made butter and cheese. Their most important implements and weapons were axes, knives, scythes, sledgehammers, blacksmith's tongs, harpoons and other fishing gear, bows and arrows, and spears.[1]

For centuries the Vikings were known for their daring adventures, which were recounted in their sagas, told and retold around the long fires at home in Iceland and Greenland by hardy sailors and storytellers.[2] A fascinating parchment map, known as "The Vinland Map," bears the inscription:

By God's will, after a long voyage from the Island of Greenland to the south towards the most distant remaining parts of the western ocean sea, sailing southward amidst the ice, the companions Bjarni and Leif Eiriksson discovered a new land, extremely fertile, and even having vines, the which island they named Vinland.[3]

The sagas differ in some details, but have much in common. One of the sagas describes the voyage of the merchant Bjarni Herjolfsson, who was en route from Iceland to Greenland when his vessel was caught in a violent storm with strong north winds and dense fog that carried him off course to the west. There he and his crew saw an unfamiliar forested shore. When the storm abated and the sun came out, Bjarni was able to get his bearings and sail his vessel to Greenland, where he described what he and his crew had seen. His description raised a number of questions. What was the new country like? Was it a good and fertile land, a place where perhaps one could settle down and live permanently?[4]

It was Leif "The Lucky" Eiriksson, son of Eirik the Red, who decided to investigate. His ship was fitted out, the women busying themselves with the big woollen square-sail, mending and strengthening it, while the men and eager youngsters carried provisions and equipment on board, including dried fish, smoked meat, butter, cheese, and water for the large barrels. They also brought axes, tongs, and a sledgehammer for a smithy, various kinds of gear for hunting and fishing, and weapons. It was rather sparse equipment for a long voyage into the unknown, but the thirty-five people on board knew how to live off the land. The next autumn a weather-beaten ship returned. Yes, the new land in the west had been found; it was a large and strange country, with riches of many kinds — pastures for cattle, forests, game, seals, walrus, and fish. Leif had built substantial houses in the new country, and he had called it Vinland.[5]

Detailed references are included in the sagas, not only about what this group found when they landed on that forested shore but to what subsequent groups found, as well: "They touched the dew with their hands and they thought they had never known anything so sweet.... Every brook was full of fish. They made pits where the land met high-watermark, and where the tide ebbed there were halibut in the pits. There

Tom Henighan

The Vikings' distinctive wooden ships and the men who sailed them were known and feared from Russia to the Mediterranean Sea and beyond.

was a great quantity of animals of all sorts in the woods.... There was no want of salmon either in the river or the lake — salmon bigger than anything they had ever seen before.... Fields of self sewn wheat grew there." One of the crew, a German called Tyrker who was also known as Leif's foster father, explored the area and found what he believed to be vines and grapes, something he said he recognized from his homeland in Europe. Many historians and botanists have questioned his description and his judgment. Were these really grapes, or could they have been another "wine berry," such as wild currants, gooseberries, raspberries, squash-berries, or cloudberries?[6]

The sagas tell us that Eiriksson's group built huts and wintered there, and as there was no frost that year, their cattle browsed outdoors. In the spring, they took a load of wood (probably a combination of driftwood from the shore and timber cut from the forest) home to Greenland, along with the unexpected and incredible stories they had to tell about what they had found. The first arrivals were soon followed by other vessels loaded with passengers. One of the expeditions brought 160 men, in addition to women and livestock.[7]

Archaeologists and historians have now confirmed that Vinland (or Vineland), one of the communities described in the sagas, was at L'Anse aux Meadows. The settlement has been uncovered at the tip of the Great Northern Peninsula in western Newfoundland, which proves the Men from the North were probably the first Europeans to realize, as early as the year 1000 AD, that North America existed. Close to one hundred men, women, and children lived at the settlement for nearly three decades while they tended their herds of cattle and flocks of sheep and goats, spun and wove clothing from the fleece, fished the rivers and the ocean (cod bones, seal bones, and whale bones have been found in the excavations), foraged for fruit and herbs in the forest, and developed gardens with the vegetables and herbs from home that they trusted to grow and flourish in that climate. These would have included turnips, carrots, cabbages, beans, peas, onions, and garlic. Meanwhile, they continued to explore the eastern shores of present-day Canada, for North American butternuts have been found at the site, although their known range is farther south in what is now New Brunswick. As there are similar European species, the Norse were familiar with butternuts and considered them a delicacy. As well, growing in the same area one can find wild grapes known today as riverbank grapes. Both of these can be harvested in late August and would have been of great value in Greenland.[8]

The Norse men and women constructed many buildings of timber frame covered with turf; they had earthen floors, low doors in the walls, and smoke holes running along the roof ridge. There were several dwellings with benches along the walls that were used for sitting or reclining during the day and sleeping at night. Remnants of long fires (like those in the homeland) that burned in the centre of the floor to provide for cooking, heating, and light have been found. They also developed small slate-lined compartments in the earthen floors next to the fireplaces that could be used as ember pits, into which the embers were swept at night and covered with ashes, making it unnecessary to light another fire in the morning to cook the first meal of the day. This technique, again, is a well-known feature of larger homes in Iceland and Greenland.[9] Ancient cairns have been discovered, which were aligned in such a way that they acted like sundials for telling time. As they could be seen from the dwellings, they would have indicated times for meals.[10]

The dwellings differed in size and comfort, suggesting there was probably a class structure in the community that may have ranged from chieftain to slave.[11] As the years went by and the settlement grew, it is obvious that some of the existing buildings had additions added to accommodate new arrivals or larger families. Four workshops and a smithy confirm that ship repairs and blacksmithing were regular skills and trades carried out by the craftsmen in the community. Bog iron was smelted in the smithy, a skill not known at that time to the Native people.

The sagas describe the encounters between the newcomers and the Native people, whom they called *Skraelings*. Some of the encounters were peaceful, while they bartered and traded, but others were fierce encounters, leading to loss of life on both sides.[12] Such conditions may have contributed to the ultimate decision of the Norsemen to leave the rich resources they had found rather than live in a continual state of anxiety.

These courageous and enterprising explorers eventually returned home with their final cargoes of wood, taking with them their memories and their stories of a rich and fertile country that became the foundation for the famous sagas. Two worlds had met and parted. It would be almost five hundred years before they would meet again, and almost a thousand years before extensive archaeological research proved that the ancient folklore and legends of the countries bordering the North Atlantic were not fiction but fact.[13]

CHAPTER THREE

The Sea Was Covered with Fish

SPICES WERE AMONG THE MOST COVETED OF trade goods to the fifteenth-century merchants of Europe. At that point in the world's history, spices such as pepper, nutmeg, cloves, ginger, and cinnamon were often as valuable as gold. They were brought overland by camel caravans from the spice-rich areas of India and the Orient to the eastern end of the Mediterranean Sea. This kind of enterprise was always dangerous and expensive, and merchants were both eager to expand the trade and willing to finance increasingly ambitious ventures to reach the spices by alternative routes. Why not sail west to the lands where they grew rather than take the long and treacherous overland route to the east? So began a series of voyages of discovery during which those early explorers who risked their lives and fortunes by sailing west found instead a vast new land mass that stood in their way — or was it perhaps an unknown and unexpected segment of a shoreline of either India or China? Hence, they gave the name "Indians" to those members of the First Nations whom they met when they landed.

One of those explorers was Giovanni Caboto, a Genoese native and Venetian citizen with long experience in the eastern spice trade. Sailing under an English banner, he is credited with "discovering" the Grand Banks in 1497. Like so many other explorers, he was attempting to find the riches of the Orient, but instead returned to England to report to the Bristol merchants who had hired him and to King Henry VII "that the sea was covered with fish which could be caught not merely by nets, but with weighted baskets lowered into the water."[1]

With this information, the merchants and traders of Bristol and Devon realized they no longer needed to rely on importing vast quantities of fish from Iceland to satisfy their customers. They turned their attention to this new and unexpected source of cod, which was so plentiful that it became known as the "Beef of the Sea" and was soon synonymous with the word *fish*. The soft gelatinous flesh of the cod dried quickly and could be stored for long periods without refrigeration, filling an economic need at the time in the markets of Europe. When those first fishing vessels arrived, the crews would fish for cod from the rail of their ships with hand-held lines and then take the catch ashore to Cabot's New Founde Lande, where it was cleaned, salted, and spread to dry. After that it was loaded in the ship's hold and transported home to England to be sold at the markets there.

Seeing Britain's success, other countries quickly followed suit, and fishing fleets from Portugal, Spain, and France struggled with England — both physically and politically — for supremacy in the area and control of this resource. It was the French fishermen who introduced a different method of fishing and preserving the catch called "greenfishing." Instead of drying the fish on shore, the fishermen gutted and salted the catch before stowing it in the ship's hold. Months later, when the vessel returned home, the fish were still moist or "green." The crews that used this method also fished from the deck with hand-held lines weighted with lead and protected from the spray and wind with small screens attached to the sides of the ship. When the hold was full, the greenfish (salted and wet) were taken back to France to be dried and sold.

Early European explorers described the codfish on the Grand Banks of Newfoundland as so plentiful that they could be caught in weighted baskets lowered into the water.

28

Exploitation of this rich resource was one of the great economic activities of Europe during the later sixteenth and early seventeenth centuries, a venture that every year lured hundreds of vessels across the ocean, drew upon and fostered seafaring support systems along much of the Atlantic fringe, and marketed its catch through a network that reached far into the European realm. Thus it trained generations of mariners, employed thousands of craftsmen and suppliers, and involved families and friends, syndicates, and whole communities in North American activities.[2]

In 1622, Captain Richard Whitbourne of Exmouth, Devon, one of the captains who by then had spent forty years trading to the Grand Banks and Newfoundland, gives us a vivid but often questioned description of the land and its fruits, vegetables, and potential for crops:

> The land of Newfoundland is large, temperate and fruitful.... Then have you there fair strawberries red and white, and as fair raspberries and gooseberries as there be in England, as also multitudes of bilberries, which are called by some whortes, and many other delicate berries in great abundance.
>
> Here also are many other fruits, as small pears, cherries, filbirds, etc. And of these berries and fruits, the store is there so great that the mariners of my ship have often gathered at once more than half an hogshead would hold.... There are also herbs for salads and broth, as parsley, alexander, sorrel, etc.... Our men that have wintered there divers years, did for a trial and experiment thereof sow some small quantity of corn, which I saw growing very fair; and they found the increase to be great, and the grain very good; and it is well known to me, and divers that trade there yearly, how that cabbage, carrots, turnips, lettuce, parsley and such like prove well there.[3]

Captain Whitbourne goes on to tell us that "The natural inhabitants of the country are willing to assist the fishermen in curing fish for a small hire ... they were able to sew the rinds of spruce-trees, round and deep in proportion, like a brass kettle, to boil their meat in." On one occasion, three of his men surprised a party of First Nations enjoying themselves in a sumptuous manner:

> They were feasting, having the canoes by them, and they had three pots made of the rinds of trees, standing each of them on three stems, boiling, with fowls in each of them, every fowl as big as a pigeon and some as big as a duck. They had also many such pots so fowled, and fashioned like the leather buckets that are used for quenching fires, and were full of the yolks of eggs that they had taken and boiled hard, and so dried small, which the savages used in their broth ... also a great store of flesh dried.[4]

The Grand Banks continued for close to five hundred years, serving the First Nations, the newcomers, and the world's hungry abroad. Surrounding it on the Atlantic Coast and in the waterways of what were to become the Atlantic Provinces was a wealth of marine life of all kinds and descriptions that sea captains, travellers, entrepreneurs, and settlers continued to marvel at. Here is just one account of the bounty in and near Prince Edward Island in the early nineteenth century:

> The rivers abound with trout, eels, mackerel, flounders, oysters and lobsters, and some salmon; and the coast with codfish and herrings in great abundance. The latter, soon after the ice breaks away in the spring rush into the harbours on the north side of the island in immense shoals, are taken by the inhabitants in small nets with very little trouble, and as salt is cheap (not being subject to duty) most families barrel up a quantity for occasional use. The lobsters are in great abundance and very large and fine. In Europe this kind of shell-fish is only taken on the sea-coast amongst rocks; at Prince Edward Island they are taken in the rivers and on shallows, where they feed on a kind of sea-weed, called by the islanders eel-grass, and a person by wading into the water half-leg deep, might fill a bushel basket in

half an hour. Many schooners are annually laden with oysters from Quebec and Newfoundland.

The plenty of fish, and the ease with which it is procured, is of great assistance to the inhabitants, and in particular to new settlers, before they have time to raise food from the produce of the land.[5]

As the explorers, trappers, traders, missionaries, entrepreneurs, and settlers moved inland, they realized that not only the oceans and the rivers flowing into it teemed with fish, but that the supply of fish in the inland rivers and lakes surpassed their wildest expectations. An interpreter and trader at the Falls of St. Mary (Sault Ste. Marie, Ontario) said in 1777: "At this place there is an abundance of fine fish, particularly pickerell [*sic*], and white fish of uncommon size."[6] And a few weeks later he noted: "We prepared our nets for fishing. The ice was three feet thick, and the snow very deep; this we were obliged to clear away, before we could cut holes in which to put our nets. For the space of two months we had uncommon success, having caught about eighteen hundred weight of fish, which we hung up by the tails across sticks to freeze, and then laid them up for store."[7]

In 1784, Robert Pagan, a United Empire Loyalist forced to flee from the new United States of America to today's Saint Andrews, New Brunswick, wrote to his wife (in Falmouth, now Portland) describing the food he was shipping to her: "By the schooner *Seafoam*, Capn. Bell, I intend to send you a kegg of pickled lobsters, & some smoked salmon, some potatoes, & turnips, some cranberries, some mackerel also a quarter of beef and a side of good mutton, which I shall procure in two or three days."[8]

From the accounts of both the First Nations and the newcomers, salmon abounded, and it was often smoked to ensure that it would keep. Here is a nineteenth-century traveller's account of the basic technique of smoking salmon, which the newcomers would have learned from the First Nations:

During our stay on the river [Nepisiguit River, New Brunswick] which lasted a month, we smoked over 120 salmon, which we packed in boxes and sent off to our friends in Saint John. The following is the receipt for that process:

Split the fish down the back and clean them, cutting out the gills at the same time; this should be done as soon as possible after they are caught, or the fish will become soft; immerse for two days in a strong pickle of salt and water, a trough for this purpose is easily hewn out of a fallen spruce or pine, or, in lieu use a dish of birch or spruce bark. After taking the fish out of the pickle, wash them in running water, then hang them in a smoke house for six days. A smoke house is built in the shape of a wigwam, and covered with birch or spruce bark; great care must be taken to keep up the fire, which is placed in the smoke house, always burning very slowly, if it gets too hot the fish becomes cooked and spoilt; it is a good plan to place the entrails of the fish on the fire to keep it cool.[9]

When John Graves Simcoe, the first lieutenant-governor of Upper Canada (present-day Ontario), arrived in 1791, he was accompanied by his wife, Elizabeth Graves Simcoe, who was an artist and also kept a diary rich in the details of everyday life. There were dozens of diary entries describing the fish to be found in Upper Canada, such as this one on April 6, 1793: "St. Denis of the 5th caught yesterday at Niagara, 500 whitefish and 40 sturgeon; this is common sturgeon, one nearly 6 foot long."[10]

Settlers often chose to build their homes beside water, both for ease of travel and for the number of fish that could be speared, netted, trapped, or caught with a baited line. Newcomers continued to be amazed at what they found:

I think I may assert, without fear of contradiction, that the angling in Canada is the finest in the world. Many thousands of trout streams and hundreds of salmon rivers discharge their waters into the gulf and river St. Lawrence. From Lake Ontario down to the straits of Belle-Isle, a distance of nearly 2,000 miles; on each shore of the river there is hardly a mile of coast-line without a river or stream. Thousands and thousands of lakes, all of which hold trout, lie hidden in the forest; in the majority of them perhaps a fly has never been cast. Trout fishing is open to everyone ... and such salmon fishing![11]

By the middle of the nineteenth century, settlers spread across the country and the fishing industry on the East Coast steadily expanded as demand for cod grew not only in Canada but in the West Indies and South America. The fishing schooners, both from Canada and abroad, now carried dories, small seaworthy craft equipped with a sail and two sets of oars for the crew of two men. The dories left the schooners at daybreak to set long lines of hooks baited with herring, squid, capelin, or salted clams. They made four trips out to the trawl, or longline, each day to check the gear. This endless round of baiting, setting, and hauling trawl ended in the evening when the "dressing" of the cod began. Each fish was gutted, beheaded, split (backbone removed), washed, and placed in the hold, where it was packed in salt. This chore ended about midnight. Then the men slept until 3:30 a.m. when they began the next day's fishing. The schooners were often out on the Grand Banks for three months, and when they returned, the catch was given to "fish makers," who washed the coarse salt from the cod and spread it to dry in the sun on racks covered with spruce boughs, known as "flakes." For three weeks the fish was watched so that it would not get wet in the rain or sunburned. When it was hard-dried, it was ready to be packaged in barrels or boxes for shipment to markets at home or abroad.

As we follow the cod from the water to the kitchen to the dinner table, we find the ingenious recipes developed by enterprising cooks over the centuries that used virtually every part of the fish: Fried Cod Roe, Fried or Baked Cod Tongues, Stewed or Fried Cods' Heads, Fish Hash (made from fresh or salt codfish), Codfish Balls, Cod Sounds (membrane lying along the backbone, first simmered in water, then baked in a casserole with onions, grated cheese, and thin strips of salt pork), Toast and Fish, Roasted Scrawd (small cod culled from the catch), Fish and Brewis, Salt Fish and Potatoes, Boiled Rounders (small codfish with soundbone intact), and many more![12] Codfish was, and is, traditionally served with potatoes, turnips, parsnips, onions, carrots, cabbage, rashers of salt pork or pork scruncheons, and drawn butter.

Drying codfish in the traditional manner at Village Historique Acadien at Caraquet in New Brunswick.

An old Newfoundland custom continues to recognize the importance of cod and other seafood. In many Newfoundland homes, even into the twenty-first century, the celebration of Christmas begins on Christmas Eve with a thanksgiving meal of Salt Fish or Cod Sounds followed by sweet raisin bread called Christmas Fruit Loaf. In this way, fishing is recognized as the main means of livelihood and, as a result, fish has its place in thanksgiving before the day of feasting.

In the 1828–1830 season, the government of Nova Scotia offered bounties on the tonnage and "Merchantable"quality (i.e., that suitable for European and South American markets) of dried cod. These bounties were designed to encourage the outfitting of vessels in Nova Scotia for employment in the cod industry and to capitalize locally on the resources.

This rich resource eventually became the major industry in Atlantic Canada, encompassing not only fishing but everything needed to support it. The latter included the building of fishing schooners like the famous *Bluenose*, launched in Lunenburg in 1921. After a season of fishing in the

Grand Banks, the *Bluenose* won the International Fisherman's Trophy and kept winning it for twenty-one years as the fastest sailing vessel in the world. The *Bluenose* is still honoured on Canada's dime. The Fisheries Museum of the Atlantic in Lunenburg, Nova Scotia, pays tribute to this rich harvest from Canada's eastern seaboard.

Giovanni Caboto did not find the rich spices he sought, but instead discovered a far more valuable resource that over hundreds (and probably thousands) of years has sustained the First Nations, newcomers to Canada, and the tables of the hungry around the world.

CHAPTER FOUR

"Come Then, Chefs, Cooks, and Boys — All You Who Make Good Cheer"

TWO TINY VESSELS ROUNDED THE SOUTHERN END of Acadia (now Nova Scotia) on an early summer day in 1604. On one of the crafts was Samuel de Champlain; Sieur de Monts, the leader of the expedition, was on board the other. De Monts had a commission from King Henri IV of France as governor of La Cadia (the land stretching from today's Philadelphia to Newfoundland) to "establish the name, power and authority of the King of France throughout the new territory," to bring the Natives to Christ, and most significantly, to "people, cultivate and settle the said lands."[1] He was now searching for the ideal location to build his first habitation. Tragically, he chose Île Sainte-Croix (now Dochet Island) at the mouth of the St. Croix River, for in the months ahead it was to become the last resting place of nearly half (thirty-five) of his total company of seventy-nine men.

Despite their preparations for winter, the members of the party were so cut off from the mainland by huge cakes of ice that it was impossible to procure fresh water and fuel. They had cut down most of the trees on the island to build their log structures, not realizing how valuable they would be as a windbreak and as fuel in the months ahead. As a result, they were forced to eat their food cold and to dole out their frozen cider by the pound. Starvation, cold, and the "dreaded disease" that we now know to be scurvy had taken their toll by spring.

In July those who survived, including Champlain, moved to the mainland and took many of their buildings with them. They called the new habitation Port Royal in honour of their king. Champlain's sketches show a larger settlement than before, with several sleeping quarters, a storeroom with a cellar (one hopes to keep their cider from freezing), a kitchen, a bakeshop with an oven, and gardens surrounded with a reservoir of water filled with trout. They had gathered some quick vegetable crops from the fertile meadows, and small game abounded: geese, ducks, partridge, and plenty of rabbits and hares. A single musket shot once brought down twenty-eight plover.[2] Despite these improvements and a more adequate supply of food, twelve more men died over the winter of 1605–06.

Champlain did not appear to know what ailment afflicted his men, or that nearly seventy years before when Jacques Cartier spent the winter with the Natives at Stadacona (present-day Quebec City), many members of his crew nearly perished with scurvy. They learned from the First Nations how to make a medicine by boiling the leaves and bark of the white spruce. In eight days they used a whole tree. "Had all the doctors of Louvain and Montpellier been there, with all the drugs of Alexander," wrote Cartier, "they could not have done so much in a year as did this tree in eight days."[3]

The Native peoples of Canada have used many berries, bark, roots, needles, and grasses to prevent scurvy among their own people (and to cure it in the case of the newcomers). If left untreated, scurvy is a deadly disease

caused by the lack of vitamin C in the diet. Over the years, the First Nations' remedies have included white pine sweet inner bark and needles, hemlock bark, the inner bark of black spruce, cranberries, the pale red berries of the false Solomon's seal of the West Coast, black-currants, gooseberries, the seed

The First Nations used many native plants and trees, including the seed pods of the wild rose, to prevent and cure scurvy.

pods or hips of the wild rose, and scurvy grass, which grows in northern Canada from the Yukon to Newfoundland.[4]

In July 1606, Jean de Biencourt, Sieur de Poutrincourt, who was searching for a new home where he could establish his family in feudal splendour, arrived with fresh supplies and fifty additional men for the tiny colony. Along with Biencourt came Marc Lescarbot, a Parisian poet, playwright, and lawyer. It may have been Lescarbot who introduced the idea in one of his dramatic presentations that feasting and celebration would cure the difficulties that had plagued the colony and that everyone feared would return in the coming winter:

> Come then, chefs, cooks, and boys — all you who make
>   good cheer,
> Scullions and pastry cooks, let soup and roast appear,
> Ransack the kitchen shelves, fill every pot and pan
> And draw his own good portion for every eater man!
> I see the men are thirsty, SICUT TERRA, SINE AQUA
> Bestir yourselves, be brisk. Are the ducks on the spit?
> What fowl have lost their heads? The goose, who cares for it?
> Hither have sailed to us a band of comrades rare:
> Let potatoes and their hunger be matched with equal care.[5]

Champlain took Lescarbot's suggestion in the hope that he could keep his men healthy, and L'Ordre de bon temps, or the Order of Good Cheer, was born. This morale booster became a well-organized evening meal, with a chief steward of the feast chosen for every day. The steward wore a gold chain around his neck and was responsible for all three meals on his appointed day. He had to hunt and fish in advance to augment the provisions of the ship and the fort, as well as instruct the cook in the preparation of the dishes.

The ship's provisions probably included peas, beans, rice, prunes, raisins, dried cod, salted meat, oil, and butter. There were hogs and sheep at the habitation, as well as hens and pigeons, so we can assume there were eggs, as well. The First Nations near the fort were the hunter-gatherer Mi'kmaqs (also spelled Micmacs), who would have been trapping and hunting beaver, otter, moose, bear, and caribou; fishing for smelt, herring, sturgeon, and salmon; and bartering seal oil. Vines, wild onions, wild peas, walnuts (butternuts?), acorns, gooseberries, raspberries, strawberries, cranberries, and maple sap were also available.[6]

Lescarbot gives us an account of some of the ingredients and the dishes that were prepared from them: "good dishes of meat as in the cook's shops that be in La Rue aux Ours [a street in Paris specializing in food]; *colice*, a hearty broth made from a cock, white sausages made from the flesh and innards of cod with lard and spice, good pastries made of moose and turtle doves."[7] Could that last dish have been an early Canadian version of the traditional *tourtière* so well-known and loved in Quebec (and other regions of Canada) today?

Great ceremony attended the evening meal, as the steward

> did march with his napkin on his shoulder and his staff of office in his hand, with the collar of the order about his neck, which was worth above four crowns, and all of them of the order following of him, bearing every one a dish. The like was also at the bringing in of the fruit, but not with so great a train. And at night after grace was said, he resigned the collar of the order, with a cup of wine to his successor in that charge, and they drank one to another.[8]

Despite the ravages of scurvy, Port Royal survived and became not only the site of the first successful colony on the mainland, but also the site of Canada's inaugural gourmands' club. There were other firsts that were to have an effect on agriculture and food, for it was here at Port Royal that the first grain was grown and a sample sent back to Europe to confirm the richness of the soil. It was to this colony that Louis Hébert, a Paris apothecary, first came. He was known to have a green thumb, and in 1617 he returned to Stadacona to become known as "Canada's first farmer."[9] In reality, this assertion was incorrect, for many of the First Nations had been farmers for centuries. Their well-established trade routes up and down the continent had brought the seeds for many crops to Canada. These included maize (corn), beans, squash, pumpkin, tomatoes, potatoes, sunflowers, and numerous others. Their tools and techniques may have been primitive by the standards of the newcomers, but

The Order of Good Cheer, as imaginatively sketched by C.W. Jeffreys in 1925, attempted to boost morale in Samuel de Champlain's precarious colony in what is now Nova Scotia.

as we have seen, their fields had been supporting their families and communities for generations and provided important items to barter with other tribes and nations.

When Hébert did return with his wife, Marie, and their family, they became the first true colonists who came to till the soil and establish a home. Marie would have used her memories of medieval cooking traditions and utensils brought from her home in France to preserve and prepare for the table the harvest from the garden and fields and the meats, fish, and game from the river and the forest.

Champlain had already established a habitation at Stadacona in 1608 and planted a garden in which European plants such as cabbages, beets, radishes, lettuce, and other necessary vegetables and herbs flourished. Quebec, the trading post and struggling colony, was at a turning point when Hébert returned, for Cardinal Richelieu, the king's chief minister and the most powerful man in France, suddenly became interested in it. The Company of New France, or Company of One Hundred Associates,

41

was formed in 1627, pledging to send out large numbers of colonists and to support them for three years.[10]

In addition, devoted men and women arrived to found missions, churches, schools, and hospitals. There had been Jesuit missionaries at Port Royal, and in 1615, three Récollet brothers came to Quebec. Soon after they went out as missionaries to the Mi'kmaqs of Acadia, the Abenaki of the Saint John Valley, and to the Hurons. A decade later the Jesuits were invited to share this work. Unfortunately, there were many occasions when the two cultures — the First Nations and the newly arrived clergy — clashed over the concept of right and wrong, life after death, God and worship, superstitions, belief in magic, feasts and ceremonials. It is thanks to the letters, diaries, and writings of the Jesuits and Récollets, and of the sisters of the Ursuline Order who arrived in 1639, that many descriptions of the people, customs, dangers, and problems in seventeenth-century Quebec survived.

In addition to the spiritual benefits, there were many unexpected financial benefits to the new colony because of the arrival of the clergy. Just one example was the discovery in 1716 by Joseph-François Lafitau, who was serving as a missionary in Sault Saint-Louis (Kahnawake), south of Hochelaga (present-day Montreal), that ginseng was a local plant. He knew this plant had been considered a medical wonder in China for thousands of years, but that it was in short supply where his fellow missionaries also served, and thus its export from Canada to China began. Natives as well as newcomers started to gather the plant and sell it to the French merchants on the Montreal market. From there it was shipped to France, then to Canton, where it was purchased by Chinese merchants. They in turn sold it to doctors and pharmacists in the Empire of China. It took thirty-six weeks for this cumbersome system to move ginseng root bought in Montreal to where it would sell for sixty times its price in Canton.[11]

Meanwhile, Champlain, fur trader, explorer, geographer, cartographer, administrator, became known as the Father of New France and went on to explore the St. Lawrence Basin and the Great Lakes, the Ottawa River, and the country of the Hurons, often guided by members of the First Nations. He has left us an invaluable record in his journals of the plants, animals, soil, foods, beverages, and medicines that were important to both the First Nations and the newcomers.[12]

CHAPTER FIVE

A Chain of Men Stretched Across the Continent

25 being Christmas, wee made merry remembering our Friends in England having for Liquor Brandy and strong beer and for Food plenty of Partridges and Venson besides what ye shipps provisions afforded.

THE ABOVE DESCRIPTION OF A CHRISTMAS DINNER in Canada was fortunately recorded by a Hudson's Bay Company fur trader, Thomas Gorst, in his journal in 1670. The guests seated at the table in the newly constructed Charles Fort (later called Rupert's House and still later Fort Rupert) included Hudson's Bay Company governor Charles Bayley, Médard Chouart, Sieur Des Groseilliers, his brother-in-law, Pierre-Ésprit Radisson, and Captain Zachariah Gillam. The ships *Wivenhoe* and *Prince Rupert* were anchored nearby in James Bay.

The two Frenchmen, Radisson and Groseilliers, had a great deal to celebrate that day. They had both come to New France as young men and had worked and travelled in the St. Lawrence region and beyond as explorers, *coureurs de bois*, and fur traders among the Huron, Cree, and Sioux nations. They realized the untold wealth in furs to be found in the forests surrounding the "Bay of the North" (Hudson Bay) and lobbied both in the New World and in the Old World for permission to trade in the region. Finally, a few months before, on May 2, 1670, King Charles II of England had granted his cousin, Prince Rupert, a royal charter that gave trading rights to the area known as Rupert's Land to the "Governor and Company of Adventurers of England Trading into Hudson's Bay." No one at that time knew the size of the land mass involved (it was actually 40 percent of present-day Canada, plus some territory that is now part of the United States of America), but the coveted "trading rights" were for furs, particularly beaver pelts.

At that time the demand for prime beaver pelts was at its height, with ready markets in Britain and the rest of Europe. The nobility was demanding fine furs for robes, jackets, capes, and muffs, and gentlemen who could afford a fine felt hat insisted that it be made of the soft downy undercoat of the beaver. As European beavers had been trapped out, it was imperative that a fresh source be found.

The fur merchants in Europe had learned from explorers such as Jacques Cartier that when he sailed into the Baie des Chaleurs in 1534 he was met by members of the Mi'kmaq nation waving furs on sticks to let him know they wanted to trade. In addition, the fishermen harvesting the Grand Banks confirmed that when they went ashore to dry their catch the First Nations continued to barter fine pelts with them. When the fishermen returned home, they often made more money from the pelts than from the fish. The pelts from Canadian beaver were particularly desirable because:

> To be of good quality, thick and heavy, the beaver-pelt must come from an animal taken during the winter, and taken in as hard a climate as possible. Then the skin carries two kinds of fur; close to the skin is a thick mass of beaver-wool, down or duvet as the French called it; on top is a glossy fur of long guard hairs. It was the beaver wool above all which the felters wanted but it was difficult to get the beaver-wool out from a prime winter's skin without also tearing out the guard hairs and thereby completely destroying the skin. English and French felters liked to get their beaver-wool from skins from which the guard hairs had already been removed and this made them dependent on coat beaver. These were skins which the Indians had worn for a season and in the process lost their guard hairs and become thoroughly greasy. The custom of wearing beaver, an art of doing so in such a way as to impart a maximum of grease, was particular to the northern Indians of Canada.[1]

This fascination with beaver pelts, to the exclusion of the rest of the animal, must have surprised the First Nations. They, too, coveted the beaver, because every part of it was important to them. The meat was tasty, with beaver tails a special treat. They skimmed off the fat as it cooked to be used as medicine. The teeth and claws were polished for ceremonial wear, and the Natives used the bitter orange-brown substance known as musk to reduce fevers and treat aching joints. Modern science has shown that Aspirin, which is used for the same purpose, contains some of the same ingredients.[2]

Alexander Henry, an experienced English trader, travelled up the Ottawa River in 1761 and observed the simple, compact rations of the voyageurs, and the way in which they were absolutely fundamental to the whole fur-trading system for, as he explains, regular food would have taken up too much space in the canoes:

> The village of L'Arbre Croche [twenty miles west of Fort Michilimackinac] supplies, as I have said, the maize, or Indian corn, with which the canoes are victualled. This species of grain is prepared for use, by boiling it in a strong lie, after which the husk may be easily removed; and it is next mashed and dried. In this state, it is soft and friable, like rice. The allowance, for each man, on the voyage, is a quart a day; and a bushel, with two pounds of prepared fat, is reckoned to be a month's subsistence. No other allowance is made, of any kind; not even salt; and bread is never thought of. The men, nevertheless, are healthy, and capable of performing their heavy labour. This mode of victualling is essential to the trade, which being pursued at great distances, and in vessels so small as canoes, will not admit of the use of other food. If the men were to be supplied with bread and pork, the canoe would not carry a sufficiency for six months; and the ordinary duration of the voyage is not less than fourteen. The difficulty which would belong to an attempt to reconcile any other man, than Canadians, to this fare, seems to secure to them, and their employers, the monopoly of the fur-trade.... I bought more than a hundred bushels,

at forty livres per bushel.... I paid at the rate of a dollar
per pound for the tallow, or prepared fat, to mix with it.[3]

Free traders (as the competitors of the Hudson's Bay Company were
called) became involved in this lucrative business, and many combined
forces by forming partnerships and companies, but it was the North West
Company that for many years challenged the powerful Hudson's Bay
Company and their decision to build their forts around the bay and let the
First Nations come to them. The North West Company realized the importance of building their trading posts in the interior of the country, where the
First Nations lived, trapped, and hunted. The rival company also recognized
the importance of adequately provisioning the men involved in the trade,
and not leaving their survival and the survival of the business to chance.

To accomplish this, the company formed one of the most innovative
partnerships ever seen in Canada, including an unlikely combination of
Scottish and English merchants, French Canadian voyageurs, First Nation
guides, canoe-makers, advisers, suppliers of survival foods, and Métis (off-
spring of a mixed white-Native marriage) labourers, trappers, traders,
and voyageurs. This partner-
ship solved the slow, complicated business of buying or
bartering for furs from the First
Nations in the northwestern
regions of Canada and moving
them to ships on the East
Coast, by which they could
then be shipped to markets

*The North West Company
partners dined in fine style
every evening as they travelled
by canoe between Montreal
and the organization's inland
headquarters at Fort William
in today's Ontario.*

Fort William Historical Park, Thunder Bay, Ontario

overseas. The North West Company developed, and maintained, a long supply route that stretched from today's Montreal to the Pacific Ocean, with an inland headquarters between the two. This plan was unique, and just as complex as the operation of a modern airline. A modern airline depends on gasoline, while the North West Company relied on specific provisions for each of the groups involved in the trade — all of which expected and enjoyed quite different fare. Their success also depended on the goodwill and cooperation of everyone involved to provide the fare in a timely manner.

The first inland headquarters for the North West Company was built at Grand Portage, and when the boundary between the United States and British territories was redrawn by the Treaty of Versailles in 1785, it moved to Fort William (at today's Thunder Bay) on the north shore of Lake Superior. Fort William became the company's trans-shipping centre, with forty-two buildings set in a rectangle and its own farm adjoining the fort to provide provisions such as grain, herbs, fresh vegetables, milk, and meat for both the regular staff and the Rendezvous that was held there annually during the summer months. The land behind the fort and on both sides of it was cleared and under tillage. Barley, peas, oats, Indian corn, potatoes, as well as other grains and vegetables were grown there. Seven horses, thirty-two cows and bulls, and a large number of sheep were kept on the farm, as well.[4]

How did this unique system work? To overcome the short summers and long winters in Canada, many of the partners of the company wintered in Montreal, spending their time assembling the trade goods, supervising the warehouses along the St. Lawrence River, and preparing for the year ahead. The rest of the partners manned the inland posts in the West and the far Northwest, trading and bartering directly with the First Nations for the pelts. They, too, were preparing for the year ahead. As soon as the ice was gone from the lakes and rivers, both groups started for Fort William. The inland traders used small *canots du nord*, which could be paddled by six men and portaged by two, and which held two tons of pelts and provisions for the thousand-mile journey. The Montreal merchants used Montreal canoes, or *canots du maitre*, which were large freight canoes, holding four tons of freight and each requiring ten French Canadian or Métis voyageurs as paddlers to cover approximately the same distance.

They [the canoes] reached lengths of forty feet, with a six-foot beam and a depth of two feet. The bow and stern curved upwards, often painted with animal or other designs. They weighed only five hundred pounds but they could carry as many as sixty men or fifty barrels of flour. They could be manufactured from cedar and pine and birch bark for as little as fifty dollars and would last for five or six years. First time travellers blanched when they saw their intended craft loaded to the gunwales perhaps a scant six inches from the water, but the Nor'westers calculated losses on voyages as low as one-half of one percent.

The canoe fleet carried a mess tent, 30 feet by 15 feet, and a separate sleeping tent and comfortable bed for each partner, carpets for their feet, beaver robes for their knees. The transport canoes went on ahead so that when the gentlemen reached the selected site for the night camp, a great fire was leaping, meat was sizzling, wine bottles were uncorked.[5]

American author Washington Irving, one of the guests of the North West Company, described the journey from Montreal:

> They ascended the river in great state, like sovereigns making a progress, or rather like Highland chieftains navigating their subject lakes. They were wrapped in rich furs, their huge canoes freighted with every convenience and luxury, and manned by Canadian voyageurs, as obedient as Highland clansmen. They carried up with them cooks and bakers, together with delicacies of every kind, and abundances of choice wines for the banquets which attended this great convocation. Happy were they, too, if they could meet with some distinguished stranger; above all, some titled member of the British nobility, to accompany them on this stately occasion, and grace their high solemnities.[6]

In addition to the partners and the comforts they needed on the journey, here is a partial list of the commodities, particularly food and beverages, listed in the "Scheme for the NW Outfit" in 1794 that would have been transported to the inland headquarters to provision the fort: "10 kegs sugar, 8 kegs salt, 32 kegs butter, 80 kegs pork, 230 kegs grease, 40 kegs beef, 400 kegs high wines, 50 kegs rum, 10 kegs port wine, 10 kegs brandy, 20 kegs shrub, 3 kegs sausages, 17 bags green peas."[7]

Meanwhile, Ross Cox, a Dublin-born fur trader who later became the Irish correspondent of the *London Morning Herald*, describes the French Canadian canoe men's rations in 1817. They present a striking contrast to the food and beverages of the partners:

> I know of no people capable of enduring so much hard labour as the Canadians, or so submissive to superiors. In voyages of six months' duration, they commence at daybreak and from thence to night-fall hard paddling and carrying goods occupy their time without intermission.... Their rations at first view may appear enormous. Each man is allowed eight pounds of solid meat *per diem*, such as buffalo, deer, horse, etc., and ten pounds if there be bone in it. In the autumnal months, in lieu of meat, each man receives two large geese or four ducks. They are supplied with fish in the same proportion. It must, however, be recollected that these rations are unaccompanied by bread, biscuit, potatoes, or, in fact by vegetables of any description.
>
> At Christmas and New Year they are served out with flour to make cakes or puddings, and each man receives half a pint of rum. This they call a *regale*, and they are particularly grateful for it.[8]

The Nor'Westers coming to Fort William from the inland posts also had to provision their teams. They soon learned that dried meat and fish, berries and greens from the forest, all took space in the canoes, and precious time could be wasted hunting and fishing. The First Nations introduced the newcomers to pemmican, made from dried buffalo, elk, or deer meat, pounded into a powder, mixed with dried berries, packed into a leather bag, then sealed with grease. Light, durable, and highly nourishing, the bags of pemmican were easily stored in a canoe, and thus pemmican became the staple diet of the canoe man. Small amounts of pemmican replaced large amounts of regular food, freeing up precious time and space to carry more furs and more trade goods in both directions.

> Pemmican was used on voyages in the far interior. This was kind of pressed buffalo meat, pounded fine, to which hot grease was added, and the whole left to form a mould in a bag of buffalo skin. When properly made, pemmican would remain edible for more than one season. Its small bulk and great nutritional value made it highly esteemed by all voyageurs. From it they made a dish called "Rubbaboo" … it is a favourite dish with the northern voyageurs, when they could get it. It consists simply of pemmican made into a kind of soup by boiling water. Flour is added when it can be obtained, and it is generally considered more palatable with a little sugar.[9]

Pemmican initially gave the North West Company a great advantage over their Hudson's Bay Company rivals, who continued to depend on bread, porridge, and meat cured with salt, instead of adapting to Native foods. However, as the story of Canadian food unfolds, we will soon learn that this dependence on pemmican, much of it produced by the buffalo hunters of the prairies and available at Pembina, the North West Company post on the Red River, would eventually be a major factor in the company's demise.

In July the two groups began to assemble at the inland headquarters — the fur brigades from the west and the merchant partners from the east. It is not surprising then that the annual Rendezvous became a legendary time of feasting and celebration. The population of Fort William grew to about two thousand persons (at the same time the population of York, the capital of Upper Canada, was about six hundred) and included the English and Scottish merchants and their clerks; the French Canadian and Métis canoe men; and the men and women of the First Nations who were guides, advisers, and providers of specialized needs such as survival foods for the chain of forts and posts stretching into the interior.

The central building at Fort William was the Great Hall, and these descriptions tell us how it appeared to two travellers of the period:

> In the middle of a gracious square rises a large building elegantly constructed, though of wood, with a long piazza or portico, raised about five feet from the ground, and surmounted by a balcony, extending along the whole front. In the centre is a saloon or hall, sixty feet in length by thirty in width, decorated with several pieces of painting and some portraits of the leading partners. It is in this hall that the agents, partners, clerks, interpreters and guides, take their meal together, at different tables. The kitchen and servants' rooms are in the basement.[10]

> The dining hall is a noble apartment, and sufficiently capacious to entertain two hundred. A finely executed bust of the late Simon McTavish is placed in it, with portraits of various Proprietors. A full-length likeness of Nelson, together with a splendid painting of the Battle of the Nile also decorate the walls.[11]

An 1844 account of dinner at Fort Vancouver, a North West Company post on the Pacific Slopes (the company firmly controlled this area, which stretched from San Francisco to the Alaska border), finds Governor (Dr. John) McLoughlin, who had served earlier as the doctor at Fort William, presiding at table:

> At the end of a table twenty feet in length stands Governor McLoughlin (known as the Father of Oregon) directing guests and gentlemen from neighbouring posts to their places, and chief traders, the physician, clerks and the farmer slide respectfully to their places, at distances from the governor corresponding to the dignity of their rank and service. Thanks are given to God, and all are seated. Roast beef and pork, boiled mutton, baked salmon, boiled ham, beets, carrots, turnips, cabbage and potatoes, and wheaten

bread, are tastefully distributed over the table among a dinner set of elegant Queen's Ware, furnished with glittering glasses and decanters of various coloured Italian wines.[12]

During the month of the Rendezvous, dignity appears to have been set aside once the sun began to set. Days were spent in the Committee House at meetings, at which the business of the trade was carried out in great secrecy, but the nights were spent dining and roistering in the Great Hall. Dinners of "buffalo tongue and hump that had been either smoked or salted, thirty pound lake trout and whitefish that could be netted in the river at the gates to the Fort, venison, wild duck, geese, partridge and beaver tails would be augmented with confectioners' delicacies that had been packed all the way from Montreal in those great canoes. They drank the wines of France and Portugal, whiskies from Scotland and the Canadas, rum by the hogshead and, on occasion, the finest champagne."[13]

Fort William Historical Park, Thunder Bay, Ontario

Cooks and bakers prepared imported delicacies for the elaborate banquets held at the annual July Rendezvous at Fort William.

Traditionally, five toasts were given, and these were presented in the following order: Mary, the Mother of all the Saints; the king; the fur trade in all its branches; the voyageurs, their wives, and their children; and absent brethren. When the dinner and toasts were over, the Great Hall witnessed one of the sights of the ages:

52

> With the ten gallon kegs of rum running low and dawn fingering the windows of the Great Hall to find the partners of the North West Company, names that mark and brighten the map of Canada, leaping on benches, chairs, and oaken wine barrels to "shoot the rapids" from the tilted tables to the floor, and singing the songs of home. Mounting broad bladed paddles, the gentlemen in knee breeches and silver buckled shoes pounded around the hall in impromptu races, shoving boisterously, piling up at the corners, breaking off only to down another brimming bumper [of spirits].[14]

However, the Rendezvous was soon over, and by August 1 both groups left for home so they would not be caught on the frozen waterways. For the partners returning for the winter to Montreal, there was the Beaver Club's fellowship and feasting to look forward to. The club was founded in February 1785 with nineteen members, all of whom had explored the Northwest. The object of the club was "to bring together at stated periods during the winter season, a set of men highly respectable in society who had passed their best days in a savage country and had encountered the difficulties and dangers incident to a pursuit peculiar to the fur trade of Canada." Despite this restriction, an additional nineteen members were accepted by 1803.[15]

The club did not have its own headquarters but met every fortnight from December to April in one of Montreal's famous eating establishments. It did have its own china, crystal, and plate, marked with the club's insignia. At the meetings the members themselves had to wear their insignia if they wanted to avoid a fine. This medal was gold and bore the words "Beaver Club of Montreal instituted in 1785," with a beaver gnawing the foot of a tree and the inscription "Industry and Perseverance." The reverse side carried the name of the member, the date of his first voyage of exploration, and a bas-relief with the motto Fortitude in Distress and a canoe with three passengers in top hats being guided through rapids by canoe men.[16]

Colonel Landman, a guest of Sir Alexander Mackenzie and William McGillivray in the early nineteenth century, gives us a vivid description of one of the Beaver Club dinners that lasted twelve hours:

At this time, dinner was at four o'clock and after having lowered a reasonable quantity of wine, say a bottle each, the married men withdrew, leaving a dozen of us to drink to their health. Accordingly, we were able to behave like real Scottish Highlanders and by four in the morning we had all attained such a degree of perfection that we could utter a war cry as well as Mackenzie and McGillivray. We were all drunk like fish, and all of us thought we could dance on the table without disarranging a single one of the decanters, glasses or plates with which it was covered.

But on attempting this experiment, we found that we were suffering from a delusion and wound up by breaking all the plates, glasses and bottles and demolishing the table itself; worse than that, there were bruises and scratches, more or less serious on the heads and hands of everyone in the group…. It was told to me later that during our carouse 120 bottles of wine had been drunk, but I think a good part of it had been spilled.[17]

Other guests at the Beaver Club confirmed that description:

They served bear meat, beaver, pemmican and venison in the same way as in trading posts to the accompaniment of songs and dances during the events; and when wine had produced the sought-for degree of gaiety in the wee hours of the morning, the trading partners, dealers and merchants re-enacted the "grand voyage" to the Rendezvous in full sight of the waiters or voyageurs who had obtained permission to attend. For this purpose, they sat one behind another on a rich carpet, each equipping himself with a poker, tongs, a sword or walking stick in place of a paddle and roared out such voyageurs' songs as *Malbrouck* or *A la Claire Fontaine*, meanwhile paddling with as much steadiness as their strained nerves would permit.[18]

The last Beaver Club dinner was held in 1827, but the event was resurrected in the twentieth century. The Queen Elizabeth Hotel in Montreal brought it back to life in 1959, and it now has nine hundred members around the world. Once a year club members dine on a five-course dinner with appropriate wines. Each course is paraded through the club, led by costumed *coureurs de bois*, voyageurs, musicians, and a representative from the Kahnawake First Nation. Now, as then, five toasts are proposed to the Mother of All Saints, the queen, the fur trade in all its branches, the women and children of the fur trade (Heaven preserve them!), and absent brethren.

Beaver hats have been forgotten by the fashion world, fur-trading empires are a thing of the past, but once a year hundreds of men and women still gather to pay tribute to an unlikely team of men and women who ruthlessly pursued a small animal across this continent. Their success depended on their food supplies and the strength, skill, and stamina of a chain of men stretched across the continent. They came from different classes, languages, cultures, and standards, but they found a common cause, and until 1821, when the Hudson's Bay Company and the North West Company merged, they were legends in their own time.

CHAPTER SIX

Bread Was the Foundation of Every Meal

AS THE FISHERMEN, FUR TRADERS, MISSIONARIES, SOLDIERS, surveyors, and eventually settlers began to arrive in the land now called Canada, they were often astonished by its incredible bounty, beauty, and harshness. They came from every walk of life, from a multitude of cultural and religious backgrounds, and they had scores of reasons for leaving their homelands, either as sojourners or settlers. Many had come to barter for furs, work on the fishing vessels, or serve in the garrisons and either chose to stay or to return later (often with their families) to take up land and make a new home in what had once been a hostile and alien environment. In addition, there were compelling reasons for many religious and cultural groups in the Old World to make the voyage to the New World. There were also the inducements of free passage and free land grants, as well as the lure of adventure or a need to break with the past.

Whatever their reasons, food was of primary concern to everyone, individual or family: finding it, preserving it, and storing it so that it was readily available to serve their specific needs, at the precise time and place they needed it. These newcomers brought with them memories of the ingredients, recipes, and foods they had known and enjoyed at home. Often they soon realized that their culinary heritage could not be transplanted to the new environment, for the challenges were simply too formidable. Confronted by a harsh (and often wildly varying) climate, new and unknown vegetation, lack of transportation except by water, and the necessity of usually having to clear virgin forest to develop gardens and fields, the new arrivals acquired an appreciation of the skills and knowledge of the

First Nations in utilizing the native plants, trees, and other vegetation for food, beverages, and medicines. Eventually, for those who stayed and prospered, they attributed their success, at least in part, to their ability to combine the knowledge and skill they acquired in their homelands with that of the Native people, and to use the best of both cultures to survive the daily challenges they faced in this, their New World.[1]

Each individual family, cultural, or religious group solved these challenges in different ways, and their histories are varied and compelling. We have here just a sampling of the perseverance and ingenuity that those early settlers demonstrated as they cleared fields, planted orchards and gardens, and attempted to ensure there would be food in the larder not only for today, but for the weeks and months ahead.

The island of Newfoundland was to become Britain's oldest colony, and along with the mainland of Labrador, Canada's newest province. For a long time, settlement and agriculture were not only discouraged but actually outlawed in Newfoundland as Britain attempted to protect its fishing interests. Because of this prohibition, the interior valleys were not explored for over a century. Despite such challenges, early English and Irish settlers persevered and began to prosper by the eighteenth century.

> Early Newfoundland settlers cleared land by burning the forests in winter, but the townspeople had to pay to have them cut down for firewood: They built themselves Cabins, and burnt up all that part of the Woods where they sat down. The following Winter they did the same in another Place, and so cleared the Woods as they went. The People of St. John's Town, who did not remove, were put to great Streights for Firing.[2]

Hundreds of scattered communities called outports developed around the coast, making contact with larger centres almost impossible. As a result, obtaining fresh food in winter was difficult and

> traditional Newfoundland food used dried or salted fish and meat as a basic ingredient. Women baked a great deal.... A small acre or two of stony soil, cleared from the

forest by back-breaking labour, was farmed mostly for root crops such as potatoes and turnips. A cow and a few sheep were kept, with the enviable half dozen chickens running around the house. Children helped with the chores — berry picking for pies, tarts and jam, and when the boys were old enough, joined their fathers on the boats, for most outports survived by virtue of the excellent cod fishing around the coast.[3]

The Habitation at Port Royal, first founded by Champlain, was the catalyst for the arrival of the Acadian settlers, who faced many challenges as the French and English battled to control the area. The Acadians were farmers who had a deep love of the land, though they had no desire to spend time on the back-breaking efforts of clearing away the forests. Instead, they chose to settle along the banks of the tidal rivers, building dikes to hold back the tides. The rich, fertile soil that was reclaimed in this way was cultivated, and abundant supplies of wheat, rye, and vegetables were grown. On their farms they raised poultry, sheep, and pigs, and salted away mutton and pork for winter use. Their cattle were of a small breed and produced very little milk, so butter and cheese were not in plentiful supply.[4]

From the earliest days of settlement the French brought with them that touch of genius that transforms humble ingredients into masterpieces of culinary art. In the minds and hearts of French cooks, whether manor-house chef or habitant housewife, would have been some firm principles — no waste in cooking and baking; everything used in meal preparation; a love of eggs, butter, cheese, and cream; and the knowledge that a little wine or spirit adds a lot of character to a dish.

The New World must have been filled with surprises for all of those first settlers, among them the food traditions of the First Nations, which were to have such an immediate and lasting effect on the new arrivals. The First Nations showed them how to tap the sugar maple trees so they would have a much-needed sweetener for cooking and baking. The Natives poured the maple sugar into birchbark moulds and stored it to be used later as a sweet, or to flavour foods such as cornmeal mush, cornmeal cake and Indian pudding. The French adapted the treat to many of their recipes for the cooking of vegetables, dumplings, puddings, and desserts. Not only did

The First Nations taught the newcomers how to tap maple trees and heat the sap until it thickened into syrup, or until it could be moulded into sugar.

maple syrup become an important ingredient, but the making of maple syrup and sugar later became a traditional cottage industry in Quebec, New Brunswick, Nova Scotia, and Ontario. "Sugaring off" parties brought family, friends, and neighbours together at the end of the maple syrup season to play card games, dance, sing and, of course, feast on an assortment of traditional treats. Many of them were made with the sugar or syrup, such as cookies, cakes, omelettes, crepes, snow taffy, baked apples, maple butter, and maple cream.

The forest yielded other new foods. For example, the Jesuits observed the Natives picking blueberries (also called soft juniper) and adding them to pemmican and to the cornmeal they were using in pottages and puddings. The settlers added them to cake dough, and the result was a moist fruit cake. The French also introduced some new fruit to the country, for Champlain planted the first grapevine in Quebec in 1608, and New France's first bishop, François de Laval, imported the first apple and plum trees.

Bread was the foundation of every meal, and in early days would have been baked in a stone, brick, or clay oven beside the kitchen fireplace, where all the cooking was done. Often a larger "out oven," shaped like a beehive and located out of doors, would replace or supplement the smaller indoor oven. Hardwood was placed inside either oven and burned for several hours to heat the clay-and stone-structure. Then the coals and ashes were raked out, the oven floor was sprinkled with cornmeal, and the round loaves were placed inside using a long, flat wooden paddle called a "peel." Some of these large outdoor ovens served the whole community, and then the womenfolk were able to bake only on a certain day of the week; sometimes bread would become stale before bread-baking day came around again. The cooks and bakers using these ovens, like bakers all over the world, were attempting to make bread without the superb leavening agents that began to appear by the middle of the nineteenth century. As a result, those early breads would have been coarse and heavy, but as the years went by and yeast made with potatoes, hops, and other agents was perfected, there emerged the beautifully plump and round loaves that can still be bought at the roadside in Quebec today. Wheat, rye, buckwheat, and oats were the grains favoured for baking. Buckwheat was often grown on lean, rocky soil where other grains could not have survived. Many methods were developed to use stale bread. It was fried, made into bread pudding or French toast, crumbled into toppings, used as croutons for the ever-popular soups, stuffed into fish and fowl, and employed to thicken gravies and sauces.

The vegetables basic to everyday cooking would have included cabbage, carrots, peas, onions, and turnips, augmented by those the First Nations had been using for centuries, such as corn, pumpkin, squash, and potatoes. Dried peas have been part of human diets since biblical times, and sometimes have been used in extraordinary ways. For example, in ancient Rome they were cooked and sold as a treat at the circus, and at times have been given away by politicians in an attempt to buy votes! Once the peas have been dried and the outer skins removed, they are easy to cook, and in French Canada they became the basis for another honoured recipe — pea soup, made originally from whole yellow peas, and later from split yellow and green peas.

The origin of the world-famous *tourtière* is hotly debated by culinary historians. Its ancestry may be traced to the ancient civilizations of Babylon, Greece, or Rome, or to the Middle Ages, or to the English pork pie. However, many believe the dish originated in Canada as a descendant of the "sea pie" of Atlantic communities, or its name may derive from the French word *tourte*, meaning "wild pigeon." Early settlers have left us accounts of the waves of wild pigeons that would arrive at certain times of the year and could be caught in nets, clubbed, or simply grabbed by hand. *Tourte* also means a pottery casserole in which pigeon pie was originally baked, so either of these uses of the word may explain the savoury pie baked between two layers of crust and usually served cold. There are dozens of variations of the recipe from region to region, and through the years ingenious housewives worked with what was available, so any combinations of beef, pork, salt pork, veal, wild game, fowl, potatoes, onions, salt, pepper, mustard, cinnamon, cloves, or allspice may have been included.

Meanwhile, people were on the move, and settlements were springing up in many locations. English settlers were attracted to Nova Scotia by free passage, free land grants, a year's provisions, farming tools, guns and ammunition, and the promise of a planned town (Halifax). Colonel Edward Cornwallis arrived in the Nova Scotia colony in June 1749 and was soon followed by twenty-five-hundred colonists.

The first winter was very difficult. There were not enough homes yet to shelter the settlers, and many had to stay on board the ships, huddled together to keep from freezing. Those on land were not much better off, for the rude shanties, formed of upright poles stuck in the ground and roofed over with the bark of trees, were not enough to keep out the cold. Their only food consisted of government rations of salt meat and hardtack, and thus, without fresh meat and vegetables to sustain their health, they developed typhus. It is tragic to note that almost one-third of the population died. But eventually Halifax became a town — a little piece of Old England nestled on a harbour in the wilds of North America.[5]

The proximity of the New England colonies in what was to become the new United States of America ensured a constant flow of settlers from the south, many bringing with them their African American slaves. When the Acadians were expelled by the British governor in 1755, thousands of these new arrivals took up their vacant, fertile farms to supply Halifax with food.

Historians believe the Highland Scots faced the greatest challenge in Nova Scotia, since they often arrived penniless. However, after cutting the timber and burning it on the land, they planted potatoes among the stumps and were rewarded with a plentiful return. In winter they would cut holes through the ice, which was often a foot thick, in order to obtain a supply of fish. They learned to hunt moose and other game, the meat of which they froze in the snow, thus providing a little variety to their meals. But they longed for the oatmeal that is so much a part of Scottish fare. The only bread to be had in the earliest days was made from grain ground on the quern, or hand mill, but this procedure was so laborious an operation that they resorted to it only when impelled by the direst necessity. The beverage served at mealtime was often a tea made by boiling the leaves of the partridgeberry.[6]

As the years passed and settlements developed, the new arrivals began to realize that they, too, could benefit not just from their farms but also from the extraordinary marine resource on their doorstep. One example of this is the community of Lunenburg in Nova Scotia, settled in 1753 by 1,453 Protestants from Switzerland, France, and Germany, whose first interest was farming their rich agricultural land. Since the town is close to the capital, Halifax, there was a ready market for root vegetables, timber, and boards. Slowly the interest of the settlers, like that of those in the nearby communities of Liverpool and New Dublin, turned to shore fishing for gaspereau (in May), cod and salmon (April to October), mackerel (June to October), and dogfish (from August onwards). These fish were eaten fresh or preserved by smoking or pickling in brine for family or local consumption.[7]

Île Saint-Jean, now known as Prince Edward Island, was "discovered" by Jacques Cartier in 1534. However, it was not until 1719 that two new-comers, fishermen from Normandy, decided to settle there. Mathieu Turin, along with his family of ten, settled at East Point, while François Douville and his family of nineteen settled at St. Peter's Harbour.[8] In August 1720, three ships carrying three hundred immigrants from the har-bour of Rochefort on the west coast of France sailed into what is now Charlottetown harbour and founded the community of Port la Joie. Soon a piece of ground was carved from the primeval forest, a few log homes were constructed, and an earthen breastwork was thrown up and mount-ed with eight cannon. Food production was of vast importance to these French settlers. One of the reasons for them being established here by the French government was to supply the beleaguered Fortress of Louisbourg on Cape Breton Island, for in 1713 Newfoundland and Acadia had been ceded to Great Britain, with the French still holding Cape Breton and Île Saint-Jean. French settlers came in considerable numbers, along with some Acadians seeking refuge under the flag they loved so well.[9]

As in many other areas in the early years, turmoil and uncertainty were caused by disputes between England and France over fishing rights and the struggle to control the Fortress of Louisbourg and the surrounding territory until eventually the British emerged victorious in 1758. The island was briefly called the Island of St. John, but in 1799 it was finally named Prince

Edward Island after the future Queen Victoria's father, and Charlottetown was named to honour Queen Charlotte, consort of King George III.

The American War of Independence had a profound effect, not only on Prince Edward Island but on all the emerging settlements in eastern Canada and Quebec. From 1783 until the end of the century, United Empire Loyalists continued to move to British North America, determined to stay, to carve out a new home on the frontier, and to prosper.

By 1818 we have a description of the island and its settlers:

> The inhabitants consisted chiefly of emigrants from England, Ireland and Scotland, the States of America, and a few from Germany. There are also about six or seven hundred of the original Acadian French settlers, who occupy three villages, and live comfortably by farming and fishing.
>
> The soil is deep and light, but very fertile, if properly cultivated; in most places there are few or no stones to be seen, except on the shores, or by digging three or four feet from them. The land produces very good wheat, barley, oats, rye, peas, &c. and the various sorts of vegetables, as in England, such as potatoes, parsnips, carrots, cabbage, peas, the different kinds of beans, asparagus, cauliflower, onions, cucumber, melons, pumpkins, radishes, lettuces, celery, &c. &c. Hops grow exceedingly well with little trouble. The English apple and cherry trees thrive very well, the garden gooseberry and currant trees yield very great crops. The land produces very good herbage, both for hay and pasturing of cattle, which thrive extremely well; the farmers, in general, have good stocks of black cattle, sheep, hogs and horses: the sheep, for the most part, produce double, and scarcely a disease is ever known amongst them.[10]

Meanwhile, in 1783 in Quebec, Governor Haldimand was prompted by the flood of refugee Loyalists to send surveyors west to lay out townships for settlement along the St. Lawrence River and later west of the Niagara River in what was to become the new province of Upper Canada.

The wife of the first lieutenant-governor of Upper Canada, Elizabeth Graves Simcoe, kept a diary, and records for us some of her culinary experiences:

> We dined in the Woods & eat part of a Raccoon, It was very fat & tasted like Lamb if eaten with Mint sauce.... His Excellency & suite eat Raccoons & Porcupines which were good the latter like pork.... The black Squirrel is large and quite black. It is as good to eat as a young Rabbit.... Wild Ducks from Lake Simcoe which were better than any I have ever tasted, these Birds are so much better than any in England from their feeding on wild Rice.

Mrs. Simcoe's diary contains scores of other references to foods found locally, including gooseberries, apples, dried apples, strawberries, raspberries, plums, wild grapes, whortleberries, watermelons, wild geese, turkey, partridge, wild pigeon, woodcock, snipe, elk, caribou, moose, venison, bear, pickerel, cod, eel, black bass, pike, herring, and rattlesnake, as well as imported foods such as shaddocks, a species of orange from the West Indies.[11]

> The Indians are particularly fond of fruit. We have 30 large May Duke Cherry trees behind the house & 3 standard Peach trees which supplied us last autumn for Tarts & Deserts during 6 weeks besides the numbers the young Men ate. My share was trifling compared to theirs & I ate 30 in a day. They were very small but high flavoured. When tired of eating them raw Mr Talbot roasted them & they were very good.[12]

In stark contrast she also describes the desperate decisions that travellers often had to make when confronted with the prospect of starvation. For instance, she noted how the lieutenant-governor and his party once started out on a five-day march to York with only two days' provisions.

> The Gov had recourse to a compass & at the close of the day they came on a Surveyor's line & the next morning saw

Lake Ontario. Its first appearance Coll Simcoe says was the most delightful sight at the time they were in danger of starving & about 3 miles from York they breakfasted on the remaining Provisions. Had they remained in the woods another day it was feared Jack Sharp would have been sacrificed to their hunger. He is a very fine Newfoundland Dog who belonged to Mr Shane.[13]

It was imperative to those settlers that they become self-sufficient as quickly as possible in order to survive the wildly fluctuating seasons in Upper Canada, the difficulty of transport, and the scarcity of ingredients and supplies. Following the example of the First Nations, the new arrivals turned to farming to ensure a steady food supply. Every family would have kept a cow or two to provide milk, butter, and cheese, and a few fowls. They would also have cleared and planted their fields, gardens, and orchards as quickly as possible to produce grain, fruit, and vegetables for their tables.

To carve cleared fields, orchards, and garden plots out of the virgin forests of Upper Canada was a Herculean task that demanded strength, skill, and courage. Using a sharp axe, the settler felled a stand of trees in the early summer and let the trunks lie where they fell until early fall when the area was set ablaze to eliminate the small branches, dried leaves, and underbrush. When the fire died down, he cut the remaining trunks into lengths and pulled them, using a yoke of oxen if he was fortunate enough to own one, into a heap where again they were set afire and reduced to a pile of potash that could be used for soap-making. The stumps were sometimes left, and the seeds sown among them, but more often the farmer used the yoke of oxen and a stump puller to remove the stumps and transport them to the perimeter where they could be piled on their sides in rows to form a fence. This was slow and difficult work, and it is believed that the average farmer cleared about three acres a year.[14]

Those who managed to make a farm out of the forest were justifiably proud. In 1794, Elizabeth Russell, half-sister of Peter Russell, the receiver general of Upper Canada, wrote to her friend Elizabeth Kiernan in England: "We are comfortably settled in our new House and have a nice little Farm about us. We eat our own Mutton and Pork and Poultry. Last year we grew our own Buck wheat Indian corn and have two Oxen got two cows with their calves with plenty of pigs and a mare and Sheep. We have not made Butter yet but hope to do so."[15]

Much of the fruit, such as cherries, plums, and grapes, for which the Niagara region became famous in later years, was native to the region. Peter Kalm, the first person to describe Niagara Falls in English from his personal observations, portrayed the bounty this way: "The wild grapevines grow quite plentiful in the woods. In all other parts of Canada they plant them in the gardens, near arbors and summer houses. The latter are made entirely of laths, over which the vines climb with tendrils and cover them entirely with foliage so as to shelter them entirely from the heat of the sun."[16]

As early as the seventeenth century, two Sulpician missionaries had described attempts to make wine from local fruit on the north shore of Lake Erie:

> I will tell you, by the way, that the vine grows here [near Port Dover, Patterson's Creek] only in sand, on the banks of lakes and rivers, but although it has no cultivation it does not fail to produce grapes in great quantities as large and as sweet as the finest of France. We even made wine of them, which M Dollier said holy mass all winter, and it was as good as *vin de Grave*. It is a heavy dark wine like the latter. Only red grapes are seen here, but in so great quantities, that we have found places where one could easily have made 25 or 30 hogheads of wine.[17]

The homes dotting the Upper Canada landscape ranged from humble shelters of canvas, bark, and boughs to well-constructed dwellings of wood, brick, or stone, with appendages such as summer kitchens, woodsheds, bake ovens, smokehouses, and driving sheds. It would not have mattered whether the home was large or small, or the family rich or poor. The kitchen, with its cooking fireplace of stone or brick, was the heart of the home in this period. A crane was built into the side of the fireplace, and from it hung the trammel, kettles, and cauldrons needed for cooking; for heating water for dishes, laundry, and bathing; for melting tallow for candles; and for a multitude of other tasks. Fortunate was the cook who had either a bake oven built into the side of the fireplace, or one outside,

Bread was not only an important addition to every meal, but was also used to thicken soups and stews, to make forcemeat, stuffing, puddings, and poultices, and to clean wallpaper.

close to the kitchen door. More often bake stones, bake pots, or earthenware ovens were pressed into service to make the daily scones, biscuits, bread, and puddings.

In these surroundings, with unlimited ingenuity and primitive handmade iron and tin utensils, such as long-handled forks, ladles, and skimmers, some extra cauldrons and pots of various sizes, a skillet, and a trivet, the womenfolk produced at least three meals daily and accomplished a round of domestic chores. A typical day would have started with lighting the fires by 5:00 or 6:00 a.m., preparing a family breakfast, clearing it away, and washing up. Sleeping areas would have then been tidied, the beds made, slops emptied, wood chopped and water fetched, rubbish and ashes disposed of, and a midday meal prepared, cooked, and on the table by noon. Once the meal was eaten, the dishes would have been cleared away, the washing-up done, utensils cleaned and polished, the kitchen put in order, candlesticks cleaned, other rooms dusted and cleaned (if needed), guests received and entertained, the evening meal prepared, eaten, cleaned away, dishes washed, and the kitchen tidied again. Depending on the day of the week, there might have been bread to knead and set to rise in the dough box beside the fireplace, clothes to make or mend, medicines to be mixed and administered, and letters to be written before bed.

Breakfast, the first meal of the day, broke the fast since tea or supper the day before. In a humble home, this meal could have been a plate of gruel or porridge and a cup of weak tea, and would have been eaten after the chores in the barns and outbuildings were finished. Breakfast would be taken at a later hour in middle- and upper-class homes, and could have included thinly sliced smoked bacon, fresh eggs from free-ranging fowl, poached smoked fish, freshly baked bread or rolls, butter, preserves, honey, and tea. The main meal of the day was dinner, taken at midday, and again the menu would vary dramatically with the economic and social circumstances of the family. One main dish, either soup, stew, or pudding, with bread and tea, could comprise the meal in a humble home. For the well-to-do, the meal could be both hearty and elaborate, consisting of soup, fish, joints of meat, vegetables, puddings (both sweet and savoury), fruit, and cheese.

The last meal of the day was variously called high tea, tea, or supper. It was served from 5:00 to 6:00 p.m. and included cold leftovers from the dinner at noon or simple fare such as biscuits, cheese, preserves, fruit, and confections.[18]

"Taking tea" was a favourite occupation in the tiny capital, as well as in the other communities in the colony, for it was an opportunity to combine a light meal in the late afternoon with good conversation and fellowship. Many times during her early residence in Newark (Niagara-on-the-Lake), Mrs. Simcoe wrote of having "taken tea" with her many friends. These occasions occurred in many locations, such as in the marquee (one of several canvas houses that Governor Simcoe bought in London, England, at the sale of the effects of Captain Cook, the explorer), in a very large bower composed of oak boughs, with the ladies of the Queen's Rangers, and at the officers' mess.[19]

As Newark grew and became a social centre as well as the political hub of the province, merchants imported and advertised teas, provisions, spirits, and tableware to serve the needs of those wishing to entertain. Rum, brandy, Geneva wine, English goods, green and Bohea tea, soup ladles, tablespoons and teaspoons, and sugar tongs were advertised in the *Upper Canada Gazette* at Newark during this period.[20] For those who did not have cash, merchants and mill owners such as Daniel Servos carried out a lively business in barter with families of the community. Customers exchanged butter, duck eggs, turnips, cabbages, peas, apples, and venison for imported provisions of coffee, salt, and sugar; Bohea, Hyson, and green teas; and spirits such as port wine and rum.[21]

It would have been at community and social events that many specially prepared dishes were served such as sweetmeats, cold tongue, chowder, pumpkin pie, mock turtle soup, and some very good cakes.[22]

CHAPTER SEVEN

"We Greatly Missed Our Tea"

O N THAT DECEMBER DAY IN 1773 WHEN a new shipment of tea arrived in Boston's harbour and a well-organized crowd, disguised as members of the First Nations, seized the ship and dumped 342 cases containing 90,000 pounds of tea into the water, the American Revolution became a reality. The Boston Tea Party, as it was dubbed, was not only an act of defiance against the British government, which had imposed a new tax on tea earlier in the year, but was also a symbol of the unhappiness that plagued all the colonies in British North America, from Quebec and Nova Scotia in the north to Virginia and Georgia in the south.

A bowl of tea was a favourite beverage at any time of the day, whether at breakfast, after dinner at noon, or with a light supper before bed. Tea combined mystery and myth, with its ancient beginnings in China in 2737 BC. It was described by Emperor Shen Nung as "good for tumors or abscesses that come about the head, or for ailments of the bladder. It dissipates heat caused by phlegms, or inflammation of the chest. It quenches thirst. It lessens the desire to sleep. It gladdens and cheers the heart."[1]

By the eighteenth century, tea had become England's national beverage and the country's subjects in the colonies were outraged with the new tax on their favourite drink and medicine. However, in 1783 and 1784, after the American Revolution ended, some fifty thousand men, women, and children remained loyal to Britain (despite the taxes and other grievances), and they streamed into the Canadian colonies to the north. The British authorities at Halifax and Quebec were suddenly faced with the monumental task of feeding, sheltering, and settling waves of refugees who

Tea was both a beverage and a medicine in colonial Canada, and this locked tea chest reflects the drink's value and importance. These chests were fitted with compartments for storing the imported teas and a bowl for blending the special mixtures.

in many cases far outnumbered the resident population. The United Empire Loyalists, as they were to become known, went on to change the face of the Canadian colonies, and their arrival led directly to the formation of the provinces of New Brunswick and Ontario.[2]

With the evacuation of New York City in 1783, the last British stronghold in the new United States of America, close to forty thousand refugees were transported to the British colonies of Newfoundland, Île Saint-Jean (later Prince Edward Island), Nova Scotia, and Quebec. For those on the ship, the voyage usually took from a week to a fortnight, depending on the weather and on whether the navigator took a "wrong tack." The army-style rations of bread or flour, salt beef and pork, butter, peas, and oatmeal were sufficient but dull, and no rum was issued. Many were sick and frightened for, of course, the greatest danger was shipwreck, particularly in the stormy Bay of Fundy. Surprisingly, only one disaster was reported. In September 1783, the *Martha* struck rocks off Sable Island near the entrance to the Bay of Fundy and "in the course of a few hours wrecked in a thousand pieces," with the loss of 115 men, women, and children. Some fifty survivors were rescued by fishing boats. Another six floated on a piece of wreckage for a couple of days, during which time two died of exposure. Eventually, the remaining four reached an island, where they lived for a week on "a few raspberries and snails" before they were found.[3]

Arrival was a mixed experience. Loyalist Sarah Frost recalled hers when the *Two Sisters* sailed into the harbour of Saint John, New Brunswick: "our people went on shore and brought on board spruce and gooseberries and grass and pea vines with the blossoms on them, all of which grow wild here." She added, as if in disbelief, "They say this is to be our city. Our land is five and twenty miles up the river."[4] Another Loyalist refugee shared her thoughts after landing: "I climbed to the top of Chapman's hill and watched sails disappearing in the distance, and such a feeling of loneliness came over me that, although I had not shed a single tear through all the war, I sat down on the damp moss with my baby in my lap and cried." That lady became the grandmother of Sir Leonard Tilley, New Brunswick's Father of Confederation.[5]

The Fall Fleet from New York City brought officers and men and their families, who proceeded to temporary locations where they lived in tents under deplorable conditions. Some of the group continued on immediately to build themselves shelter more substantial than a tent. One of these was Sergeant Benjamin Ingraham, whose eleven-year-old daughter, Hannah, recalled the day they moved into their new house:

> One morning we waked to find the snow laying deep on the ground around us, and then father came walking through it and told us the house was ready and not to stop to light the fire then, and not to mind the weather, but follow his tracks through the trees, for the trees were so many we soon lost sight of him going up the hill; it was snowing fast, and oh, so cold. Father carried a chest and we all carried something and followed him up the hill through the trees.
>
> It was not long before we heard him pounding, and oh, what a joy to see our gable end.
>
> There was no floor laid, no window, no chimney, no door, but we had a roof at last.

A good fire was burning on the hearth, and mother had a big loaf of bread with us, and she boiled a kettle of water and put a good piece of butter in a pewter bowl, and we toasted our bread and all sat round the bowl to eat our breakfast that morning and mother said, "Thank God, we are no longer in dread of having shots fired through the house. This is the sweetest meal I have tasted for many a day."[6]

The Ingrahams soon had a door, a floor, a window, and a chimney, and were as snug as they could have hoped for under the circumstances. Others were less fortunate, particularly those such as Mary Fisher and her family who, for one reason or another, had failed to erect some sort of rude shelter or cabin and continued to live in the tents. The Fishers, along with thousands of others, had landed at St. Ann's (later Fredericton). This enormous influx led to the division of Nova Scotia, and in June 1784 the colony of New Brunswick was created. As Mary describes it:

We pitched our tents in the shelter of the woods and tried to cover them with spruce boughs. We used stones for fireplaces. Our tents had no floor but the ground. The winter was very cold, with deep snow, which we tried to keep from drifting in by putting a large rug at the door. The snow, which lay six feet deep around us, helped greatly in keeping out the cold. How we lived through that awful winter I hardly know. There were mothers that had been reared in a pleasant country enjoying all of the comforts of life, with helpless children in their arms. They clasped their infants to their bosoms and tried by the warmth of their own bodies to protect them from the bitter cold. Sometimes a part of the family had to remain up during the night to keep the fires burning, so as to keep the rest from freezing. Some destitute people made use of boards, which the older ones kept heating before the fire and applied by turns to the smaller children to keep them warm.[7]

Death by freezing and exposure was not the only threat that confronted the Loyalists. The danger of starving to death was every bit as real. True, they were entitled to government rations. The daily ration per person was a pound of flour, half a pound of beef, and an "infinitesimal quantity of butter." In addition, each received per week a pound of oatmeal and one of peas, and occasionally a little rice. Children under ten were entitled to half the amount. Such a ration, while not exactly luxurious, would certainly keep a person alive; the problem was they did not always get it. There were all sorts of difficulties involved in the distribution of these provisions, which had to come all the way from Britain — troubles created by logistics, supply, graft, and bureaucracy.

Needless to say, the Loyalists were often hungry, even on the verge of starvation, during the winter of 1783–84. In desperation the men made long trips on snowshoes and hauled supplies back on hand sleds or toboggans from distant warehouses. They fished through holes in the ice; they hunted moose and deer. Even so, many did not survive until spring.[8]

Spring finally came and with it relief from the interminable cold, but not from hunger. "A full supply of provisions was looked for in the spring," Mary Fisher recalled,

> but the people were betrayed by those they depended on to supply them. All the settlers were reduced to great straits and had to live after the Indian fashion. The men caught fish, hunted moose and shot pigeons; they ate fiddleheads, grapes and other wild plants. Some ate weeds, which proved to be poisonous, and several died as a result. In the spring we made maple sugar. Men started to clear land but had to desist from hunger. Others had to dig up the potatoes they had planted and eat them. It was a bleak period, but eventually a schooner arrived with cornmeal and rye. The winter was over — most of the refugees had survived, but a substantial number lay in their graves on the riverbank.[9]

Despite the challenges, there were some happy accounts in Mary Fisher's narrative, and these included the discovery of some large patches of pure white beans, marked with a black cross. These had probably been originally planted by the French, but were now growing wild. The Loyalists called them "Royal Provincials' bread," and later "the staff of life and hope of the starving." Mary also reports that "The first store was kept by a man named Cairnes. He sold fish at one penny each and butternuts at two for a penny. He also sold tea at $2.00 per lb. which was to us a great boon. We greatly missed our tea. Sometimes we used an article called Labrador, and sometimes steeped spruce or hemlock bark for drinking, but I despised it."[10]

Meanwhile, on Île Saint-Jean the new arrivals fared slightly better. William Schurman, his wife, Elizabeth Hyat, and their family of five boys (ages two to thirteen) were able to set up storekeeping in a log cabin room in Central Bedeque near Summerside. From his account books, George Leard, writing in the *Loyalist Gazette*, tells us that:

> Food purchases were a small item and it would appear that the most important were tea and pepper. These are in almost every account. Flour was bought from the miller, or ground in some poor way at home. Salt, so important in diet and food preservation, must have been obtained from schooners landing it for the fishermen, because it does not appear in the accounts till 1795, when it sold at eighty cents a bushel. Sugar was not charged till 1794, when it was twenty cents a pound. This was likely West Indian brown. Maple sugar was the staple sweetener up till that time, supplemented of course with molasses, which sold at eighty cents a gallon in 1787.
>
> Tea, the most popular beverage, sold for ninety cents in the cheaper quality called Bohea with Shoushand tea selling in 1795, at two dollars the pound. Coffee is not mentioned except in the first year, when it sold very reasonably for thirty cents a pound. Nutmegs at ten cents a piece, and a stick of cinnamon for twenty cents, made spices luxuries in the earliest accounts. However, by 1800, ginger and allspice were sixty cents a pound and pepper seventy.
>
> Schurman took butter on account from Bedeque women and gave a shilling, a pound, no more, no less,

for practically the whole time he was in business, from 1784 to 1819. It was good value sometimes, yet during the war years, 1812–1814, when it took ten to twelve pounds of butter to buy a pound of tea, it must have seemed like a starvation price. In the meat department which was a barrel of pickle at the back of the shop, beef seldom varied in price at ten cents a pound, with pork two to four cents dearer, and lamb and veal between eight and nine cents.[11]

In Upper Canada (later Canada West, and eventually Ontario), the experience was again slightly different for the seven thousand Loyalists and their First Nations allies who had walked from Vermont, western New York, and Pennsylvania and settled on the north shore of the St. Lawrence River. The Loyalists were without food, clothing, shelter, and land. They were moved by bateaux (long, flat-bottomed cargo and passenger boats crewed by six men and holding two tons of goods) from Quebec up the St. Lawrence to fourteen newly surveyed townships and settled by religious and military groups on land drawn by lot.

Archives of Ontario

An encampment of the United Empire Loyalists at Johnstown (later Cornwall), a new settlement on the banks of the St. Lawrence River, June 6, 1784. From this base camp the soldiers and families of the King's Royal Regiment of New York moved to their new land along the river.

To the west of them, along the west bank of the Niagara River, Butler's Rangers under Colonel John Butler had been building houses and sowing crops since 1780, and in 1782 sixteen farmers with their families had cleared 236 acres of land. Peter Secord produced two hundred bushels of corn, fifteen of wheat, seventy of potatoes, and four of oats on twenty-four acres; John Depue grew two hundred bushels of corn and fifty of potatoes on sixteen acres; and Michael Showers produced forty bushels of corn, six of oats, and fifteen of potatoes on twelve acres. The Rangers prepared the Government Farm for planting Indian corn. In 1784 they had established Butlersburg, later Newark, and eventually Niagara-on-the-Lake.[12]

There were success stories. William Jarvis, a Loyalist militia officer later appointed secretary and registrar of Upper Canada, writes to his father-in-law, the Reverend Samuel Peters, on November 22, 1793:

> I shall leave my family well provided for. I have a yoke of fatted oxen to come down, 12 small shoats to put into a barrel occasionally which I expect will weigh in from 40 to 60 lbs., about 60 head of dung-hill fowl, 16 fine turkeys, and a doz. ducks, 2 breeding sows, a milch cow which had a calf in August, which of course will be able to afford her mistress a good supply of milk through the winter. In the root house I have 400 good head of cabbage, and about 60 bushels of potatoes and a sufficiency of excellent turnips.
>
> My cellar is stored with 3 barrels of wine, 2 of cider, 2 of apples (for my darling), and a good stock of butter. My cock-loft contains some of the finest maple sugar I ever beheld, 10,000 lbs. was made in an Indian village near Michellemackinac. We have 150 lb. of it. It was my intention to send you a small keg of it, but I was taken ill. Also plenty of good flour, cheese, coffee, loaf sugar, etc. In my stable I shall have the ponies and a good slay; the snugest and warmest cottage in the province. Thus you see I shall have the best of companions abundantly supplied with every comfort in the wilderness, where few have an idea only of lonely existing. In fact I am early

provided with every requisite for a long and severe winter which is close on our heels.[13]

The St. Lawrence settlers arrived too late to plant crops in 1784 and had to appeal to the government for extra supplies to see them through the first year. In 1787, just as they began to become established, they suffered crop failures and threats of famine as the Crown rations were ending. Leeks, buds of trees, and leaves were ground up to eat, and 1788 became known as the "hungry year" because of the shortage of food. One of the Loyalists reported:

> While many difficulties were encountered in the early settlement, yet we realized many advantages. We were always supplied with venison; deer was plentiful, partridge and pigeons in abundance, plenty of fish for all who wished to catch them, no taxes to pay, and an abundance of wood at our doors. Although deprived of many kinds of fruit, we obtained the natural productions of the country — strawberries, raspberries, gooseberries, blackberries and plenty of red plums. Cranberries were found in abundance in marshes. The only animal we brought with us was a dog named Tipler that proved almost invaluable in hunting.
>
> After the first year, we raised a supply of Indian corn; but had no mill to grind it, and were, therefore, compelled to pound it in a large mortar, manufacturing what we call "Samp," which was made into Indian bread, called by the Dutch, "Suppawn." The mortar was constructed in the following manner: We cut a log from a large tree, say two and a half feet in diameter and six feet in length, planted firmly in the ground, so that about two feet projected above the surface; then carefully burned the centre of the top, so as to form a considerable cavity, which was then scraped clean. We generally selected an ironwood tree, about six inches in diameter, to form a pestle. Although this simple contrivance did well enough for corn, it did not answer for grinding wheat. The Government, seeing the difficulty,

built a mill back of Kingston, where inhabitants for seven
miles below Brockville got their grinding done.[14]

Merchants like Richard Cartwright in Kingston and Robert
Hamilton in Niagara, who had been supplying the fur traders and the
military, began selling food, clothing, housewares, and rum to the
Loyalists and taking wheat, corn, potash, and pork in return. By 1787
the 300 residents of Marysburgh were raising 219 pigs — their faith was
in salt pork and in trade! It was this very Great Lakes trading system that
gave rapid rise to the development of many of the communities in Upper
Canada, swelled by new arrivals from the Maritimes, the new United
States, and Europe, especially Britain.

Upper Canada had another influx of Loyalists when, in the 1790s, New
Brunswick was becoming crowded. Many moved their families again up the
St. Lawrence, through Lakes Ontario and Erie, to the Long Point country.
They, too, had to get rid of the great forests of beech, maple, white and yellow pine, and walnut to clear fields for crops. One settler describes the daily
round as "working from dawn to dark and then walking 3 miles to the river,
catching fish by the light of the 'fire jacks,' using the bone of a pike as a
hook." The fish, buds and leaves of trees, and milk from one cow brought
from New Brunswick kept the family alive until August when a little crop
of spring wheat headed out sufficiently to allow a change of diet. The Long
Point settlers were not eligible for three years of rations, because this migration was their second, so they all suffered hardships.

All kinds of edible items were consumed — pigweed, lamb's quarters,
groundnut, and the plant called Indian cabbage. The bark of certain trees
was cut in pieces and boiled, as were also the leaves and buds of the maple,
beech, and basswood. Occasionally, a deer was shot and divided among the
members of the rejoicing community. Frequently, also, great flocks of wild
turkeys were seen in the marshy lands, and it did not require an expert shot
to bring down the unsuspecting birds. Fish were also easily caught so that
as soon as the first year or two had passed the settlers had abundance for
themselves and for many strangers "within their gates." Tea was a luxury for
many years, with hemlock and sassafras used as substitutes. As historian
L.H. Tasker has written:

Still, a rude plenty existed. As to meat, the creeks and lake supplied fish of several kinds — black and rock bass, perch, carp, mackerel, pickerel, pike, and white fish, and above all speckled trout; the marshes — wild fowl, turkeys, ducks and geese; the woods — pigeons, partridge, quail, squirrels, rabbits, hares and deer. As to other animals in the woods, there were many (too many) wolves, bears, lynx, wild cats, beavers, foxes, martins, minks and weasels. Bastards and cranes also were found by the streams. As to grain, they soon had an abundant supply of Indian corn, wheat, peas, barley, oats, wild rice, and the commoner vegetables.

The ingenious housewives of those times tried to make up for the various articles of food, which they could not produce by the invention of new dishes, and to make the ordinary *menu* as palatable as possible by some change or addition. One of the most appreciated of the "delicacies" was the pumpkin loaf, which consisted of corn meal and boiled pumpkin made into a cake and eaten hot with butter. It was generally sweetened with maple sugar.

Another "Dutch dish" was "pot-pie," which consisted of game or fowl cut up into small pieces and baked in a deep dish, with a heavy crust over the meat. On such fare were developed the brawn and muscle, which in a few years changed the wilderness into a veritable Garden of Eden.[15]

From these tentative and uncertain beginnings, the United Empire Loyalists became the founding families in many communities in eastern and central Canada, for they were not just travelling through looking for a better place to settle or to make their fortune. They came from a farming tradition and wanted to be farmers again in their new homes.

Food traditions of the eighteenth and early nineteenth centuries have stayed surprisingly constant among the Loyalist descendants. The beehive ovens, cauldrons, danglespits, and butter churns have been replaced by modern equipment, but the traditional foods of their ancestors are still enjoyed, particularly on special occasions. Hearty soups and stews, pancakes, roasts of beef and pork, well-known root vegetables such as potatoes, carrots, turnips, and onions, pots of baked beans, cakes, cookies, puddings of bread, rice, custard, dried fruit, and oatmeal, and fresh fruit pies grace their tables in various combinations and on the pages of community cookbooks.

When the Loyalist Bicentennial was celebrated in 1984, many communities sponsored contests and special events to highlight their favourite foods. Recipe books were published, and newspapers ran special food columns about Lobster Cake, Hare Soup, Brown Bread Ice Cream, Fish Stew, and Spice Cake with Boiled Icing.[16] Several Maritime communities marked the Loyalist landing with pancake breakfasts and country suppers that featured baked beans, scalloped potatoes, homemade bread, and desserts, all washed down with lashings of tea made with the little leaf that helped to spark a revolution. Tea has become one of the most popular beverages, not only in Canada, but around the world.

CHAPTER EIGHT

Victorians at Table: I Looked Forward to Every Meal

W HEN QUEEN VICTORIA CAME TO THE THRONE in 1837, Canada was still an emerging nation, with Upper and Lower Canada on the brink of rebellion against the government of the day. There were a few cities — Quebec, Montreal, Halifax, Saint John, and the newly minted Toronto (formerly the Town of York). The villages and towns were strung out in a long line from Gaspé to Lake Huron, often with the forest at their backs. It was a time of uncontrolled emigration, often on crowded, disease-ridden ships as thousands of people were dumped into the ports of Halifax and Quebec City. The new arrivals were often forced to depend on the charity of the inhabitants until they could establish themselves or find transport farther inland where they could seek employment on a farm, in a lumber camp, or on a construction gang that was building a new canal or a short railway line.

Eating on the move for the newcomers was often a challenge, as we learn from the accounts of those who experienced it. The quality of food and service at the inns and taverns varied widely, even within a few miles, something John Howison, travelling in the Kingston area, found in the nineteenth century: "Most of the taverns in Upper Canada are indeed a burlesque upon what they profess to be. A tolerable meal can scarcely be produced at any one of them; nay, I have visited several which are not even provided with bread." But compare this to what he found a short distance away: "After waiting a quarter of an hour, we were conducted into the second room, and there found a table amply furnished with tea, beefsteaks, cucumbers, potatoes, honey, onions, eggs, etc. During this delectable repast, we were attended by the hostess, who poured out tea as often as we required it, and having done so, seated herself in the door-way, and read a book."[1]

Despite the uncertainty of their food, beverages, and service, the inns and taverns were a welcome port in the storm along the transportation routes. Before the arrival of the railways in the 1850s, there was a tavern roughly every mile or two along the major roads in what was to become Southern Ontario, and a Nova Scotia travel guide listed twenty-nine on the busy route between Halifax and Digby.[2]

Unfortunately, many of the inns and taverns became notorious for brawling and drunkenness in their barrooms, and even outside their premises, fuelling the temperance movement and the opening of temperance hotels. Travellers headed for the temperance hotels lured by advertisements such as the one that appeared in the *Cobourg Star* on August 31, 1859:

ST. LAWRENCE TEMPERANCE hotel
Corner of Division and James Streets, Cobourg.

The above hotel, lately opened for the reception of the public in the building known as McConnell's block, is pleasantly situated near the centre of business. As the proprietors are determined to make it a First Class House, no expense will be spared to make it comfortable, and every attention will be paid to the wants of their guests. A variety of temperance drinks always on hand. Warm meals or luncheons and suppers at all reasonable hours. The stable accommodation is the largest in town, the stable being 1200 foot in length. An attentive ostler in attendance.

The temperance movement, the temperance hotels, and "those damned cold water drinking societies," as Colonel Thomas Talbot condemned them, may now have faded from memory, but the tangible evidence of their existence lives on in Canadian hotels and restaurants where pitchers or glasses of water are served at your table even as you are being seated.

By the middle of the nineteenth century in larger centres such as Halifax, Quebec City, Montreal, Toronto, Kingston, and even Cobourg, new hotels were opening to serve a more elite and sophisticated clientele. Unfortunately, few of the early-nineteenth-century bills of fare have survived, for in many hotels, whether temperance or not, everyone was served the same food. There were fixed times for meals, rich in fat and sugar, with breakfast at 7:30 a.m. with "beef-stake, fried pork and buckwheat cakes"; dinner at one with roast of beef or pork, wild game or fowl, vegetables and pudding; supper at 7:00 p.m. was a lighter meal often made of leftovers from dinner at noon. All three meals were washed down with strong lashings of tea.[3]

Thomas Montgomery's Inn, Toronto

The cooking fireplace in the Victorian home, hotel, or inn remained popular long after stoves became available.

It was a land in transition as the colonies swelled in population. New Brunswick was building dozens of ships every year, Nova Scotians were to be found on every ocean. Inland, the trees were falling fast, and new fields, new villages, new towns were appearing. Everywhere there was vigorous local life. Every colony wished progressive reform; none wanted change in allegiance. Confederation was the solution the politicians explored at their now-famous meetings in the shady village of Charlottetown (population seven thousand) in September 1864. We learn from the newspapers of the day — *Ross's Weekly* or the *Protestant* — that it was not all dry speeches, debates, and compromises, and this notion is confirmed by Harry Bruce in *Canada 1812–1871: The Formative Years.*

Yes, those same stiff-necked characters in the famous group portrait … those fellows with the mutton-chop whiskers and the dark, heavy, discreet narrow-legged woollen suits … with their cheeks full of potatoes and their apparently glum, Victorian, Sunday-morning faces … those same men, the whole rollicking bunch of them, they stayed up all through the night of September 7–8, 1864, at the Grand Ball at Province House in Charlottetown.

They arrived at 10, and they danced the local women around the hall, and they boozed it up, and they made florid speeches, and they didn't even start to eat till one in the morning. Then, somewhere around 5 a.m., they all made their way down through the warm island fog to the harbour and climbed aboard the steamship *Queen Victoria* for a trip to Nova Scotia.

There they would continue their "deliberations." They were founding a nation, and all through that astonishing, euphoric and frequently comic summer and autumn of 1864 they were proving that man does not found nations on bread alone.[4]

By 1865, Saint John's *Weekly Telegraph* was crudely describing the historic Charlottetown and Quebec conferences as "the great intercolonial drunk of last year." The *Perth Courier* referred to Confederation as "the measure of the Quebec ball-room and the oyster-supper statesmen," and even while the Quebec Conference was still underway, the *Berliner Journal* was so bold as to suggest that, no matter what the delegates did on their forthcoming trip to Canada West, they could not possibly expect any worse hangovers than they had already acquired.[5] Hangovers aside, it is obvious there was far more warmth, passion, intemperance, and colour to the founding of Canada than one would expect from this Victorian colony.

Meanwhile, the floods of newcomers to Canada continued as letters "home" from those already established praised its opportunities. As the century progressed, what was really happening on the dinner tables of the nation?

The 1877 *Home Cook Book* gave suggestions to those needing guidance — and who had the means to make or produce the ingredients and the time to prepare the dishes. Under bills of fare were included menus for three breakfasts, two lunch parties, two dinners, two teas, and two suppers, as well as four alternatives on how to vary cold lunches for washing days, or other days of extra labour. There is also an economical dinner recommendation for every day of the week.

There must have been scores of housewives in Victorian Canada like Anna Leveridge, who in 1883 brought her seven children from England to make a home with her husband, David, in the backwoods of Hastings County, Ontario, where he had found work in a lumber camp. Her letters home describe the joys and hardships of her everyday life and confirm how little help the publications of the day with their bills of fare would have been to Anna or many of her contemporaries:

> The shanty cost quite a bit to build, about 40 dollars, and it cost us quite a bit to move up here, so that we are got pretty bare again....
>
> I should feel lonely indeed if it were not for my neighbours.... I go in now and then and get a good dinner or tea, which is all the same, for they eat meat and potatoes three times a day. They killed three fat pigs a little time ago. Then they pack it in salt in large barrels and it lasts them till they hunt deer. Then they live on them. I tried to get some meat of them, but they will not part with any, so we have to live as we can. We don't get very fat.[6]

Anna and David walked to church, a journey of four and a half miles, accompanied by one son, Arthur. Edward, another son, had grown out of his boots, and "they could not get him any more yet, until they were out of debt." She went on to say "The children all round go barefoot all the summer, and most of the women too, Mrs. Foster and Mrs. Hewton and all other Canadians."

There were some good meals, for on that occasion she tells us: "We had a famous dinner, to which I did ample justice, my walk having made me ravenous ... stewed chicken, mashed potatoes, and custard pie, i.e., custard flavoured with ess [essence of] lemon on a short crust, on soup plates, and the whites beaten up and put on the top." On Christmas Day, Anna's neighbour, Mrs. Tivy, sent "a large piece of pork, nearly a qr. [quarter] of a pig."[7]

For those living in the growing towns and cities, Christmas was the time for festive meals and entertaining. Merchants' shelves and counters would have been loaded with spices, lemons, oranges, English cheese, dried fruit, nuts, and other exotic imported items. Local Christmas markets, such as the one in Saint John, New Brunswick, advertised "500 turkeys, geese, etc., all fine looking birds, many with labels. One magnificent turkey carcass weighing 23 pounds is christened the 'Beaconsfield,' the 'Marquis of Lorne' rolls up 20 pounds, and 'Sir John A Macdonald' 18½ pounds."[8]

Christmas Eve, often called the Holy Eve, brought French Canadians first to worship and then to their homes for special services, singing, and symbolic foods in the hours after midnight. This was, and still is, a time of reunions, with midnight mass followed by a Reveillon, with pastries, wine, and other delicacies such as *tourtière*, the centrepiece of the feast. Other favourite foods included head cheese, green-tomato relish, and potato candy at this celebration in Quebec and everywhere else the French had settled.

For Canadians of British ancestry, the traditional Christmas feast was held on December 25 and included roast turkey or goose, seasonal vegetables, and rich desserts such as mince pie and plum pudding, all old favourites and sure to please the gathering. This menu appears to have survived for over two centuries, as Canadians who kept diaries confirm, for in 1800, Joseph Willcocks, a resident of York (Toronto), describes Christmas Day in his diary: "Went to Church. Weekes dined with us. We had for dinner, soup, roast beef, boiled pork, Turkey, Plumb Pudding and minced pies."

The Galt Cook Book, published in Toronto in 1898, recommended a similar menu with several additions:

BILL OF FARE FOR CHRISTMAS DINNER
Oyster Soup

Roast Turkey   Cranberry Sauce

Mashed and Browned Potatoes

Onions in Cream Sauce   Tomatoes

Chicken Pie   Rice Croquettes

Plum Pudding   Foaming Sauce

Mince Pies Lemon Tarts
Salted Almonds Celery
Crackers Cheese
Fruit Coffee[9]

F.J. Shipman, the proprietor of the Seldon House in Owen Sound, Ontario, offered an appealing menu for Christmas in 1891.[10] The nineteen-course meal consisted of Blue Points on the half shell, soup, fish, pickles and relishes, beef, duck, young turkey, wild turkey, English partridge, black bear, English hare, venison, vegetables, English plum pudding, assorted cakes, kisses, bon-bons, fruit, cheese, nuts, green or black tea, coffee, port, and sherry. This menu, like so many others, was printed in both English and French, no doubt to persuade the guests there was a French chef in charge of the kitchen!

As well as serving local residents on those special occasions such as Christmas, local hotels hosted the growing number of fraternal and benevolent organizations and the dinners and banquets they sponsored.

The Victorians loved picnics, either indoors or outdoors, with the ladies supplying a bountiful collation of hams, fowls, meat pies, tarts, and cakes, while the gentlemen were expected to provide music and games, carry baskets, and if outdoors, pick flowers, climb trees to free kites, bait fish hooks, and offer any other services required.

Fortunately, travellers in the last half of the nineteenth century left first-hand accounts of meals at many hotels. The scholarly Englishman, George Tuthill Borrett, staying at Montreal's St. Lawrence Hall in 1864, discovered that the way to impress a waiter was to pretend to order almost everything — even if you didn't want it. Here is his description of his first breakfast:

> I found myself in about two minutes surrounded by a multitude of little oval dishes, on which were fish, steaks, chops, ham, chicken, turkey, rissoles, potatoes (boiled, roast and fried), cabbage, corn, cheese, onions and pickles, besides plates of hot rolls, buns, crumpets, toast and biscuits, flanked by a great jug full of milk and an enormous vessel of coffee. However, in the midst of my bewilderment, which seemed to puzzle the waiter, who had taken my order as a thing of every day occurrence, my friend the banker turned up, and with his help I succeeded in demolishing a considerable portion of the formidable array of dishes.[11]

As the Victorian period drew to a close, Canadian food traditions were a study in contrasts. Hotel dining rooms and newly opened restaurants were expanding their services in larger cities and attempting to entice ladies to patronize the establishments.

The impressive Terrapin Restaurants were opened in the Crystal Block, Notre Dame Street, Montreal, and at 89 King Street East, Toronto, and in 1863 the bill of fare covered thirty pages, with an equal number of pages of advertisements in both cities.

TERRAPIN RESTAURANT
Crystal Block, Notre Dame Street, Montreal,
AND
No. 89 KING STREET, EAST, TORONTO.
THE MOST ELEGANT, SPACIOUS &
COMFORTABLE ESTABLISHMENTS IN CANADA

LADIES' AND GENTLEMEN'S ORDINARY
DAILY FROM 12 TO 3 O'CLOCK, P.M.
BREAKFAST 8 TO 10 A.M.
SUPPER 6 TO 8 P.M.
Full Board, $4.00 per Week.
Dinner, $2.00 per Week.
LADIES' ICE CREAM & REFRESHMENT
SALOON.
The Proprietors have fitted up the Upper Part of
the Building adjoining their Restaurant, having a
private entrance from Notre Dame Street, in the most
sumptuous and costly manner for the accommodation
of Ladies and Families, as an ICE CREAM and
REFRESHMENT SALOON — where can be
procured all delicacies of the Season.
DISHES OF GAME, &C.
Boned Turkey, Jellied Hams, Tongues and Game,
Chicken and Lobster Salads, Oysters, &c., furnished to
Families and Parties in the City, or sent to the country
at the shortest Notice.
ICE CREAM AND JELLIES
HAVANA CIGARS
Of the finest brands, direct from the Importers, for sale
by the Thousands, Box or in smaller lots.
MEERSCHAUM PIPES, CIGAR HOLDERS,
AND FANCY GOODS
IN GREAT VARIETY.
CARLISLE & McCONKEY,
PROPRIETORS.[12]

As the Victorian period drew to a close with Queen Victoria's death in
1901, we have a description of meal preparation by our fellow Canadians
in the Arctic written by a visitor:

The preparation for dinner, as I watched them on blizzardy
days when we did not fish, started soon after the eleven

o'clock lunch. Two women would go out together, one climbing up on the platform to select fish for the meal, the other standing below it with a whip to keep the dogs at a respectful distance from the food. The fish chosen were those judged fattest, for these were preferred to others where the desired fat had to be supplied from our store of white whale oil.

At home the fish were rolled out gently over the floor planking. They were hard as glass and required the same care against breakage. After an hour or so on the floor, when the fish were soft enough to indent slightly when the women pinched them, the heads and tails were cut off and placed as tidbits in a pot for the children's dinner, which was earlier than ours. The rest of the fish was cut into three- or four-inch segments and the entrails removed and set aside for the dogs. Since the river was convenient to our house, water was fetched and enough poured into each pot to cover the fish segments. The pots came to a boil slowly. At the very first bubbling, they were removed from the fire and set aside to cool.... With our fish at Tuktoyaktuk there were standard preferences, for example, species of fish, part of the fish, fatness. The women went through a friendly and complicated process in selecting pieces for each diner's taste. In the family they were familiar with the preferences of all of us; with visitors they inquired solicitously. When the piece had been selected, the server would squeeze it so that nothing would later drip from it, for we ate without plates, picnic fashion, and sat on a bed platform covered with fur bedding that must not get damp under any circumstances.

The extreme heat produced by the cooking began to decrease while we had dinner. In two hours or so it would be something like 70° F. at our shoulder level as we sat listening to stories, singing songs, or conversing.... As we had our nine o'clock supper of cold fish leftovers, the warmth remained constant. We then went to bed and slept naked…. By the end of January, 1907, I was convinced that I was healthier on the Stone Age regimen than I had ever before been on any diet or in any way of life…. I was looking forward to every meal.[13]

The Victorian period lives on in the memories of many Canadians as a time of prosperity, opulence, and gracious living. While that may have been true for some families, many others were still very much the pioneers, struggling to survive and prosper, to improve their everyday lives and the quality and quantity of food and beverages on their dinner tables.

CHAPTER NINE

Rupert's Land Became the Breadbasket of the World

WHEN CHARLES II GRANTED THE COVETED AND exclusive trading rights for all the lands draining into Hudson Bay in 1670, no one knew the extent of the territory involved. For almost two centuries, until 1869 when the new dominion government purchased Rupert's Land for £300,000, that still remained largely a mystery. During that period, both the Hudson's Bay and North West Companies exported hundreds of thousands of pelts and left behind mountains of trade goods, while explorers, adventurers, and cartographers attempted to plot the size and shape of the land and water that blocked their way to the Western Sea, and thence to China.

The fur-trading posts often developed farms and gardens to augment the staple diet of pemmican as Alexander Henry explains in his book *New Light on the Early History of the Greater Northwest*:

> The amount of flesh or fish required to provision even a small trading post was staggering. In one winter at Alexander Henry the Younger's Pembina [Manitoba] post, seventeen men, ten women, and fourteen children "destroyed" to use Henry's own phrase, 63,000 pounds of buffalo meat, 1,150 fish of different kinds, some miscellaneous game, and 325 bushels of vegetables from the garden. It added up to about a ton of meat and fish for every man woman and child in Pembina.[1]

Small communities grew up around trading posts like Pembina. The residents were guides, canoe men, *coureurs de bois*, clerks, and traders, many of whom married Native women. Their resulting families, called Métis, combined the best of the French, Scottish, and other European traditions of their fathers with the food traditions of their Native mothers — all the cultures mingled freely over their cooking fires.

Into the midst of the fur traders, the earl of Selkirk arrived on the Red River in 1812 with the first group of agricultural settlers, Scots who had lost everything in the Highland Clearances. Selkirk brought with him a concession of forty-five million fertile acres in the Red River Valley of present-day Manitoba, North Dakota, and Minnesota. Miles Macdonnell, governor of the Red River Settlement, issued a proclamation on January 8, 1814, forbidding the export from the colony of pemmican and other dried provisions (jerky and pounded meat).[2] This edict was a blow to both of the fur-trading companies and led to the conflicts known as the Pemmican Wars. The North West Company lost, for without this irreplaceable commodity to use on their long canoe trips to the interior and as a staple food for the First Nations over the winter, the trade was crippled and many historians believe this led to the demise of the North West Company and its union with the Hudson's Bay Company in 1821.

The newcomers who accompanied Selkirk brought their own traditional Scottish food, like Black Bun, Haggis, Honey Cakes, and Buttery Rowies. Unfortunately, the rigours of homesteading and the lack of ingredients forced them to put aside their culinary traditions temporarily. The river was the centre of the colony, and farms were allotted in strips of land fronting on the river, for ease of transportation and irrigation. The main settlements were Pembina, Upper and Lower Fort Garry, Point Douglas, Selkirk, Kildonan, St. Boniface, and the growing town of Winnipeg. The new arrivals quickly learned from their Métis neighbours how to survive by organizing buffalo hunts in the spring and fall, not only for the meat but also for the robes that could be made from the hides.

By the middle of the nineteenth century, signs of change were in the air. Civilization was encroaching, and steamships were beginning to appear more frequently on the waterways. The age of the canoe and Red River cart was soon to be supplemented by the construction of the railway. The Canadian Pacific Railway (CPR), completed in 1885, brought westward immigrants who were to change forever this untamed expanse of isolated trading posts and scattered communities.

The food traditions of what were to become the provinces of Manitoba, Saskatchewan, and Alberta were about to be influenced by successive waves of people from every walk of life and every corner of the globe. Despite their diverse backgrounds, they shared a common bond. They were all searching for the fertile soil that would ensure secure futures for their families.

With the construction and opening of the CPR, both the government and the railway (with millions of acres adjacent to its track) began intensive advertising in the United States and overseas to lure families as homesteaders to the forests, tundra, and prairies. How could anyone resist such superlatives as those expressed in the *Manitobian*, which were used to describe the agricultural potential of the new province?

> Whatever exaggeration there may have been with reference to other matters, there never could have been any with reference to the fertility of the soil. The land of Manitoba is probably so rich and fertile as could be found in this wide world. Wheat ripens there in 90 days and 50 bushels to the acre have been realized from the virgin soil…. A visit to the garden of a new settler had shown a crop of 1,000 bushels of fine potatoes, peas, parsley, onions, leeks, cucumbers, radishes and other vegetables, growing most luxuriantly. A bed of sunflowers had attained a height of 11 feet, and there were excellent strawberries, raspberries, huckleberries, and gooseberries.

As well as the First Nations, the Métis, and the Red River (Scottish) settlers, new arrivals from French Canada and Ontario were soon flooding into what in 1870 was to become the new province of Manitoba, It was soon to become a cultural crossroads as British, Icelandic, German, Chinese, American, Ukrainian, Polish, Belgian, Swedish, Norwegian, Italian, Greek, Danish, Dutch, Czech, and Slovak, as well as Mennonite and Jewish settlers, each claimed 160 acres for a $10 filing fee.[3]

In the late nineteenth and early twentieth centuries, newspaper advertisements, brochures, booklets, and broadsides were circulated to lure settlers, merchants, and businesses to western Canada.

Archives of Manitoba

The government built Immigration Halls in centres such as Winnipeg, Edmonton, and Prince Albert and supplied thousands of meals every month to newcomers. The food was simple but nourishing, with soups, stews, bread, and biscuits the basis of their fare. More than a million settlers arrived between 1895 and 1910 and travelled as far as they could by rail and then completed the journey on a wagon pulled by oxen or on foot. As they made the long trek across the prairies to their newly acquired homesteads, they stopped at the isolated homes along the way for food and shelter, and so the tradition of western hospitality was born. The first home of the newcomers was often a one-room sod or log shanty. The cookstove was often set outdoors in good weather, and everything possible was used for food.

Several factors combined eventually to turn this vast territory into the breadbasket of the world. They included the rapid growth of the great industrial cities in both North America and Europe with their demands for food, improved transportation on both land and water, and the incredibly rich soil of the area. Added to this was the miraculous preservation by Ontario farmer David Fife of a few grains of wheat he had received from a friend in Scotland.

Fife, his parents, and his brothers had arrived in Otonabee Township, Canada West (Ontario), in 1820 to take up a land grant. By 1842, Fife was farming his own two hundred acres and was unhappy with the wheat seed available to local farmers. He asked a friend, Will Struthers, a clerk in a Glasgow seed house, to watch for some seed that could successfully survive the northern climate and the short growing season on Canadian farms. Losses to early frost, rust, and other diseases also frequently proved to be disastrous. When Struthers sent a sample of Galician wheat from Gdansk, Poland, Fife did not know if it should be planted in spring or fall, so he sowed a little in each season. His wife, Jane, is credited with rescuing three heads from their wandering herd of cattle, which were munching in the experimental plot. By 1843, Fife realized the potential of this new, rust-free, disease-free variety and was supplying samples to some of his neighbours and harvesting forty-eight bushels for every bushel sown. Within a few years the wheat's special qualities, combined with the superior flour it produced, led to its adoption by farmers across Ontario and many American states. By the end of the century, Red Fife, as it became known, was famous in all the wheat markets of the world.[4]

Two new provinces sprang from the breadbasket when, in 1905, Saskatchewan and Alberta were created. *Saskatchewan Homemakers' Kitchens*, published in 1955, the jubilee year, pays tribute to the farmers, the farms, and the famous hospitality of western Canada.

The history of the West would not be complete without a record of the young men who, never having done any cooking until their homesteading days, learned in their solitary shacks to make Flapjacks and Baking-Powder Biscuits, the latter often being cooked on the hot stove lids. The staple groceries for every homesteader were flour, dried beans, prunes, corn syrup, and perhaps canned milk. This diet, supplemented with eggs and salt pork, was reasonably adequate nutritionally, except for vitamins, but the early pioneers were not concerned about nutrition and were so full of light-hearted optimism that "prunes" became "CPR strawberries" in their colourful vocabulary.

Not all of the pioneers were bachelors. Some of them were accompanied by their womenfolk, and these courageous women often baked bread for all their unmarried neighbours. A few of the earliest cooks employed the salt-rising method for making bread, but they soon learned to use hops to make "starter," which kept from week to week. When the cheap and reliable Royal Yeast Cakes appeared on the market, homemakers were released from the uncertainties of using homemade bread starters, and for many years the yeast cakes, first round and later square, were found in every home.

Such recipes as Bread and Butter Pickles, Steamed Carrot Pudding, and Shepherd's Pie may have come from the cookbooks of the grand-mothers of Saskatchewan pioneers. These same grandmothers may have compiled many new recipes for utilizing rhubarb, the versatile fruit that was brought west by the first settlers and which has been the homemakers' standby through all the intervening years.

Cranberries could be baked into mock cherry pies, while saskatoons, those wild, succulent, flavourful berries were good in preserves and pies. Lamb's quarters (called pigweed in many other parts of Canada) made a tasty vegetable if picked while young and tender, washed, boiled in salt and water, and served hot. Dandelion leaves sprinkled with salt and pepper, bacon fat, and vinegar made a good salad. Of course, wild rice and Winnipeg goldeye were special treats.

Homesteaders from Germany introduced sauerkraut with its high vitamin C content and encouraged their neighbours to eat it to prevent scurvy. Easy to grow, cabbages soon became a familiar sight in every garden, and in August the sauerkraut cutter was shared among neighbours. The cabbages were shredded and packed into crocks between layers of salt. Approximately ten pounds of cabbage to one and a half cups of salt were put in the container in layers until the crock was full. A plate or wooden lid was placed on top and weighted with a stone to hold it down as the container's contents fermented. The sauerkraut was ready to eat in about a month, but it would keep for several months in a cool, dry place.

Many women became concerned about the need to provide or support programs about community life, health, education, recreation, and other matters of mutual interest. In Saskatchewan in 1907 the Prosperity Homekeepers' Society was formed near Rocanville, and in 1909 the Open Door Circle emerged in Mair. Other groups were encouraged to form along the CPR line, and in January 31, 1911, forty-two interested women representing eighteen communities held a three-day conference in Regina under the auspices of the University of Saskatchewan. The conference resulted in a constitution, with the object being "the promotion of the interests of the home and community" and the name "Homemakers' Clubs." They launched projects that supported clinics, hospitals, community halls, educational programs, libraries, exhibits, and festivals. Their work was similar to, and often in co-operation with, the Women's Institutes in other provinces.[5]

The drought and depression in the 1920s and 1930s brought devastation to many communities. One prairie wife recalled: "There was no water, no toilet, no jobs for the young, and the nearest doctor was seven miles away by horse."

In many homes, food was limited to what the farmer could produce — homegrown flour, boiled wheat porridge, garden vegetables that survived the drought, eggs, home-cured meat, and coffee made from roasted barley, dandelion root, or dried bread crusts. Many townspeople and farm folk depended on relief and shipments of food from other provinces.

There was so little currency that doctors and ministers of the church were often paid with produce. One year almost every parishioner at a certain church left turnips at the parsonage — in lieu of money. The minister said nothing, but invited the church officials to his home for a meal. His wife served: Turnip Soup, Turnip Loaf, Mashed Turnip, Turnip Salad, and Turnip Pie. History does not record whether the church officials found some money, after all.

The Great Depression lasted until 1939, and then the farms began to flourish again. Later, the discovery of oil and gas, potash, and uranium strengthened the economic base and helped make Saskatchewan a well-to-do province. Its fields of ripening wheat have earned it the name "The Breadbasket of the World."[6]

Despite the hardships, Winston Churchill's famous words "This was their finest hour" come to mind, for during this gruelling period new clubs were organized, membership grew, services were not only maintained but expanded, Youth Training Courses, Homecraft Clubs, and Summer Short Courses were promoted. Many families moved from the drought-stricken areas to more northerly parts of Saskatchewan. This again was a pioneering experience, and women who had familiarity with Homemakers' Clubs established new branches that grew to be among the most successful in the province.[7] In 1955 there would be 330 Homemakers' Clubs with a membership of more than five thousand women.

To the west, in the rich grassland and rolling hills of what had become the province of Alberta, change was everywhere. The Hudson's Bay fur-trading post, Fort Edmonton, where countless voyageurs, trappers, and traders had been launched into the fur-rich Northwest, had become the capital.

Bunny Barss reminds us in her many books about Alberta food traditions that

> it was the sun ripened grasses and wide open spaces that lured the first ranchers and cowboys to Alberta and the flat prairies and rolling parklands attracted homesteaders too. They planted grains where there had been only tough prairie sod and when those waving fields of grain were harvested, they served up splendid spreads of food, succulent roasts, crispy fried chicken, homemade breads and pickles, mouthwatering pies and cakes fresh from the oven.[8]

One of the best-known "splendid spreads" that appeared annually on any farm in Canada where grain was grown was the one laid out at a threshing bee. Instead of owning a large and expensive threshing machine, many farmers relied on a hired thresher who, along with his machine, came with two or four teams of horses or a portable steam engine for power. The approach of the threshing bee sent not only the farmers but also the womenfolk in the family into high gear. A visitor from England, Isabella Bird, describes this social phenomenon:

> When a person wishes to thresh his corn [in England wheat was called corn], he gives notice to eight or ten of his neighbours, and a day is appointed on which they are to meet at his house. For two or three days before, grand culinary preparations are made by the hostess, and on the preceding evening a table is loaded with provisions. The morning comes, and eight or ten stalwart Saxons make their appearance, work hard till noon, while the lady of the house is engaged in hotter work before the fire, in the preparation of hot meat, puddings and pies; for well she knows that the good humour of her guests depends on the quality and quantity of her viands. They come to the dinner, black (from the dust of a peculiar Canadian weed [i.e., from smut]), hot, tired, hungry and thirsty. They eat as no other people eat, and set all our notions of the separability

of different viands at defiance. At the end of the day they have a very substantial supper, with plenty of whisky, and if everything has been satisfactory, the convivial proceedings are prolonged till past midnight.[9]

The western provinces and their rich natural resources continued to attract new arrivals whose culinary traditions added greatly to local culture and to community meals as they shared their recipes at bazaars, socials, and potluck suppers, as well as at threshing time. Treasured recipes for Bleenies (Russian Pancakes), German Coleslaw, Kourabiédes (Greek Shortbread), or Krammerhuse (Icelandic cookies shaped into cones), the last filled with sweetened whipped cream and garnished with fruit, mingled with specialties such as Ukrainian Perogies, Polish Cabbage Rolls, and Sour-Cream Pies, while their creators basked in the compliments of their peers.

National Gallery of Canada, Ottawa

Manitoba Party, *painted by William Kurelek in 1964, highlights the famous cooking, baking, and hospitality, both at home and at community events, in western Canada.*

Meanwhile, the chuckwagon cooks became famous. They were attempting to provide three hearty meals a day — often from one large pot — for the cowboys working on the trail or on the wide-open range. The chuckwagon cook was boss of the wagon and the space around it. There were unwritten rules regarding manners and deportment. When riding into camp, a cowboy always stayed downwind, and woe betide the unlucky one who stirred up a cloud of dust or tethered his horse too close to the wagon. A visitor to the outfit would not dream of helping himself to a snack or a cup of coffee until invited to do so. When a meal was ready, the cowboys held back until the cook yelled, "Come 'n get it," or gave some other signal for them to help themselves. Then they would fill their plates, sit down on their bedrolls, and begin eating. They did not wait for others to serve themselves, nor did they make polite conversation. "Eat now and talk later" was the rule. Hungry men could go back for seconds, but they never took the last portion of food unless everyone else had been served first. Generally, they ate with their hats on; only when eating at a proper table in the presence of a lady did they remove their headgear, though if they left it on the faux pas was not regarded as offensive. Only a greenhorn broke these rules, and then just once.

In the days of the open range, a well-run chuckwagon was highly regarded. Not only did it attract good cowboys, but it reflected a well-managed ranch, as well. It can be said truly that chuckwagon cooks made a significant contribution to our history and deserve a place of honour in our folklore.[10]

By the middle of the twentieth century, chuckwagon outfits (wagon, horse, driver, outriders, and equipment) were competing in chuckwagon races at fairs, exhibitions, stampedes, and other special events. The entrants are required to break up an entire camp — including a burning stove — load all the paraphernalia into a wagon, do a series of figure eights around barrels, and then ride once around the track.[11]

The Calgary Stampede draws visitors from around the world. One of the greatest pleasures of fairgoers is to enjoy some of the simple traditional foods — Pancakes, Flapjacks, Griddle Cakes, or Hot Cakes served with maple syrup, mock maple syrup, or homemade jams; Bannock or fried bread; Beef-on-a-Bun dressed with onions and sour cream — that have delighted the residents since the early days of settlement.

For serious diners, the following menu appeared in *A Collage of Canadian Cooking* in 1979:

STAMPEDE BRAND BARBECUE
Tossed Bronco Salad
Rolled Rotisserie Roast Beef
Rum Trader Beans   Saddle Bag Spuds
Homesteader Bread
Old Fashioned Ice Cream[12]

As the chuckwagon cooks said, "Come 'n get it!"

CHAPTER TEN

All Aboard!

O N JULY 21, 1836, THREE HUNDRED GUESTS watched the first Canadian train roll along the flimsy wooden tracks from Montreal to St. John, a prosperous village on the Richelieu River. At the end of its sixteen-mile journey "the guests enjoyed a magnificent collation as they feasted and consumed madeira and champagne galore in the brand-new railway station in St. John."[1]

This railway was built to move freight and goods and appears to have been a dismal failure in that regard, but a great success with passenger traffic, as Montreal families were eager to join excursion parties. They would travel at an astonishing twenty-five miles an hour and then unpack their picnic baskets and sit near the rails to eat.[2]

Fourteen and a half miles of straight line from the hamlet of La Prairie to the village of St. John, the railway appears to have been the catalyst for many short lines in the first half of the nineteenth century. The most unusual was probably the London and Port Stanley line, which appears to have been built mainly for social purposes. It opened on October 1, 1856, having cost £205,000, to take passengers for a day "at the seaside" in Port Stanley on Lake Erie. Masonic Lodge picnics, Oddfellows' picnics, Grand Union Temperance picnics, Irish, English, and Scottish picnics, Presbyterian, Anglican, and Catholic picnics were the order of the day, but turning a profit it was not, and this ill-fated line would finally become an element of Canadian National Railways (CNR) in the twentieth century.[3]

Despite this uncertain beginning, British North America appears to have been thrown into the grip of railway mania as a flurry of construction aimed to draw together the communities scattered across the country. As the nineteenth century progressed, the challenge of constructing longer railways and linking many of the existing ones was too great to resist. Dreams of lines to link the provinces and the United States and ultimately to span the continent from east to west were all to become realities before the century ended.

No matter how long or short the line to be constructed, the survey party went first to begin the task of selecting a route and creating the roadbed. The ideal route was the most direct one possible — which also avoided excessive grades and curves.[4] The survey crews looked after their own supplies and were very vulnerable to shortages, as survivors can confirm:

> In the spring, the freshets took their toll of the supply canoes, which were tracked by hand lines up swollen streams. If a party came to disaster, no one might know of it for days or even weeks. Sometimes the pack parties deserted, declaring the passage to be too dangerous. There were no medical services; if a worker became seriously ill, the rigors of his evacuation often were enough to kill him.[5]

In 1911 when the Moose River Basin was surveyed, Surveyor Ells's Gross Section Book gives us a brief list of his supplies: "beef 20, pork 15, corn 2 dozen, beans 15, peas 11, toilet soap, string, tea, coffee, bread, clock, lard, bacon, soap."[6] This crew probably included eighteen men: a chief, a transit man, a picket man, five axe men, a level man, a rod man, two chainers, a topographer, a cook, two cookees (who helped the cook), and two dog drivers for the dog teams.

Once the route was chosen, construction could begin, and it appears the construction crews for the early short lines were often local men. However, this trend was to change as the projects became larger and more complex. When the Canadian main line of the Grand Trunk Railway was started in 1853, it was estimated that twelve thousand unskilled labourers would be needed, and the contractors thought they could be recruited in Canada. This goal proved impossible, for Canadians did not want to work in the winter, did not know how to work frozen ground, had no interest in team tasks that were absolutely essential in railway construction at that time, and perhaps, more important, believed that joining a railway construction gang was about as respectable as running away with a circus.[7]

Thus began the tradition of recruiting workers from abroad for large construction projects in Canada. A report dated November 1, 1884, confirms the size of the Chinese construction crews working on the western end of the Canadian Pacific Railway: "On Kamloops Lake Section, I have in all about 1600 Chinese, besides a good force of whites."[8] Later the same report continues:

> Above Kamloops ... we have now on this portion about 650 Chinamen and 200 whites. I have arranged to increase this force to 1300 for the winter, and I have supplies for that number being delivered at several different points. We passed by a number of gangs of Chinamen by the way, both during the day when they were hard at work with pick and shovel and in the evening when they were at their camps. Each camp has its Chinese cook paid by the gang, who prepares all the meals. I saw one cooking rice in large tin pans and it looked to me both white and good. Another was chopping meat for a stew.[9]

What if you were organized into one of the gangs that was not made up of Chinese workers? What would your cook have as provisions for the month? Here are the supplies for one gang working on the prairies: "2 sacks flour, 25 bacon, 65 ham, 1/2 barrel corned beef, 26 sugar, 10 tea, 5 coffee, 1 keg syrup, 30 oatmeal, 25 beans, 11 split peas, 25 dried apples, 10 baking powder, 1 package yeast cakes, 20 rice, 11 hops, 1 packet salt, 1/2 pepper, 1/4 mustard, 10 bars soap, 11 wax candles, 1 quarter gross matches, 1/2 doz. mixed pickles, 1 case tomatoes, 6 cheese, 1 tub butter, 1 pail lard, 6 currants, 1 box raisins, 1 doz. corn, 1 doz. peas, 1 doz. canned milk, 1 case canned apples, 1 case canned plums."[10]

In eastern and central Canada, beginning in the late nineteenth century and continuing into the twentieth century, one of the largest cultural groups to join the construction crews was Italian men. These crews often lived in the most primitive of camp accommodation, or in boxcars.

Each had a small coal stove in the centre of the room or boxcar, with wooden bunk beds around it to accommodate twelve men. The men were earning about $2 a day, and this accommodation cost them $1 per month. In order to save money, the Italians preferred to cook their own food rather than eat in the railway boarding trains.

The camp cooks could find catering companies that promised specialized foods such as "pea soup for French Canadians, macaroni with parmesan cheese for Italians, roast mutton and tripe for Englishmen, caraway seeds for Finns," and so forth. Despite this facility, "Italians liked to grub in pairs. Two of them would lay in a month's supply as follows:

> 1 large wooden box macaroni $3.50
> 1 bag potatoes $2.00
> bread, 1 loaf each per day $4.50
> 1 pail lard, l0 lbs. $2.50
> smoked bacon, side, 22 lbs. $4.00
> tea, incidentals, etc. $2.00

Thus, two Italian workers, cooking for themselves, would live quite well, and for less than $10 each per month."[11]

In the late nineteenth and early twentieth centuries, catering companies began to provide an increasingly important service to both construction contractors and railway maintenance crews. Contracts could be negotiated for provisions only, or for a complete service that included a clerk, a cook, cookees, and hot meals cooked and served on the spot. One of these companies, headed by F.C. McCracken and Murray Crawley, signed a contract on May 2, 1914, with J.J. Scully, general superintendent of the CPR at North Bay, Ontario, for boarding, maintenance, and construction gangs in the Algoma District. This contract had formerly been held by the Harris Abattoir Company, Limited, and involved two thousand men in sixty different camps, scattered over eleven hundred square miles of territory.

McCracken and Crawley soon realized their spare equipment would serve only five camps, they could not buy on the spot, and stoves would have to be custom-made.[12] The dilemma was finally solved by their rival, Harris Abattoir, selling them the existing equipment at reasonable prices, and they were relieved to turn their attention to finding

The Skillet

December, 1934.   Published at the Head Office by Crawley & McCracken Co., Limited   Volume I.

The Biggest Cook undertakes A New and Pleasant Task.

THIS time, for the purpose of promoting good fellowship and acquainting our operating staff with the policy of the Company, we have inaugurated a House Organ, which will be published from time to time as the necessity arises or a sufficient number of items of interest accumulate. So that our new employees may learn a little of the background of our Company, this issue contains the history of the Company over a period of twenty years.

"THE BIGGEST COOK"

There are few great business executives who cannot point to a moment of reckless daring in their early careers when they gambled against long odds and won—to establish themselves on the road to leadership in their sphere.

It was on May 2nd, 1914, that F. C. McCracken and M. D. Crawley made the daring stroke that was to establish them as the leading catering firm in Eastern Canada, and laid the foundation for the present firm of Crawley & McCracken Company, "Canada's Biggest Cook." On that day they closed a contract with J. J. Scully, general superintendent of the Canadian Pacific Railway Company, at North Bay, for boarding maintenance and construction gangs on the Algoma district of the C.P.R.

Neither man had looked over the territory or knew much about it, but they firmly believed that they had the right idea of the catering business, and they were not afraid to take a chance. So, gritting their teeth, they plunged in, taking over a contract formerly handled by Harris Abbatoir Company, Limited.

R. D. Lehan Engaged.

As soon as the name of the successful tenderer was announced, R. D. Lehan, of

There was only one thing they could do; purchase from Harris Abbatoir, their rivals for the contract. Harris Abbatoir had them at their mercy as to price, and could have struck a crippling blow at the new enterprise, but to their credit they sold the equipment at a very fair figure. Today Mr. McCracken counts among his best friends the head of the Harris Abbatoir. In those early business deals a friendship was forged which has continued for many years.

The Toss of a Coin.

An agreement was soon reached for the purchase of everything but the ranges. Finally, after hours of bargaining, Crawley and McCracken offered 60 cents on the dollar for them, while the Harris Abbatoir held out for 65. Again his gambling instinct rose, and Mr. Crawley offered to match pennies to see whether they paid 60 or 65. He lost and the turn of the penny cost his company several hundred dollars, but nothing to what the loss would have been had he failed to secure the ranges.

Trained Organization Essential.

The equipment was only the first step. Building up a staff was even more important. No one can succeed in the catering business

profit per meal was exactly 55/100 of a cent, which meant a profit of 1·65/100 cents per man per day.

Depressing Times.

The winters of 1914, 1915 and 1916 were depressing ones for the struggling firm, but they refused to give up. Railroad work was done entirely in the summer months, with the result that camps had to be closed for the winter. It was an expensive proposition to retain summer help in semi-idleness, yet the company feared to let the staff go in case their services could not be secured when needed in the spring.

In 1916 they secured the contract to feed the construction workers on the Canadian Northern Ontario Railway, now the Canadian National, then being built through Northern Ontario, and they have fed C.N.R. gangs in Ontario ever since.

In 1918 the Consolidated Boarding & Supply Company decided to close out their interests in Canada. Through the efforts of Mr. McCracken a Canadian Company named Crawley & McCracken Co. Ltd.

In December 1934, Crawley & McCracken Limited, "Canada's Biggest Cooks," published the first issue of The Skillet *to serve its staff and alert the public to the success of the firm.*

and training staff for the camps. This task was not an easy one, for railway work was often done entirely in the summer months, with the camps closed in the winter, and it was a challenge to find competent temporary staff.[13] Crawley & McCracken Limited — "Canada's Biggest Cooks," as the firm became known in 1918 — strove valiantly to live up to its name, for it was also the successful contractor in 1916 to feed the construction workers on the Canadian Northern Ontario Railway

(CNOR), then being built, as well as the CPR line in New Brunswick and the CNR gangs in the Montreal district. The company provided its staff with recipes for a wide range of dishes, including Blanc, Chocolate, and Pineapple Mange; Butterscotch, Maple Nut, Snow, and Lemon Pudding; Fresh Strawberry Whip; Brown Sugar, Butterscotch, Lemon, and Custard Sauce; Lemon, Chocolate, and Rhubarb Custard; Raisin and Blueberry Pie; and English Tarts.[14]

Despite the firm's best efforts, however, it was far from a perfect world out in the camps. Labour disputes could affect vital supplies, as J.E. Cahoon, vice-president and general manager of Crawley & McCracken, described to the officials of the Temiskaming & Northern Ontario Railway (T&NOR):

> We are worried about the impending packing house strike and think that you should be made aware of the serious situation that can develop. Our camps may have meat for a few days after the strike takes place but, if it lasts for long, there will be no meat for the men. We will be reduced to the position of just serving what food is available. There will be no meat, butter, eggs or shortening for baking and no fat for beans. It may mean porridge and milk, and whatever fruits etc. are available.
>
> Under the restricted diet, it is natural that the men will not be in condition to do a day's work, as they could do if given full meals. They will not fare better in case they decide to quit work and go home, because the meat shortage will also exist at their homes.
>
> The men in the camps should be advised of the impending situation instead of letting them face it suddenly, as it would create confusion and unrest. Representatives in charge of the men should prepare them for the trouble and ask for their co-operation and support.[15]

These challenges continued as correspondence thirty years later confirms:

May 29, 1946

This letter is to advise you that the men in my gang are complaining about the board. I took the matter up with the cook, asking to have same improved, and the answer was that he cannot get supplies.... I cannot understand how the cook can feed this gang of men without adequate supplies.... And about the sweets such as syrup, jam, molasses, apples, prunes, etc. We have not seen any on the table for the last 2 weeks. Kindly check up and see if these orders can be filled more fully in the future. If not I expect to have trouble with my gang.

August 8, 1946

This cook was sick upon arrival and did not get up to make breakfast on July 31st, with the result that there was a very poor breakfast and these sixteen men quit. There is no eggs. Milk or bacon or seemingly anything that can be cooked for breakfast to take the place of these.

Extra gang foreman advises that he now has only eighteen men in the gang, and Edwards has only sixteen men despite inquiries at Kirkland Lake Rouyn and Timmins we have been unable to secure labourers. Can any thing be done at North Bay as our whole program is being interrupted. I have noticed that when the meat supplies come in the butts were addressed to the Ditcher and gas shovel gang while we get the ribs so that we have stew, stew and more stew.

When sweets come in, there is only enough for one or two breakfasts and then no more for a week or more. There has been no toast for the breakfast since the gang went out this spring and there are very few greens.[16]

Labour shortages also affected the staff, despite wages having risen from $40 a month in 1903 to $150 per month for cooks and $60 a month for cookees by 1945 when the T&NOR suggested hiring women as cooks to the catering company. There was some reluctance to act on this suggestion, as this response suggests:

> You called this morning in connection with using Women as Cooks and Cookees on boarding outfits in event of you finding it impossible to secure suitable male help for these positions.
>
> Should you find it absolutely necessary to employ Women for this work, it will be in order to do so. You understand of course, in view of the difficulty in providing suitable sanitary arrangements for Women, and also the possibilities of they being injured, it is most undesirable that we should have Women employed on these Gangs.[17]

Once the trains were running, the catering companies often retained contracts to provision the maintenance crews, while the train crews usually looked after their own meals, except under extraordinary circumstances. In cases of accidents or emergencies, the railway would pay for their meals if they could be fed by local farmers or settlers living near the track. As a general rule, the train crews carried their own lunches, packed at home to last for a few hours, or a few days, if it was to be a long run.

The engine crews had one great bonus when it came to meals, for they could clean up a stoking shovel and cook on it — bacon, eggs, steak, and fried potatoes could all be on the menu. If they brought soup or stew in a jar, or a bottle of tea, it could be set up on the engine and would soon be warm enough to eat or drink.[18]

Steam trains could travel approximately 120 miles before they needed servicing with water, fuel, and maintenance. At these divisional points the train crews were expected to rest for the next leg of the journey. In 1896, Charles Hayes, general manager of the Grand Trunk Railway, became concerned about living conditions for his crews at the destination points, often remote and desolate railway towns, and persuaded D.A. Budge, secretary general of the Montreal YMCA, to investigate. Budge was appalled by the dreadful food, drafty shelter, absence of entertainment, and the fact that crews were often expected to sleep in abandoned boxcars.[19]

Hayes's concerns and Budge's bold experiment marked the start of an era. In more than two dozen Canadian railway towns, railway Ys would become an important part of both the physical landscape and the social fabric. While a few were located in Canada's larger and more prosperous communities such as Moncton, Montreal, Toronto, and Stratford, more than half were in Northern Ontario's remote railway divisional towns strung along the CPR line and what would become the Canadian National Line — Sioux Lookout, Ignace, Kenora, Chapleau, Cartier, Schreiber, Hornepayne, and White River were some of these — while others were in the British Columbia mountain towns of Field, Cranbrook, and Revelstoke.

"The Railway Ys form a remarkable group, offering as they do comfort and cheer to those who man the trains running through the wilds of B.C. and northern Ontario," boasted H.B. Stevens, chief dispatcher of the CPR, on opening the White River Y in 1909. "In erecting these buildings, the CPR has set a worthy example for other corporations." Now tired crews could relax in reading, lecture, or games rooms, or repair to restrooms, with beds and bathrooms with tubs and showers, or prepare their meals in lunchrooms on gas stoves.[20]

What of the passengers on the trains? As we have seen, the first short runs gave the passengers an opportunity to pack picnic lunches to consume in the coaches, beside the tracks, or at their destination. With the building of the longer railways and the opening of the transcontinental lines, hampers of food brought from home or sandwiches purchased at station counters, from nearby hotels, or from platform vendors would not suffice, particularly for the well-to-do, who were accustomed to being served.

George Pullman of Chicago recognized as early as 1864 the importance of making railway passengers comfortable — and the profit that could be made by doing so. Pullman designed elegant dining cars, where the first-class passengers enjoyed lavish meals prepared by his chefs. Advertisements read:

THE CANADIAN PACIFIC RAILWAY DINING
CARS Excel in Elegance of Design and Furniture and in
the Quality of Food and Attendance Anything Hitherto
Offered to TRANCONTINENTAL TRAVELLERS.

The fare provided in these cars is the best procurable and the cooking has a wide reputation for excellence. Local delicacies such as trout, prairie hens, antelope steaks, Fraser River salmon, succeed one another as the train moves westward.

The wines are the company's special importation, and are of the finest quality.[21]

Meals in the dining car were advertised at 75 cents during the first years of transcontinental service. It is interesting to note that on CNR in August 1940 it was still possible to have a table d'hôte luncheon that included a choice of tomato juice or consommé or dessert, a choice of an omelette, salad, or sandwich, two hot vegetables, rolls, and a choice of tea, coffee, milk, iced tea, or iced coffee for the same amount.[22]

One of the important offshoots of the dining-car service was the CPR hotel system, which stretched from the Empress Hotel in Victoria to the Lord Nelson in Nova Scotia and included two fishing resorts at the French River and at Kenora in Ontario. Passengers on the CPR, "The World's

This Dining Car Service Menu for Canadian Pacific Railway details the dinners available in 1941 for $1 and $1.25.

Greatest Travel System," were assured that the sleeping-car conductor would be pleased to wire ahead, without charge, to any of the company's hotels for reservations.[23]

Many travellers on transcontinental trains, however, could ill afford the cost of dining-car meals, and it became common for restaurants to spring up at divisional points where a passenger could obtain a quick and cheap meal while the locomotive was being changed, watered, or fuelled. Passengers were always fearful of moving too far from the platform and the steps to the train in case it glided off, for the conductor would call "All aboard!" and even as he uttered the words the train would begin to move.

Cafés near the station had their specialties. One might be renowned for its roast beef, another for its great breakfasts. If you boarded a train that had no diner in the 1920s, you would hope for a long stop near a good café. At High River, Mrs. Robinson's had raisin pies that made you drool thinking of them. The Lethbridge train would stop in the town for ten minutes, and folks would rush to Mrs. Robinson's for a slice of pie.

Once, about twenty people trooped into the café, and Mrs. Robinson ran out of raisin pie. The conductor and the engineer came in and said they wanted some so badly that they would wait until a new batch came out of the oven. "What about your schedule?" somebody asked.

"Don't you go having no conniption over the schedule," the engineer said. "We'll make her to Lethbridge okay."[24]

These restaurants were usually privately operated, but the railway had to establish its own restaurants in the mountains, where it was impractical to haul the extremely heavy dining cars over the steep grades. The westbound Pacific Express and the eastbound Atlantic Express were timed to arrive at these points at mealtimes. Although they had not been ready for operation when the first transcontinental went through, temporary quarters in the form of dining cars pulled to the side of the tracks were used until the work on the line was complete.[25]

Other alternatives to the dining car were also provided for the floods of passengers on the railways. "Newsies" such as Denny Hollows from North Bay were popular on many railways. Mr. Hollows started on the T&NOR in 1928 at age fourteen and was soon earning $70 a week.[26] Hartley Trussler describes the newsies he remembers and how their wares could augment a lunch from home:

It was amazing all the stuff he had for sale and it was all kept in a couple of trunks or cases between two seats in the end of the smoking car. I will never forget the smell of the oranges and bananas as he strolled down the aisle with his wicker tray filled with fruit and chocolate bars all nicely displayed so you could not resist the temptation to buy. In those days we country kids only smelled oranges at Christmas or some special occasion; and the pop or soft drinks. What a treat it was to get a drink of cream soda or orangeade. It was pure nectar to us. And the smell of the cigar smoke, another aroma which was rare to we kids. Cigarettes were not as common then; people who could afford to smoke, smoked 5 cent cigars and on the train was where they indulged.[27]

An innovation introduced by the T&NOR in 1912 was the *Agumik*, an air-conditioned restaurant car. This pioneering effort provided service and comfort at a moderate price. *Agumik* means "Place of Eating," and the car was indeed a good place to eat. Prices ranged from 10 cents for a peanut-butter sandwich to $1.25 for a steak. The *Agumik* was built in the railway shops, and the dining counter was set up like a very long soda-fountain counter running the length of the car, with the staff and equipment on one side, and stools and the patrons on the other. The Polar Bear Express that runs from Sault Ste. Marie to Moosonee (Ontario) offers its own menu and appears to cater to the younger passengers travelling with their parents, or to adults with slim pocketbooks and simple tastes.[28]

Eating on the rails has changed a great deal in the past 150 years in Canada. Whenever a group of people gather to reminisce about their experiences travelling on our railways, the elegance and superb cuisine of the dining cars are always remembered with a great deal of nostalgia tinged with regret at their disappearance. The modern substitutes, even in first-class coaches, are treated with disdain by many who believe we have lost an important part of our culinary heritage.

CHAPTER ELEVEN

From Sea to Shining Sea

For centuries the West Coast of Canada remained a mystery to much of the world, especially to the Europeans, despite the probing and speculating that went on to find the elusive Northwest Passage across or around the continent. As the search continued, Captain James Cook and his crew were among the first newcomers to visit the shores of present-day British Columbia. Cook became famous in the history of maritime exploration for his magnificent accounts of his expeditions, for once they were printed, they aroused keen interest around the world. He became famous also for his innovative measures in preventing scurvy among his crew. Cook was one of the first sea captains to order his men to eat "Sour Krout" (salted cabbage) and Portable Broth (green vegetables and fresh meat) on their three voyages around the world between 1768 and 1780. In the spring of 1778 on his third voyage as he was searching for that elusive northern passage, Cook's vessels sailed into Nootka Sound on Vancouver Island. Cook and his men were met by the First Nations and leave us this description of a meal in preparation:

> I was in one of these Houses about the middle of the day, and saw them cook their Dinner, which was done after the following Manner; they took a wooden Box, pour'd some Water into it and put it by the side of the Fire; their Method of making a Fire is, by first forming a round hole in the Ground, which they line with Stones; upon these Stones they lay the Fuel and make the fire; having placed the Box

in a convenient situation by the Fire with the Water in it, they put in their Flesh or Fish, or whatever they have to dress, and then keep plying it with a Succession of hot Stones, which they are supplied with from the Fire, and by this means keep the Water simmering till the contents are done to their palates. When I saw them perform this Operation, they cook'd some Flesh, which I believe was part of the Carcass of a Porpuss, however they laid it down upon the bare Ground and cut it up in convenient Junks for cooking; when they put it in the Box, it was in many places so cover'd with dirt that you cou'd scarcely see the colour of the Meat, however with these honest fellows it was very well, dirt and Meat went altogether.[1]

In *The Flavours of Canada*, Anita Stewart enlarges on Cook's description of meal preparation by the Native peoples on the West Coast:

Canada's only indigenous cooking method, bentwood box cookery, was developed during the ancient times, long before European contact. It was women's work, a ritual completed with pride. Handmade cedar boxes were filled with water to soak and tighten for three to four days. A fire was lit and potato-sized beach rocks were placed in it to heat. The hot rocks were then picked out of the fire with a split alder branch, washed briefly in one box, then placed in a second filled with water and salmonberry shoots. In moments the water foamed and boiled. Seafood was added — prawns, scallops, clams, chunks of halibut or salmon — and a woven mat was placed over top to hold the steam. Within minutes the pure, sweet taste of the sea were retrieved from the box and the feast began.[2]

The nations of the northern West Coast, the Nootka, Haida, Tlingit, and Tsimshian, built their communities, each with its own chief, along the shore and close to their livelihood. There was salmon in abundance, bear, deer, and mountain goats in the dense forest, while whales and porpoises

The First Nations continue to prepare fish for family and friends in traditional ways and to give fish as a gift to a new acquaintance or an old friend.

roamed the coastal waters. They erected giant poles (called crest, or totem, poles) in front of their homes as the genealogical record of the family to confirm their status and position in the community. It was imperative that the chiefs maintain their reputation as strong, wealthy leaders, and this goal was often accomplished with a traditional potlatch.

The potlatch was generally planned a year in advance, the clan chief directing his family, quite conceivably an entire village, to prepare not only enormous quantities of food but a huge supply of blankets, boxes, and all manner of useful and valuable items. When this mass of material was accumulated, the chief would invite the headman of a rival clan and his people to the feast. Here everyone dressed in their finery, and the host would distribute gifts to his guests — the dozens of blankets and boxes and other articles that he and his clan members had gathered together throughout the year. A sumptuous feast was presented, with more than anyone could eat. To climax the potlatch, the host might take one or more of his shield-shaped coppers (a sheet of copper used as a symbol of wealth or distinction), valued at perhaps a hundred blankets, and hurl them into the sea. The host herewith displayed to the assembled throng his utter disdain for material wealth. The ostentatious exhibition was frequently accompanied by the killing of one or more slaves for, as property, they now meant nothing at all to their owner. It was a glorious occasion, a time for receiving gifts, of feasting, of being honoured by a powerful and beneficent leader.

There was one catch, however, to the potlatch. The guest chief knew that within one year all of the things he had been generously given, all of the displays and destruction of property, must be reciprocated, and reciprocated with lavish interest. The potlatch was, in fact, a form of insidious economic warfare waged with the calculated design of ruining one's rival. And it worked. Some headmen went bankrupt, others went mad, and a few ventured upon suicidal expeditions of war.[3]

In 1884 the federal government outlawed potlatches on the grounds that "the institution was wasteful and destructive." The Potlatch Law, as it became known, remained on the statutes of Canada until 1951.

Meanwhile explorers and adventurers continued to penetrate the channels along the coast, among the Arctic islands, across the tundra, and into the labyrinth of mountains from the west, while the servants of the North West Company and the Hudson's Bay Company approached from the east, where many of their forts now had communities growing up around them, with gardens and fields to supplement the traditional rations.

It was the young Scottish-born North West Company trader and explorer Alexander Mackenzie who read Captain Cook's accounts and persevered until he successfully reached the Pacific. With a mixture of grease and vermilion, Mackenzie wrote the following words on a rock overlooking the open sea:

> Alexander Mackenzie, from Canada, by land,
> the twenty-second of July
> one thousand seven hundred and ninety-three.

The Rocky Mountain barrier had been penetrated, and when Mackenzie's book about his travels was published in 1801 and was read by the English-speaking world, it galvanized countless explorers and traders to make their way across the mountains to the coast, as well.

Meanwhile, events in the United States were to have a profound effect on this coastal region when gold was discovered in California and armies of fortune hunters arrived. They soon pushed north from one valley or river to another until they struck gold on the Fraser River in 1858.

This was the "birth" of modern British Columbia, a territory that was a fascinating mixture of First Nations, explorers, adventurers, fur traders, and merchants. There were two settlements, Victoria and Esquimalt, with a total population of about two hundred. Vancouver Island was a separate colony, and surveyor general Despard Pemberton leaves a prophetic description of the area's future:

> The fertility of the soil in the neighbourhood of the gold-bearing rocks is very remarkable, and is indicated rather by production from ordinary seed of gigantic roots, and vegetables and fruits, than by crops of grain. Turnips as large as hassocks, radishes as large as beets or marigolds, and bushels of potatoes to a single stalk, are nothing astonishing....
>
> Indians everywhere grow potatoes and carrots as far north as Queen Charlotte's Island; their plan is to repeat the crop until the ground is exhausted, and then to clear some more. The potatoes are excellent; and potatoes and salmon their standing dish....
>
> With a market close at hand, and high prices for everything he can produce, the farmer's prospects are extremely promising; and in consequence of the dearness of labour in every department, the larger his family the wealthier he is.[4]

Those "gold-bearing rocks" mentioned by Pemberton, and the dream of one lucky strike with an instant fortune, lured thousands of prospectors and miners to the goldfields of British Columbia after the strike of 1858. Among them was Ah Hung, merchant and agent for a San Francisco company, who was prospecting not for gold but for new business. Mr. Hung was Canada's first "official" Chinese arrival, and when he wrote about his experiences in the *San Francisco Daily Globe* on May 16, 1858, he described receiving a job offer as a cook for $20 a day! Drawn by such enthusiastic reports of *Gum San*, "the Land of Gold," as Canada was briefly known, three hundred Chinese men arrived two months later from San Francisco by ship, and a few months after that, arrivals landed directly from Hong Kong.[5]

The *Victoria Daily Colonist* estimated that four thousand Chinese arrived in 1860, and many went to the goldfields to earn a dollar a day. Those with a little capital began small businesses to serve the growing population of single men. These included restaurants, laundries, market gardens, and fishing companies, where the fish were caught by rod and line, then salted, dried, and shipped inland to the protein-hungry miners. Import firms such as Kwong Lee (also from San Francisco), "Importers and Dealers in all Kinds of Chinese Goods, Rice, Sugar, Tea, Provisions," established their headquarters in Victoria and used pack trains of mules and horses to move their goods to the "instant" communities springing up in the goldfields. One of the most famous of these towns was Barkerville, which suddenly became, in 1862, the largest community north of San Francisco and west of Chicago.

The fur trade, and since 1821 the Hudson's Bay Company, had ruled the area, but suddenly change was needed, and the new colony of British Columbia was created in 1858, with Queen Victoria naming its capital New Westminster. Governor James Douglas, who had worked as a young man in the fur trade, ruled with an iron hand as he decreed that the lawlessness of the mining camps to the south would not spread north of the border. He also requested a company of Royal Engineers and, in response, the British government sent 150 officers and men. They were accompanied by thirty-seven women and thirty-five children, and when the engineers were disbanded five years later, many of them chose to stay as pioneer settlers in the mainland colony.

Perhaps Douglas's greatest achievement was ordering the building of the famous Cariboo Road, which stretched from Yale to the Fraser River and north for 480 miles into the Cariboo country. Swinging around mountain curves, clinging to precipitous cliffs high above whirling waters, it was the boldest enterprise in road building ever undertaken in a pioneer community in British North America. On the earlier pack trails, the cost of freight had been enormous, and the prices of goods carried to the Cariboo country were fantastic: $50 for a pair of shoes and $90 for a hundredweight of potatoes. The completion of the Cariboo Road changed this situation and opened a regular postal and stage service, with express coaches drawn by six-horse teams and travelling day and night in relays of twelve to thirteen miles. Pack trains of mules carried heavy freight; strangest of all, twenty-one camels were tried but proved to be a failure. Their smell frightened the horses and created havoc along the way.[6] Roadhouses were built every ten to twelve miles along the road to serve as hotels and supply depots. There travellers could buy a hot meal, have a drink from a bar, sleep on a hay mattress, and stock up on flour, beans, bacon, potatoes, coffee, tea, and hay for the next part of the trip.

Viscount Milton and his friend, Dr. Cheadle, left this rather rueful description of hotel life in the Cariboo district of British Columbia in 1863 at the height of the gold rush:

> Our quarters at Cusheon's Hotel were vile. A blanket spread on the floor of a loft was our bedroom, but the swarms of lice which infested the place rendered sleep almost impossible, and made us think with regret on the soft turf of the prairie, or a mossy couch in the woods. The fare, limited to beefsteak, bread and dried apples, was wretchedly cooked and frightfully expensive. Beef was worth fifty cents or two shillings a pound, flour the same, a "drink" of anything except water was half a dollar, nor could the smallest article, even a book of matches, be bought for less than a "quarter," one shilling. Before we reached Williams Creek we paid a dollar and a quarter, or five shillings, for a single pint bottle of stout.[7]

At the goldfields the diet for the miners was Caribou Turkey (bacon) and Caribou Strawberries (beans), sometimes supplemented by fish or wild game. Enterprising cowboys drove cattle from California and Oregon to feed the miners, where they received top prices for their beef.

After the mining operations slowed down, cowboys and roadhouse operators concentrated on ranching and established some of the big British Columbia cattle ranches. Work was hard and "grub" was plain — plenty of hot biscuits, fried salt pork, beans or rice, and always stewed prunes to "keep a fellow in good order."[8]

In 1865, Matthew MacFie described a ranch established three years earlier and owned by a Mr. Davidson on 1,860 acres, with 175 acres under cultivation (mostly barley and oats): "There were about fifteen acres of potatoes, two acres of cabbage, one of turnips, one of onions, and several of corn, beans, parsnips and carrots. The ranch also had some of the best livestock in the province, eight yoke of working oxen, six to eight horses, and a good selection of farm implements, including a reaper, mower and threshing machine, which could thresh 1,000 bushels a day." MacFie also stressed that farming lost favour because of the proximity of the gold strikes. A gold rush was a serious hindrance to agricultural development, because workers refused to stay on the farm.[9]

As the goldfields were depleted, the miners turned to the coal mines, or prospecting for jade. A very large number of Chinese miners resorted to fishing, market gardening, food industries such as the canning factories, domestic service, and the construction of the railway. By the late 1870s, there were four hundred Chinese cooks and servants in Victoria providing the only domestic service available to the well-to-do in that growing town. By then the two colonies, Vancouver Island and British Columbia, had united, and they joined the new Dominion of Canada in 1871. Two years later, Prince Edward Island entered Confederation.

Stuart Cumberland, FRGS, was commissioned by a syndicate of Australian, Indian, and English newspapers to cross Canada by rail as soon as the CPR's last spike was driven on November 7, 1885: "I am positively the first person to go over the line of rail between the Pacific and the Atlantic in a journalistic sense," he claimed. He was pleasantly surprised at his reception in New Westminster:

> The principal hotel in New Westminster is most comfortable, and the table is excellent as well as abundant. Salmon cutlets and sturgeon steaks deliciously cooked, hot rolls, with pats of guinea gold butter, and jugs of fresh, thick cream and well-made tea and coffee graced the breakfast table; and the midday dinner included oyster soup, marrowbones, roast and boiled joints, and fat tender chicken. The vegetables were a treat in themselves, whilst luscious fruits of various kinds were in abundance at every meal. The charge per day was, I believe, from $1.50 to $2.00, a considerable reduction being allowed permanent boarders. Next to the Driard House at Victoria the hotel at New

Westminster was decidedly the best house I "struck" from the Pacific to Manitoba.[10]

By the end of the nineteenth century, elaborate, illustrated brochures were being issued in an attempt to lure immigrants to the new province. Typical of these was *Information for Immigrants*, issued in 1875 by G.M. Sproat, agent-general in London, England, for British Columbia. To refute descriptions of Canada as the land of ice and snow, the author met the challenge head on: "The great snow question. British Columbia has not a snow winter. There is snow, but not much snow.... British Columbia has not a snowy winter such as Eastern Canada and the Northern States of the Union have. The British Columbia winter is the winter of England and of France."

The advertising appears to have worked, for Canadians continue to note the parallels between the two. "A little bit of England" and "more English than England" are phrases that are often applied to British Columbia. We should not be surprised that tea and British Columbia or tea and Victoria have become almost synonymous, despite the growth and culinary diversity of the province.

The newly arrived British colonists built beautiful homes on large properties in Victoria. Every housewife had one day of each month set aside when her friends would join her in the drawing room for afternoon tea. The drawing room was the "special" room of any house where the best furniture, china, and pictures were displayed — no children were allowed there except by special permission. The usual tea at these occasions consisted of thinly sliced bread with butter and rock cakes. Before departing, it was customary for the guest to leave her calling card, which indicated that she would like her hostess to come to tea.[11]

The Empress Hotel, one of the magnificent hotels constructed for the Canadian Pacific Railway's guests, opened in Victoria in 1908 and began serving afternoon tea in the Palm Court with its splendid dome of Japanese glass. The tradition lives on, not only in the romantic elegance of the Edwardian lobby but in scores of other tearooms, tea gardens, farms, hotels, inns, restaurants, and cafés in and around the city.

From the nineteenth-century immigrants of Chinese ancestry in British Columbia, one of the largest and most varied Oriental cuisines in North America has grown, while in Vancouver one of the largest Chinatowns in

Canadians of Chinese ancestry have made important contributions to our food industries for more than 150 years, and wherever we travel in Canada, there is a Chinese restaurant serving an excellent meal at a modest price.

North America has arisen. Newcomers from Japan have, over the past century, also established their place in the province's cuisine, popularizing Japanese food long before it was fashionable anywhere else in Canada.

In 1986, when British Columbia hosted Expo 86 in Vancouver, the world came to visit and learned of the province's beauty, resources, and lush natural vegetation. Vancouver was the focus of the exposition, and many residents in the interior of the province felt they were being ignored. To counteract this criticism, then-premier Bill Bennett had the Coquihalla Highway built, a stunning ebony trail that runs from the outskirts of Hope to the Okanagan cities of Kelowna and Kamloops. This road, along with the Trans-Canada Highway, opened the interior of the province to the rest of the planet.

For Expo 86, Susan Mendelson wrote the *Expo 86 Cookbook*, and it, too, introduced the world to the cuisine of the host city and province. In her introduction, she tells us:

> Just as the sixties health food craze started on the West
> Coast, so have many recent food trends that you now find

in large metropolitan, centres everywhere. The emphasis on food in Vancouver is on simplicity, lightness and freshness. This is reflected in the fresh salads and fish dishes that are served in our restaurants and homes. Diversity and sophistication are also stressed. Hot and cold hors d'oeuvres offered at most Vancouver parties now allow the diner to taste a little of everything — all without breaking the budget. Specialty food stores can be found in increasing numbers, reminding Vancouverites of the city's varied ethnic make-up; and burgeoning produce markets keep us supplied with fresh fruit and vegetables from around the world.[12]

Susan and her partner, Deborah Reitberg, opened the Lazy Gourmet in 1979, specializing in new food ideas for their customers. It was in their store that Nanaimo Bars were first sold commercially, and in her book she gives us several variations on this Canadian favourite.

The Okanagan Valley has now become famous for producing some of Canada's best fruit and vegetables (much of it organic), and it is the location of organic vineyards. Saltspring Island, with its incredibly moderate climate and ideal growing conditions, has become the home of many organic growers. It is a Mecca for all those interested in this growing movement, spurred by our concern for our environment and our food supply in the future.

The temperate climate, long growing season, and sheltered valleys make anything edible possible! As a result, fruit, vegetables, wine, edible flowers, artisanal beers, honey, and mushrooms are available locally and (usually) at all seasons of the year. Organic farms are multiplying and thriving, and their products continue to grow in popularity. Salmon, idolized by the First Nations, has become a favourite food of all West Coast residents and is usually the centrepiece of every special occasion.

CHAPTER TWELVE

"You Feed Your Pigs and Cattle More Scientifically Than You Feed Your Families"[1]

WITH THE TRAGIC DEATH OF JOHN HOODLESS, fourteen-month-old son of Adelaide Sophia Hunter Hoodless, in August 1889, a happy wife and mother was transformed into a domestic crusader. When doctors in Hamilton, Ontario, told her that her youngest child was stricken with "summer complaint" from drinking impure milk, Adelaide realized that if she, an educated woman, did not understand the scientific principles of running a household, how did those manage who did not have her advantages?

Adelaide began to lecture and lobby for the development of educational programs to train girls and women in the practical science of running a household. She also advocated an organization for women similar to the Farmers' Institute, which had emerged in 1884 under the guidance of the Ontario Ministry of Agriculture. She became a well-known speaker, often accusing the men in her audience of lavishing more affection, money, and concern on the farm livestock than on the farm family. She also opened a cooking school in Hamilton and began to advocate for a school of domestic science (now the Macdonald Institute) at the Ontario Agricultural College at Guelph, Ontario.

On February 19, 1897, a meeting was held at Squire's Hall in Stoney Creek, Ontario, to hear Adelaide's message. Despite the weather, 101 women and one man travelled by foot and by horse and buggy to attend, and before the evening was over, they had unanimously endorsed her crusade and formed the first Women's Institute (WI) in the world. No one present that night could have dreamed that this fledgling organization would pioneer in the field of women's issues, the strengthening of family life, and the enrichment of rural communities — not only in their own province but across Canada and internationally.[2]

Erland Lee (a founding member of the Farmers' Institute) and his wife, Janet, lived nearby and worked tirelessly to ensure the meeting's success. They were to be rewarded by watching two other groups form before the end of the year: Whitby WI in York County and Kemble WI in Grey County. Within five years there were forty-four groups in Ontario, and the Agriculture and Arts Amendment Act of 1902 recognized and confirmed "The formation of Women's Institutes for the purpose of improving rural home life, and of imparting information in regard to women's work upon the farm." The growth of the movement and its educational programs was phenomenal in the years leading up to the outbreak of World War I in 1914, with 843 branches and 25,000 members.[3] In 1915 a Junior WI was formed on Manitoulin Island, the first of many, thus recognizing that this growing educational program for homemakers should include girls and women of all ages.

In the 1920s, many branches became interested in historical research and began scrapbooks that recorded the early history of their communities (often reaching back to the First Nations), detailing the homes, farms, crops, livestock, stores, industries (such as dairies and cheese-making factories), churches, and schools. By 1947, when the movement was celebrating its fiftieth anniversary, these scrapbooks became the foundation for the Tweedsmuir Histories, which Lady Tweedsmuir, wife of Canada's governor general, encouraged every branch to develop. Many of them contain a message from Lady Tweedsmuir:

FOREWORD

I am so glad to hear that the Women's Institutes of Ontario are going to compile village history books. Events move very fast nowadays; houses are pulled down, new roads are made, and the aspect of the countryside changes completely sometimes in a short time.

It is a most useful and satisfying task for Women's Institute members to see that nothing valuable is lost or forgotten, and women should be on the alert always to guard the traditions of their homes, and to see that water colour

sketches and prints, poems and prose legends should find
their way into these books. The oldest people in the village
will tell us fascinating stories of what they remember, which
the younger members can write down, thus making a
bridge between them and events which happened before
they were born. After all, it is the history of humanity
which is continually interesting to us, and your village histories will be the basis of accurate facts much valued by historians in the future. I am proud to think that you have
called them "The Tweedsmuir Village Histories."

— Written by Lady Tweedsmuir.[4]

*The Women's Institutes, begun in the late nineteenth century in Ontario,
have often been called universities for rural women. They have expanded
around the world to educate girls and women in domestic science and bring
them out of their kitchens to support community projects with innovative
fundraising events.*

These books are invaluable research tools, since they record in detail the everyday life of rural Canada. What was grown in the gardens, fields, and orchards of Canadian farms, how many general stores there were in the village and what was on their shelves, who was raising dairy cattle, beef cattle, sheep, hogs, and chickens? All this and more filled their pages, collected by dedicated curators of the Tweedsmuir Histories, and at regular intervals, Tweedsmuir Teas were — and still are — held to display the volumes to the communities and to attract new members to the group.

Originally, a few women would gather in a member's parlour to hold a meeting and discuss everyday household tasks such as churning butter, baking bread, or "putting down" preserves. A visiting speaker might discuss some aspects of food preparation or preservation. As time went on, many branches expanded both their activities and their horizons to benefit the whole community by developing or supporting libraries, hospitals, museums, and school programs; undertaking cemetery preservation; installing streetlights; and overseeing a host of other improvements. The members became successful fundraisers, organizing box socials, garden parties, bazaars, bake sales, special catered events, and community meals. Many members coordinated food tables at rural school fairs, introduced hot lunches in schools, and catered for plowing matches, a tradition still carried out today.

To support their expanding educational programs and community services, many WIs developed cookbooks to sell as an educational device, as a showcase for their culinary skills and, of course, as a means to raise funds. These books are much more than a collection of recipes, for they give us a unique, first-hand account of everyday life in the homes of rural Canadians. They usually begin with a brief history of the WI, such as this introduction to *Out of Country Kitchens* by Quebec Women's Institutes:

> Quebec Women's Institutes have been active in Quebec since 1911, when the first meeting was held in Best's Hall, Durham, Quebec. Institutes originated in Stoney Creek, Ontario, in 1897, through the efforts of Adelaide Hunter Hoodless, Erland Lee and a group of interested country women whose concerns for a better understanding and quality of life in rural homes and municipalities led to the

forming of this organization that today, comprises around nine million members in sixty-eight countries.

Consequently one of Quebec Women's Institutes' main concerns has always been good nutritious food for their families. Today wherever W.I.s are active and food is mentioned you know it's bound to be excellent. Over the years they have offered workshops on various aspects of food production, prizes at country fairs for food and also for young gardeners. Their earliest association here in Quebec has been with the Department of Agriculture and these liaisons are still maintained today as well as their interest in all aspects of agriculture and food production.

All too often in this modern day and age we find lovely recipes in magazines, newspapers, etc. but they require ingredients that are not always available in rural areas. With this in mind the members of Quebec Women's Institutes have compiled this cookbook of simple and easy recipes of just plain good cooking.[5]

Many of the cookbooks contain advertisements and illustrations for local merchants and industries (some also appear in the Tweedsmuir Histories). There are not only recipes, complete with the name and community of the contributor, but menus and quantities for large gatherings and community meals, such as a Ham Supper for 225 or Tea Refreshments and Dainties for 300 people. There are sections on homemade medicines, with recipes such as "Grandpa's Recipe to Cure Arthritis" or "Cough Syrup," antidotes for poisons, substitutions for missing ingredients, and much more.

Many of these recipes reflect the historical, cultural, and regional preferences of Canadians. Recipes from the First Nations, such as Venison Jerky, Wild Duck, Bannock, Fried Rabbit, and canned wild meat such as deer, moose, buffalo, appear in *Burriss Family Treasures*, published by Burriss WI, Burriss, Ontario.

Favourite Recipes, published by the Pickardville WI in Pickardville, Alberta, features Chuck Wagon Beans and other local favourites, while a contributor from British Columbia sent the recipe for Nanaimo Bars. *Popular Recipes*, compiled by the WIs on Prince Edward Island, contains recipes for Lighthouses (a type of cookie) and an array of dishes that highlight seafood. *Favourite Recipes*, published by Lyons Brook WI in Pictou, Nova Scotia, embodies the area's historical beginnings and presents recipes for Scottish Oatcakes, Rolled Oats Bread, Oatmeal Cookies, Oatmeal Drops, and Butterscotch Squares. It also showcases a love of seafood, including salmon, oysters, finnan haddie, codfish, tuna, and more!

Despite Canada's cultural and regional preferences, there are some amazing similarities in the recipes and the dishes that have been, and continue to be, served for a century or more right across Canada. Gum Drop Cakes, Squares, and Cookies, for example, appear in almost every book, along with a basic pudding recipe with many names, including Half-Hour Pudding, Altogether Pudding, Poor Man's Pudding, Hurry Dessert, Liberal Pudding with Conservative Sauce, or Conservative Pudding with Liberal Sauce!

Many of the cookbooks highlight the foods of celebration on Canadian tables, with a host of birthday and anniversary cakes, while a few, such as the *Cook Book*, published in 1951 by Tara WI in Tara, Ontario, ventured into the realm of religion, with Hot Cross Buns, Easter Garland Coffee Cake, Paradise Pudding, and Divinity Fudge. Christmas is universally covered, with puddings, cakes, cookies, and pies featuring carrots, plums, mincemeat, dried fruit, and spices in abundance.

In the last half of the twentieth century, a surprising number of recipes appear to have been influenced by, or based on, the food traditions of Canadians of Chinese ancestry, and include Orange Soy Sauce for Fish Fillets, Mock Chop Suey, Cantonese Chicken, Chicken Chow Mein, Hong Kong Casserole, Sweet and Sour Spareribs, Sweet and Sour Short Ribs, Pork Fried Rice, Sweet and Sour Tuna, Sweet and Sour Meat Balls, Chinese Meat Balls, Chop Suey in Casserole, Sweet and Sour Pork Chops and Cabbage, Canton Tuna Caserole, Oriental Beef, Chinese Broccoli and Beef Salad, and Chow Mein Cookies.

Many recipes tell a story about the donor, the family, or the rigours of everyday life, such as "Grace Cameron's Cake always served to my aunt's threshers," from *Country Cooking*, published by Zion WI in Durham, Ontario, or the "Tired House Wife Cake" from *Cooking Favourites of Barkway WI*, Gravenhurst, Ontario. Perhaps the ultimate is "Stay-a-Bed Stew," which appears in *From Our Kitchen to Yours*, published by Auburn WI, Auburn, Ontario.

Many Women's Institutes prepared and published cookbooks to support fundraising. These publications are a priceless record of everyday Canadian life.

The Junior WIs in many communities also published cookbooks. The *Cook Book*, published in 1932 by the Tara Junior WI, is an excellent example of a clear, concise guide for the beginning homemaker. She does not need to fret about what time of day to begin making her bread. "Take two cups of potato water at noon," the recipe explains. If buns are to be made, "set about three o'clock in the afternoon," so they will have risen twice and be ready to bake in the morning.

For close to a century, the culinary and social history of Canada can be traced on the pages of these WI cookbooks, from Victoria Pudding to Prince of Wales Cake to Queen Elizabeth Squares. There are recipes — Apple Less Apple Pie or Poor Man's Pudding or Poor Man's Rice Pudding or Ham Bone Dinner — to feed a family during the Great Depression when the larder was almost empty. And there are many versions of Macaroni and Cheese, as well as tips on how to stretch a small can of tuna to serve a family of eight.

These cookbooks, priced at 25 cents per copy, as was the Elm Grove Women's Institute *RECIPE BOOK*, published in 1945, provided an affordable treasure that the thrifty housewife could not overlook. There are recipes for Canada War Cakes, War Fruit Cakes, and plain War Cakes. In the 1960s after the advent of television, Colourvision Cakes and TV Squares appear. In the 1980s whole chapters are devoted to "Something Quick," featuring convenient recipes, shortcuts, and helpful hints for microwave cooking.

The names of many recipes raise questions. What is a Featherbed? How do you make a Lighthouse? A Shipwreck? Cry Babies? Sex in a Pan? Angel Wings? Food for the Gods? How can we resist reaching for a bowl, a spoon, and the ingredients?

Just as the Women's Institutes around the world have changed and expanded to meet the needs of their members and their communities over the past century, so have their cookbooks and the astonishing wealth of information they contain. They are indeed a true reflection of their motto: For Home and Country.

CHAPTER THIRTEEN

Edith Had Got the Nutmeg!

At times of both happiness and heartbreak, families, friends, and neighbours unite to commemorate the life, death, or union of those they love. In addition to the ceremonies that recognize their loved ones, Canadians have long traditions of food and beverages that are served to mark various occasions.

Nicolas Denys described the bounty of one dish at a seventeenth-century Mi'kmaq wedding feast: "The bridegroom brought in the meat in a huge bark dish, divided it and placed it on as many plates as there were persons, as much as they could hold. There was in each [small] plate enough meat for a dozen persons."[1] Two centuries later, Mary Gapper, an English visitor staying with her two brothers, who had taken up land near Thornhill, Upper Canada, recounted a visit on October 28, 1829, to Dr. Peter Diehl and his bride, Ann Macaulay, at York:

> We called on Dr. Diehl who begged to introduce us to his bride. We were accordingly ushered into a little parlour where she sat with her bridesmaids in bridal state. There was wine and bridescake on the table and another plate of little white rolls. We talked of the weather, the state of the roads, and our journey. The party exclaimed at our robustness when we said that we had come and intended returning the same day. The bride said she could have no enjoyment living so far from neighbours.

Then came Mrs. Sheriff Ridout and her daughter. I thought that the silence, which ensued, would never be broken. I am not sure that Mrs. Sheriff had spoken yet, but the bride inquired of the young lady in a half whisper if she had heard that Edith had got the nutmeg. This I learned was concealed in the cake and the happy person who cut the piece containing it was the next to be married. They all seemed to think being married excellent fun, except the bridegroom who looked rather more serious about it.[2]

The following year, on May 13, Mary herself was the bride when she married a neighbouring farmer, Edward O'Brien, and her sister-in-law, Fannie, reported the event:

After breakfast the little bridesmaid distributed the gloves to the gentlemen. We then went to equip ourselves and jumble off to church in the lumber waggon, the pleasure waggon being broken. We arrived there at eleven o'clock and found the carpenters busily employed, but they soon laid their work aside.

Mr. Mathews performed the service most impressively and Mary and Edward behaved very properly on the occasion. Little Pug was very pleased with her dress, which was a French white, bonnet and tippet. She looked very pretty and behaved very well at first, but before we left the church she was restless and amused herself by pushing up nails.

On our return home we found a large cake (made by Edward's desire in the largest milk pan he could get) and wine on the table. Mr. Mathews stayed to dinner and between five and six returned to York in a thunderstorm. Mary and Southby remained with us the evening.[3]

From Mary's *Journal* we also have a description of a truly Canadian custom known as a *shivaree* (also *chariviari, chivaree,* and *chivari*):

November 25, 1828 — A hard frost. After the rest of
the party were gone to bed, Mama and I were startled
by an unusual uproar ruffling the wings of the night.
The dogs caught the alarm and added their barking
to the sounds of horns, guns, and shouting which came
from the distance. On enquiring the cause of the
uproar, we were told that it was a *chivaree*. That is a custom, brought from Lower Canada, of assaulting the
dwelling of a newly married pair with every species of
noisy uproar that can be devised, for the purpose of
extorting whiskey.[4]

The custom of extracting either a treat or money from the bridegroom by loud serenading so that the visitors can go off and buy food
and drink for themselves appears to have been first mentioned in the
Quebec Gazette on January 12, 1786. That means the tradition may
indeed have originated in Lower Canada as Mary noted. In fact, J. Long
gives an account of the practice in 1791 in *Voyages and Travels of an
Indian Interpreter and Trader*.

Sometimes I distinguish myself at a *charivari*, which is a
custom that prevails in different parts of Canada, of assembling with old pots, kettles, &c. and beating them at the
doors of new married people; but generally, either when
the man is older than the woman, or the parties have been
twice married: in this case they beat a *charivari*, hallooing
out very vociferously, until the man is obliged to obtain
their silence by a pecuniary contribution, or submit to be
abused with the vilest language.[5]

In *Canadian Prairie Homesteaders*, we learn that after a *shivaree* in western Canada the guests were invited into the home of the newly married
couple to visit, dance, and play cards. The neighbour ladies would bring
along refreshments, fresh buns, jelly rolls, matrimonial cake, and dough-
nuts.[6] Not only did the custom spread across Canada, but it is still carried
out in many modern rural communities.

In 1840, Joseph Beete Jukes, the geological surveyor of Newfoundland, was delayed in his work in St. Mary's because of a stiff knee, and records a wedding that he attended:

> I was taken by priest Father D to a wedding at a fisherman's house close by. The company, consisting of young men and women with a few of the seniors, assembled about nine o'clock, and sat round the room drinking grog for some time. Presently a fifer struck up a tune, and reels and jigs began. There was much bustling of women in and out of a back room; and about half past ten the bride was said to be ready, the music ceased, a table was brought forward, the priest put on his scapular, and the bride and bridegroom came forward and knelt before the table. The priest opened his book, asked them the usual questions in English, and rapidly read a number of Latin prayers, and the ceremony was completed. Instantly there was a struggle among the men around for the first kiss, but as the bride was not yet off her knees, and the bridegroom was kneeling beside her, he had the best chance and won accordingly. A plate of cake was next produced and put upon the table: the bride and bridegroom came forward, took a piece of cake, and deposited several dollars on the table before the priest. Each one in the room then came forward and took a piece of cake, leaving a dollar before the priest, who stood behind the table thanking them as they came up. I had nothing but two-dollar notes in my pocket, of which I laid down one, when Father D took it up, looked at it, shook his head and said "Ah, sir, upon my word that's too much! A five pound note!" When all had made their contributions, they stood round while he counted the money and declared its amount … nearly 15 pounds…. Supper was now brought in, consisting of tea and hot cakes; after which there was more dancing and grog-drinking, nearly to the break of day.[7]

Marie Nightingale, in *Out of Old Nova Scotia Kitchens*, describes the customs of the first German settlers in that province when they celebrated the most festive of all occasions — the wedding:

> Guests lingered in those days often as long as a week, but more usually two or three days. The hostess used to press upon her guests that they must not leave until all the food had been eaten. That took a long doing, since bounteous supplies were laid in for the wedding feast — roasts of mutton and geese, hams, soups, puddings, pies and cakes.
>
> Always there was a fiddler to play his lively tunes for the polka and the Old-Fashioned Eight, or "Stamp your Sauerkraut." Quantities of liquor were also consumed — sometimes as much as 25 gallons for one wedding![8]

The newcomers from Belgium to Manitoba in the late nineteenth and early twentieth centuries brought with them the tradition and the recipe for the cookies called Belgian Lukken. They were, and are, usually served as a special treat along with wine to guests before a wedding or at Christmas. These delicious cookies are a combination of butter, sugar, flour, eggs, and either brandy or rum, and are baked on a krumkake iron until golden brown.[9]

Food was not just a part of the wedding feast for our ancestors, but often an element of the courtship, as well. Karl Hansen, a young Danish bachelor and homesteader in the Thunder Bay District in the early twentieth century, was invited to celebrate Christmas with his neighbours, the Andersons, where he met

Many young unmarried women slept with pieces of wedding cake under their pillows, hoping they would dream of their future husbands.

Agnes, his future wife. He shares his memories of "walking out" with her:

> As soon as possible, I started to sow my cultivated land. I planned a big garden, where we could grow plenty of vegetables for our own consumption. Instead of a dairy cow we had a goat, as well as a suckling calf and a horse, and, as our livestock was not that numerous, we had not spent all of our time looking after them. Agnes and I just loved to fish for trout, and there were plenty of these small delicious fish. Sometimes we caught so many that we could use them for three meals a day, and neither of us got tired of eating trout. The major part of this, the first summer, was spent at the cabin, from where Agnes and I went on pleasure tours. If we were not out fishing we would be out picking berries, or we went on a tour back home to the post office.
>
> It was busy in our new home. Our mother was busy in the kitchen helping Agnes with the cooking. The whole Anderson family was present to celebrate the wedding in our new home. Everything went calmly and humbly. Only the family was present, no drinking, we only filled our stomachs with good food, a little more than we were used to. We had a happy day together. At last the lady and the landowner were alone on the estate. We had been that way so very often before, but there was a big change happening in our lives that evening.[10]

The *Canadian Cook Book*, first published in Toronto in 1923, has a brief section on "Wedding Refreshments":

> The serving of wedding refreshments may follow the type outlined for a formal luncheon; otherwise a choice is made of the buffet service or the arrangements suggested for the afternoon tea or reception. The hour of serving and the number of guests are usually determining factors in the service chosen. In any case, the bride's cake should form the

central table decoration. When the guests are to be seated, place cards should be used, the bride and groom being placed at the middle of one side of the table.[11]

This popular cookery book continued through many printings, and by the thirteenth edition of 1941, we find detailed recommendations for those planning a wedding reception, with a variety of menus:

Assorted Sandwiches
Curled Celery   Olives
Tutti Frutti Ice Cream   Raspberry Ice
Wedding Cake   Assorted Small Cakes
Fruit Punch   Tea   Coffee

OR

Chicken à la King   Water Cress Rolls
Celery Olives   Pickled Cherries
Pistachio Ice Cream   Apricot Ice
Wedding Cake   Assorted Cakes
Bonbons   Salted Nuts
Punch   Tea   Coffee[12]

Our Canadian ancestors were not only traditional folk, but they held many beliefs and superstitions about ingredients, prepared foods, and beverages, as well. These were all central to foretelling the future, warding off evil, or bringing good fortune. When Mary Gapper O'Brien recorded in her *Journal* "that the bride inquired … if she had heard that Edith had got the nutmeg," that tradition lives on. In *Pioneer Recipes and Memories*, published on Manitoulin Island in 2004, the wedding-cake recipe still calls for one nutmeg! This book was inspired by Carrie Wilson (1891–1973), and many of the recipes in it are from a handwritten, indexed book that she kept.[13]

While some hopeful young women may have depended on the nutmeg to foretell their future, Norwegian girls settled in Manitoba relied on an almond. An old Norse tradition tells of families putting an almond in the Yulegrot bowl. Whoever got it was the next one married (or, some say, will have good luck in the new year). Yulegrot contains milk rice, raisins, salt, sugar, cinnamon and, of course, an almond, and is gently cooked for about two hours before serving.[14]

Many cultural groups served a light or dark fruitcake at a wedding, and traditionally the unmarried women take a piece of this cake home with them to put under their pillows, confident they will dream of their future husbands that night!

When members of a community passed away, whether First Nations or newcomers, friends and neighbours rallied around to honour the deceased and to support and assist the living. Champlain may have been the first newcomer to record this tradition in the culture of the founding peoples. In 1608 he noted that, following the death of a chief, the Natives would hold a banquet three times a year and sing and dance on the grave. A few years later, in 1613, he described a cemetery on the Ottawa River in which the tombs were like shrines and had embellishments that denoted the needs of the departed. If the deceased were a woman or a girl, a kettle, an earthen pot, a wooden spoon, or a paddle might be depicted.

On September 28, 1635, Father Le Jeune provided an account of the Feast of the Dead in which he related how he and Father Buteux discovered a band of Natives holding a feast near the graves of their dead relatives. The Jesuit said that the Natives gave the departed the best part of the banquet, which they tossed into the fire.

Newcomers to Canada appear to have brought with them the traditions of their cultures and their communities. One of the most positive ways many of these newcomers showed their support was to provide ready-made dishes of food delivered to the door of the mourning family. Arrangements also had to be made to feed, water, and care for the horses of the mourners, many of whom travelled long distances and stayed for several days upon hearing of the death of a relative or friend. When the service was over, whether at home, at a place of worship, or at the graveside, and the deceased had been buried, everyone was invited back to the house for "refreshments," and long hours would be spent with old acquaintances and friends. A funeral rated a good supply of liquor. Although there was a great display of mourning until the deceased had been properly buried, things cheered up somewhat on the return from the cemetery. A generous table was laid with barley bread and

Bees and their habits are important parts of Canadian folklore. For example, if there is a death in the family, the hives should be draped in black, a mournful tune should be hummed, and the name of the departed should be announced so that these messengers will take the news to heaven.

cheese, loaf cake, and always a funeral cake, which was a plain cake flavoured with cinnamon.[15]

Old Hemmingford Recipes, published in 1977, celebrated the centennial of the incorporation of Hemmingford Village, Quebec, and includes the favourite recipes of some of the families that settled there as early as 1800. "An early settlers' recipe" for Funeral Pie calls for sour cream, raisins, eggs, salt, spices, lemon juice, and cornstarch baked in an unbaked pie shell.[16]

Greek settlers coming to Manitoba brought with them the tradition of preparing Kolliva (also Kolyva) for the mourning service, held forty days after the passing of a loved one. This dish contains wheat, symbolizing everlasting life, and raisins for sweetness. Almonds, pecans, zwieback (crisp buns), and sugar are added to the recipe, which takes several hours to make. When it is ready to serve, a cardboard cross is pressed into the centre and then the depression is filled with silver candy or coloured sugar.[17]

Canadians of Chinese ancestry hold nine-course banquets to celebrate rites of passage such as weddings and funerals. When they pay their respects at a funeral home, they are handed a white envelope as they leave, containing money and candy. The candy represents sweetness after the bitterness of their loss and is always eaten before they return home.

In many communities in Canada, Quing Ming has been, and still is, celebrated in the spring by those of Chinese ancestry. On this day all Chinese restaurants close so that everyone can visit the cemetery to clean the graves, plant fresh flowers, set off firecrackers, pour liquor over the graves, and then enjoy a picnic right there beside their ancestors.[18]

Many cultural groups do not have a traditional mourning food or foods but simply embrace the fellowship of a light meal together after the service. In many Canadian communities that meal will include assorted sandwiches, relishes, cookies, squares, cakes, tea, coffee, and cold beverages during the summer months. This tradition gives everyone an opportunity to honour the deceased and remember his or her favourite foods, which are often featured on the laden table.

CHAPTER FOURTEEN

"I'd Rather Work for a Dollar Less in a Real Camp Where the Food Was Good"

For centuries countless Canadians have lived, worked, studied, and eaten their meals, not at home but, as we have learned, in a variety of locations — fur-trading posts; military garrisons; lumbering, mining, and railway camps; schools; prisons; religious residences; and many others. Men, women, and children from all walks of life have had incredibly diverse experiences with food, often ranging from adequate to appalling, because they were at the mercy of faraway governments, superior officers, harvests, budgets, tides, weather, roads (or the lack of them), and neglect.

We know that many of the explorers and fur traders learned from the First Nations how to forage and hunt in the wild, and often depended on them for survival foods. The military and the surveyors who came later acquired their supplies in a variety of ways. Just two examples of the strict regulations that were often in force are found in military and surveyors' records.

The garrisons were built at strategic locations to control and repel the enemy of the moment, without consideration of how they would be provisioned. Whether in the heat of battle or performing the monotonous round of drill and sentry duty, the logistics of supporting one individual soldier, let alone a whole regiment, were enormous. It required a massive bureaucratic organization to ensure that barracks and storehouses were built and maintained; sufficient supplies of food, medicines, tools, ammunition, and clothing were on hand; and that the myriad details relating to troop movements, pay and allowances, promotions, and discharges were all well organized. In the years immediately following the American Revolution, the provisioning of the army in Canada was handled primarily from Britain. Items such as salt meat and flour were contracted for in Britain, packed, and then shipped to Canada.

It was impossible to control the quality of the food, and eventually commissariat branches were established in Canada that employed a contract system with local merchants and individual producers. The actual process of feeding the men appears to have occurred as follows. The soldiers' morning meal, served between 7:30 and 8:00 a.m., usually consisted of tea and bread. The main meal of the day was served at 1:00 p.m. Each soldier, on a rotational basis, would take a turn collecting his squad's share of meat, peas, and bread from the commissary, plus any vegetables that had been gathered from the garden or purchased locally, and he would cook the meat in large kettles in the regimental cookhouse. The food would then be carried to the men's barracks where it would be served out. The "cook of the day" required no particular skills for preparing the daily serving of beef or pork stew. While the meal may have been a monotonous serving of stew day after day, at least the soldier could count on one regular meal per day.[1]

In addition to military rations, a soldier's food supplies could be augmented by game shot by hunting parties and fish from local streams or by gathering wild rice, fruit, and nuts. If the troops had sufficient currency and access to civilian stores, they could also purchase supplies to add to their rations.

The early surveyors in Canada faced a formidable challenge as far as food was concerned. The surveyor general outlined the terms and conditions under which surveyors and their crews were expected to run true lines through forests and swamps and over hills, mountains, and tangled underbrush. In a letter dated March 24, 1809, the terms and conditions of the road survey through Middleton, New Brunswick, were outlined:

> For this survey your pay will be 7/6 per day, with an allowance in lieu of rations of 1/3 Prov'l curr'y per day.... The Chainbearers will be allowed 2/ per day, the axemen will be allowed 1/6 per man per day, all Provincial currency, and you will be allowed for each, ration furnished to your 1/3 provincial currency, per man per day. The ration to be of the following species 1 1/2 lbs. Flour, 3/4 lb of pork and 1/2 pint of peas. You are to understand that

this allowance to you of 1/3 Prov'l curr'y per man per day for each ration, is to cover all expenses whatsoever, such as transport, Batteau hire, camp kettles, axes, Tommthawks, Tents, bags, Snoe shoes.[2]

Provincial currency in the above passage refers to Halifax currency: £1 was equal to $4, and 1 shilling was equal to 20 cents. Surveyors, too, would have lived off the land wherever and whenever possible to supplement the never-ending rations of salt pork, bread, and dried peas.

In the first half of the nineteenth century, lumbering vied with agriculture as the most important industry of the Canadas. Perhaps that is why the Canadians who took control of the quality and quantity of their meals were the lumbermen. If they didn't like the food, they simply moved on. As a result, the camps with the best cooks got the best men.

The first commercial logging camps in Canada often had one building (or shanty) that served as both bunkhouse and cookhouse. The loggers may have taken turns cooking for themselves, or they may have lured an inexperienced lad to prepare "the great trinity" of bread, salt pork, and beans that they then ate standing up. On one of his CBC Radio broadcasts, host Miller Stewart quoted an elderly Bobcaygeon, Ontario, lumberman: "The eatin' was the meanest part — nothin' but beans, salt pork, potatoes, flapjacks and bannock. We never seen a pie, we never seen a cookie. Nothin' sweet but blackstrap. But the tea they biled in the kittles — it was real good."[3]

The challenge was, of course, the isolation of the camps and the difficulty in moving supplies to them by either land or water. These realities made salt pork a staple item on the table for a very long time right across Canada.

The lumbermen in the early camps were often a mixture of farmers in need of cash, young men in search of adventure, and professionals who moved from camp to camp in search of better food and better wages in that order. As the industry grew, and with it the demand for better meals, the lumber companies separated the function of the cookhouse from the bunkhouse. The cook, with the help of one or more cookees, and the bull cooks (men or boys who chopped wood and other chores), prepared from three to five meals a day. Working over a gigantic wood stove or two, or a huge fireplace stoked by wood, the cook was surrounded by great cast-iron pots, kettles, and Dutch ovens. The division of buildings also resulted in

In the bachelor camps needed to build roads and railways, log trees, and mine gold and silver, the skills and knowledge of the cook were the most important assets to keep the men on the job.

the famous cookhouses where the men sat down to eat, served by "flunkeys," each one of whom could serve up to forty men. There was a rule of silence at the table, and lumbermen insisted that they ate those meals in less than ten minutes. Some believe that silence was imposed from the earliest days when cooking, eating, and sleeping were all done in one room by the whole crew.

Joshua Fraser, writing in the *Backwoods of Canada* in 1883, waxes eloquently about the cooks and the fare:

> And you would be amazed at the general excellence of the cooking that is done by these fellows. Where will you find such bread as is made in their immense pots, buried in and covered over by the hot ashes at the end of the *camboose* [an open fireplace]? Not a particle of the strength and fine flavour of the flour is lost by evaporation, as in the case of a stove or open oven: It is all con-

densed in the bread. Then it is strong and firm, and yet — and this is the mystery to me — it is light and porous as that of any first-class housewife's.

And what shall we say about the beans? They are simply *par excellence*. They are baked in the same kind of pot as the bread, the lid being hermetically sealed to the rim by the dough, and then buried in the hot ashes. The beans are first thoroughly sifted, washed and boiled, and then large slices of fat pork mixed in with them. The pot is then placed in its deep bed of hot ashes, and as in the case of the bread, not a breath of steam or of the essence of the beans is allowed to escape. The fat pork, becoming dissolved by the heat, and of course, neither fried not boiled as in other processes, becomes amalgamated with the beans, and when the whole is considered sufficiently cooked, a mess is ready, which, for succulency of flavour, and savoury richness of nutrition, will completely throw in the shade the famous pottage for which Esau bartered his birthright.[4]

The cook was almost always a man in the early days. However, by the end of the nineteenth century and the beginning of the twentieth, women were often working in the camps. Sometimes they were the wives or family of the camp owners or managers, to ensure there was no "hanky panky."

Elinor Thomas, writing in *A Loving Legacy*, describes the enormous stove her mother, Lurena (age fourteen), her Aunt Greta (age twelve), and her grandmother, Annie Wilson, had cooked on in the Crow Bridge Camp of forty men on the Crow River in Quebec in 1916: "The stove did not have the usual four burners; this monster had eight. Two huge ovens, two hot water reservoirs, one on each side, and a warming oven big enough to lie down in."[5]

On this monster, Lurena baked all the bread and biscuits, while Greta baked the pies — 1,036 pies in twenty-four days! Their day began at three in the morning in preparation for a five-o'clock breakfast of boiled beans and salt pork, which had simmered on the back of the stove all night, lots of freshly baked bread, butter, molasses to spread on the bread, pies, and strong lashings of tea.

The men who were going into the bush to cut logs were
given a lunch to take with them. This was meat sandwiches; more salt pork until freeze up, when they could keep
beef frozen. Lots of pie, again, and tea. The lunch, carried
in cloth bags, had frozen solid by lunch time, and had to
be thawed out over a campfire until it was soft enough to
eat. The tea was brought expertly to a "first roll-over boil"
in a honey pail, and drunk from "shanty dishes" — enam-
el bowls without handles, which warmed the hands
cupped around them.[6]

The place selected for the fire to thaw out the lunches and boil the tea
was called "the dinner hole," and for many men good memories remain of
this place in the forest. The dinner hole was a restoring oasis of warmth,
nourishment, relaxation, and comradeship in the middle of the grinding
toil and cold of the old-time lumberjack's day. Food was quickly sacrificed
to appetites generated by four or five hours of chopping, sawing, and log-
rolling. The blazing fire thawed numbed toes in cold weather and dried
wet mitts in mild. There was time for conversation and an after-dinner
smoke, pleasures that were forbidden in the camp cookery. When the men
returned to their axes, saws, and cant hooks, a new group took over.
Chickadees, whiskey-jacks, and squirrels seized the ground to search out
and carry off fallen crumbs and discarded rinds. Long before nightfall the
fire died and winter's silence descended over the dinner hole.[7]

Good and varied food became a condition of labour, because competition for workers proved at an early date that food quality was something
an employer could control. The name of the lumberman who first lured
timberbeasts from his competitor's camp with the aroma of better pies is
long lost in the woods. But food is what counted. "The camp that served
the best meals got the best men. It was as simple as that."[8]

As a figure in logging folklore, the cook is bigger than Paul Bunyan,
who never put in an appearance in New England, while the fabled cook
certainly did. Paul's own cook was his cousin, Big Joe, who was from three
weeks below Quebec and made Hot Cakes on a griddle so large you could
not see across it when the steam was thick. It was greased by boys who
skated over it with hams on their feet.[9]

Lorne Fleece Collection

Three times a day "good food and plenty of it" was imperative to a well-organized, happy camp.

By the middle of the twentieth century, variety and quality in food supplies was growing, and in May 1943 a camp near Longlac, Ontario, received foodstuffs that included hip beef, pork butts, wieners, beef sausage, cheese, shortening, butter, eggs, bacon, smoked ham, potatoes, carrots, fresh beef, and spaghetti, so the cook and cookees had a varied larder to work with. In addition, the men received empty syrup barrels, so they could make "Finnish Beer," a thirst-quencher concocted from raisins and molasses.[10]

Folklorist Edith Fowke, in *Lumbering Songs*, captures the importance of good food to the men in the camps. The following song is from "Anstruther Camp," Buckhorn, Ontario, about 1900:

> Then at length the cook calls, "Supper boys!" We crowd
>   into our seats —
> It is a sight for all sore eyes to see those brave boys eat.
> And then the supper it being over, we talk of the days gone
>   by,
> And Jack will say to Jim, "Old boy, did you get enough of
>   pie?"[11]

Emil Engstrom, a logger working in British Columbia in 1914, recalls "the small fly-by-night logging camps were paying up to five dollars a day, but that was too much for me, I'd rather work for a dollar less in a real camp where the food was good."[12]

Very few written records appear to have survived of the recipes used by the cooks and cookees in the lumber camps. A *Cookee Book* is a rare example, and the first recipe is for Teakettle Soup, which contains a bowl of boiling water, a dash each of Worcestershire Sauce, butter, salt and pepper, and a piece of hard bread![13] How long would Emil have stayed at that camp?

CHAPTER FIFTEEN

Ladies Please Provide Versus Men Serve Oysters!

Food was a fundamental foundation used for fundraising by our ancestors, and remains so in many Canadian communities today. In the nineteenth century, the project that many organizations attempted was — as it continues to be — the assembling of recipes and publication of a cookbook offered for sale at a modest price. *The Home Cook Book*, "compiled by Ladies of Toronto and Chief Cities and Towns in Canada" and published in Toronto in 1877, is believed to be the first such fundraising cookbook, with the proceeds to benefit the Hospital for Sick Children. It was obviously a resounding success, for although by 1885 Canada's population was only about four and a half million, over a hundred thousand copies were sold![1]

With this project as a model, many other organizations such as the Women's Institutes followed suit, as we have seen. They were soon joined by, or in competition with, a multitude of others wanting to raise funds, including the Women's Temperance Auxiliary of Sparta, Ontario, with the *Spartan Cook Book* in 1908, and St. Luke's Church in Winnipeg, Manitoba, with *St. Luke's Cook Book* in 1910. The former organization had worked to remove the liquor licence from the Sparta Hotel and was now raising funds for the "purpose of furnishing in the house of entertainment, a drawing room, equipped with daily papers and good periodic literature, and of making the general surroundings of the place such, that it would not only be a hospitable home for the traveller, but also a centre of social and educational interest to the community at large."[2] The latter organization tells us that "This book is published for the purpose of applying the proceeds of its sale to The Organ Fund of St. Luke's Church Winnipeg. The recipes in the book are either original or else they have been tried and found successful by those whose names are appended."[3]

Although many organizations did publish cookbooks, others chose to organize, publicize, and present events that involved the fellowship of actually eating or drinking whatever food or beverages were being featured. One of the first of these appears to have been the Tea, or the Afternoon Tea, which would be held in someone's home or in the local hall, church, or other public building. Anna, the seventh duchess of Bedford, is credited with introducing this light meal to her friends in the Royal Court in the early nineteenth century. She would invite a few friends to her room for tea and biscuits when she experienced a "sinking feeling" around five in the afternoon. The United Empire Loyalists and the settlers from Great Britain also brought with them their love of tea, and the custom of "taking tea" was often described by Elizabeth Simcoe in her diary. *The Home Cook Book* gives detailed instructions for Afternoon Tea served in the home:

> Guests arrived in the five minutes before the hour, or the five minutes after. The tea is brought in punctually and placed on the hostess' table in the corner, where are the urns of black, green and Russian tea for those who like each, a basket of wafers, delicate sandwiches of chicken or thin sliced meats, and a basket of fancy cake. If the English style is followed, the cups of tea are carried to the guests on a tray, and a tiny table to rest the cups on placed in the reach of the group.[4]

Why not take this comfortable tradition that every woman in the community knew and understood and transform it into a fundraiser? By the end of the nineteenth century, Teas of all sorts were being held in the villages and towns to raise funds for churches, lodges, societies, associations, Women's Institutes, and the Ladies' Aid, to support worthy causes of all kinds.

Marion Leithead grew up in Winnipeg in the early twentieth century and recalls that, as a small child, she helped her mother, Ida Leithead, polish her grandmother's silver tea service in preparation for the St. Andrew's

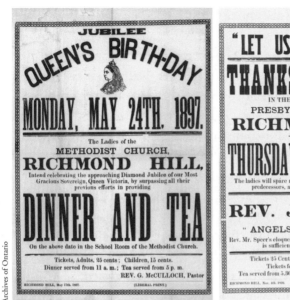

Archives of Ontario

The tradition of "taking tea" in the afternoon began as a pleasant and informal way to entertain but soon became a popular fundraiser, either on the lawn or in the parlour, at home or at church, in towns and cities across Canada.

Presbyterian Church Tea. Like many other churches at the time, St. Andrew's was using the Parable of the Talents, as told by Jesus in the New Testament. Each member of an organization was given a small amount of money and, by using her talents, was to make it grow into a larger sum. Ida would make quantities of Seville Orange Marmalade with her "talent" money and take orders for it. When the Tea was over, Marion's task was to fill her little wagon with the jars of marmalade that had been ordered and pull it along the streets of Winnipeg, delivering them to the correct addresses and collecting the money.[5]

Communities across Canada developed their own regional fundraisers based on local food or on the foods they loved and knew would be available in large quantities. These included Baked Bean Suppers, with a menu that consisted of beans baked with salt pork, salad, rolls and butter, assorted pies, and coffee. In eastern Canada, Lobster Suppers and Seafood Suppers were — and still are — great favourites. Ham Suppers were popular at any time of year, particularly in the fall when the hogs were slaughtered, or in the spring when canned ham was served along with potato salad, cabbage salad, jellied salads, and strawberry shortcake. In many communities, Turkey Dinners, complete with mashed potatoes, butternut squash, jellied cranberry rings, celery sticks, and assorted pies brought out the local residents, while in the west, Fowl Suppers, with roast chicken, mashed potatoes, gravy, cabbage salad, pies, cakes, and tarts helped to raise funds for current projects.

Perhaps the most curious of all the fundraising meals were the Oyster Suppers that first appeared in Ontario in the nineteenth century and continue in some communities today. There has been speculation for over a century about this phenomenon. Were oysters plentiful and cheap? Were they packed and shipped only in fifty-pound barrels and therefore required a crowd to host a meal? Was it the influence of the United Empire Loyalists and/or the new arrivals coming from Great Britain, all bringing their love of oysters with them?

By the last quarter of the nineteenth century, we find the wives of the United Farmers' Organization in Stouffville, Ontario, "providing an Oyster Supper once a year. Oysters must have been plentiful and cheap as this seems to have been common entertainment."[6] On March 2, 1899, in Tweed, Ontario, an Oyster Supper and lecture was announced in the *Tweed News*:

> On Monday evening Mar. 6th an oyster supper and lecture will be given in the Presbyterian Church when Rev. Mr. Potter, who is so favourably known in Tweed, will deliver his popular lecture "Sawdust without butter." Immediately after the lecture, which will begin at eight o'clock sharp, oysters will be served in the basement of the church. Admission 25 cents, children under twelve 15 cents. Everybody come.[7]

The following week, on March 9, the *Tweed News* tells us how successful the evening was:

> The lecture and oyster supper held in the Presbyterian Church on Monday evening passed off very successfully, both parts of the programme being much enjoyed by

those present. Mr. Howard Stutchbury, baritone soloist in St. James' Cathedral, Toronto, and late of Old Trinity, New York, who was secured at a late hour by the lecturer, Rev. Mr. Potter, sang two solos and two encores, which were very much appreciated. The lecture "Sawdust without butter," delivered by Rev. J.G. Potter, who is well and favourably known here, was probably not of the nature expected by the audience, but was, nevertheless, abounding with good strong points and was listened to with much interest by the audience. After the lecture, oysters were served in the basement, which was scarcely large enough to accommodate all present.[8]

Reports of Oyster Suppers continued into the twentieth century:

One remarkable occasion took place at Wenona Lodge on Sparrow Lake, Muskoka, Ontario, after the return of the soldiers from the first World War. The Women's Institute provided an oyster supper, popular fare in those days and the famed Plunketts of the "Dumbells" provided the entertainment.[9]

In the tiny Ontario village of Greenwood, the genesis for the annual Oyster Supper was a meeting in the Greenwood General Store in 1948 held by the board of Greenwood United Church to discuss fundraising. The group of men was unanimous in the decision that an Oyster Supper in the basement of the church was the perfect solution. A nearby community, Mount Zion, had been successfully hosting Oyster Suppers for over a decade. Why not here?[10] The following year the first Oyster Supper was held, and it became an annual event. The difference in Greenwood was that the men of the community took the lead, as we read in the story by correspondent Betty Pegg in the *Stouffville Tribune* in 1969:

Men Serve Oysters ... The Oyster Supper sponsored by the men of our congregation last week was a real success. It is a pleasure to watch these men work with such congenial effort; someone was heard to say it was a real pleasure to wash those nice church dishes so many times in one evening. Several one-time residents of our village made a special effort to come back for that supper date.[11]

Two years earlier the same newspaper gives us some history and tells us of the success of the 1967 Dinner:

Recently a crowd of 300 people turned up at Greenwood United Church and enjoyed a full oyster supper with all the trimmings. This is the most popular function of the year.

Every 19th century kitchen was adorned with a barrel of oysters in one corner. The oysters, brought in fresh from the eastern seaboard, were packed in wet sawdust and apparently remained fresh enough to be enjoyed for several weeks. Served as fritters for breakfast, soup for lunch and stew for dinner, every pre-confederation menu had a complete complement of shellfish.

Suddenly they went out of style for everyday use and appeared on first-class hotel menus. Probably price had a great deal to do with their demise and their unfamiliarity to modern day shoppers has inspired the notion that we no longer enjoy them.[12]

The roles and responsibilities of men and women throughout all of the nineteenth century and a good portion of the twentieth century were clearly defined in rural Ontario and many other parts of Canada. Food selection, preparation, and presentation were considered "women's work." For men to buy groceries, prepare recipes, set the table, serve meals, or wash dishes was virtually unheard of, except in bachelor communities, until the advent of the Oyster Supper. Here, roles were completely reversed in many communities, as the men chose the date, booked the location, prepared the advertising (broadsides and notices in local weekly newspapers), ordered the ingredients (often driving many miles to pick up the oysters), and set the tables. They then took the tickets, welcomed the guests and served them, cleared the tables, and washed and put away the

For close to sixty years the gentlemen of Greenwood, Ontario, have lured a capacity crowd to their annual Oyster Supper.

dishes. The one contribution expected of the womenfolk was the baking and donating of pies for dessert.

One man would often emerge, either by volunteering or being selected by his peers, to be the chief cook for this event, and he would continue to hold the position for many years. In Greenwood, for example, the chief cook for over forty years was Bill Brown, a local farmer. About three o'clock on the day of the Oyster Supper he would begin to combine and slowly heat the gallons of oysters brought from market in Toronto and the donated milk from nearby farms. Home-churned butter, salt, pepper, and large quantities of crackers rolled into crumbs would be slowly added to the cauldrons of soup that were gently simmering over a portable Coleman gas stove in the makeshift kitchen in the church basement. When the edges of the oysters began to curl, the chief cook knew the soup was ready. The challenge was to keep it hot, but not allow it to scorch, until all three hundred guests were served![13]

The popularity of Oyster Suppers in rural Ontario does not appear to be waning as we begin the twenty-first century. Not only have they been a continuing tradition for over a century, but they are still organized for fundraising or special events. In 1993, in honour of the launching of

Origins: The History of Dummer Township by historian and author Jean Murray Cole, the Dummer Township Historical Society Committee sponsored an Oyster Supper in the Dummer Township Hall in Warsaw, Peterborough County. The committee decided to revive the popular tradition of Oyster Suppers in Peterborough County after reading descriptions of past suppers in the book they were about to launch.[14]

Meanwhile, in Greenwood, the annual Oyster Supper continues, a true combination of good food and good fellowship for that rural community, as former residents return year after year to enjoy oyster soup, ham, hot vegetables, an array of pickles and relishes, rolls and butter, and a wide selection of homemade pies, while they watch those men work!

"Ladies please provide" was a theme that accompanied the advertising for many fundraisers, since the expectation was that the womenfolk would provide the food while the men would provide the cash to purchase it. Several events capitalized on the concept of an auction as a fundraiser. In many Canadian communities, beginning in the early twentieth century, Box Socials became a popular time of fellowship and an opportunity to raise funds for the organization sponsoring them. They were often held in the local school or community hall in conjunction with a euchre party, a crokinole party, or a dance.

The women of all ages in the community would decorate a box (shoeboxes were a great favourite) to look like a ship, a house, a garden, or whatever, and then fill it with enough refreshment for two people. Food could consist of sandwiches, crackers and cheese, relishes, pickles, cookies, tarts, squares, and/or pies. The boxes were then smuggled with great secrecy into the event. At the appropriate time an auctioneer took over and the bidding began by the gentlemen in attendance. There was, of course, fierce competition if a young man saw someone else bidding on the box he suspected belonged to a girl he cared about. Finally, when all the boxes were sold, the couples paired up to eat supper together. The successful bidder also had the privilege of walking his partner home that evening, so this was an important investment.

The Pie Social was a popular entertainment in rural areas of Nova Scotia, as well as in other provinces. Each lady would bake her favourite pie and carefully pack it in a basket to share with the gentleman who "won" her with the highest bid. Sometimes envelopes with the lady's name sealed inside were decorated in unique ways to entice the men to bid high as they were auctioned off. It was a matter of pride among the womenfolk to be able to claim the highest bid of the evening. However, never let it be said that secrets were always kept, for the unmarried girls made sure the "right" boy would recognize her envelope. And why not? It also became the privilege of the "winner" at a Pie Social to escort the lady home.

Four kinds of pies were most sought after at the Pie Socials: coconut cream, chocolate, lemon meringue, and butterscotch. However, fruit and berry pies were made in season, while pumpkin and squash pies were popular in the fall after the crops had been harvested.[15]

In addition to the many single events planned and presented in communities both large and small, Canadians have developed a number of fundraising events that span several days or weeks. Their common theme is a local food or beverage, and they are often called festivals, although they are usually not based on a specific historic or religious event. The whole community takes part, either as presenters or participants, all striving to publicize and showcase the community and its resources — and to make money (it is hoped) right there in the community.

In Aurora, Ontario, a Peach Festival was described in the *Aurora Banner* in 1872. It is interesting to note that the Peach Festival also featured ample supplies of oysters and ice cream. The latter would have been handmade in wooden ice-cream makers and eaten as it came out of the container.

THE PEACH FESTIVAL

The Peach Festival held last Thursday and Friday was continued on Saturday, owing to the great encouragement given on the first two days, and the large amount of provisions on hand at the close of the second day. Too much credit cannot be given to the ladies of the Presbyterian Church, and their friends, for the abundant and substantial, and even elegant display of cakes, fruits and flowers, which tempted and gratified the eyes, the olfactories, and the palate of the visitors who especially on Friday, in the best of good nature, crowded the hall to its utmost, and reluctantly left it, even at midnight. The peaches were luscious and abundant; the oysters, on the second and third

days, were largely patronized, as they deserved to be; and
the ice cream could hardly be surpassed. Grapes, pears,
apples, melons & etc., added to the variety, whilst nuts,
taffy and other sweetmeats attracted the hungry-eyed little
folks and cakes, pies, tarts of every description, with sandwiches, tea and coffee, lured the more simple appetites of
the elderly.[16]

In British Columbia, the Penticton Peach Festival is celebrated in late
July or early August and lasts for a week, while in Tupperville, Nova Scotia,
an Ice Cream Festival is celebrated. Fish and Seafood Festivals are featured on
both coasts — lobster, oysters, scallops, and salmon are all festival themes,
while the Northern Pike Festival runs all summer in Nipawin,
Saskatchewan.[17] Festivals that celebrate potatoes (Prince Edward Island),
bread and honey (Ontario), pumpkins (Nova Scotia), corn and apples
(Manitoba), or sourdough (Yukon) draw large and enthusiastic participants.

Manitoba is home to at least two well-known winter celebrations. The
first is the Festival du Voyageur in St. Boniface, which began in 1970 and
honours the French Canadian voyageurs of the fur trade, remembering
their music, food, clothing, and way of life. The Northern Manitoba
Trappers' Festival, held annually in February in The Pas (four hundred
miles north of Winnipeg), features both traditional foods and traditional
cooking skills. Lunch is served in the basement of the community hall,
and for $5 you can enjoy breaded walleye, fried to a golden brown, home-
style baked beans, pan-fried potatoes (with onions), and a ball of Bannock
twice the size of your fist. If you are still a little peckish, add a bowl of beef
stew chock full of root vegetables.[18]

If you want to compete at the festival, brush up on your culinary skills.
When was the last time you built a fire? Filleted a fish? Whipped up a batch
of Bannock or cooked it over an open flame? Okay, it's likely been a while.
And that's why the Trappers' Festival is the perfect cooking school: you'll
learn to separate a fillet from a fish with half-frozen hands and to cut lard
into a mixture of flour, baking powder, and salt — no small feat when done
outdoors in temperatures that are more than a few degrees below freezing.

And, hey, if you can make it here, you can make it anywhere. Just
think how easy things will seem later, back in your own kitchen, when you

fire up the gas range, pull out the pastry board, and have a Henckels knife at your disposal.[19]

Many Canadian provinces have vineyards that produce wine from local harvests. Commercial vintners have partnered with communities to host a variety of festivals featuring grapes and wine, wine and cheese, food and wine, and a variety of other delicious combinations. One of the newest is the Icewine Festival that has emerged in recent years. This famous winter wine festival began with a Riesling icewine made by Walter Hainle in British Columbia in 1973. Ontario vintners soon followed and, like their western colleagues, have won many international awards for this unique beverage. Grapes for icewine must be picked at temperatures between −8°C and −10°C, usually very early in the morning. This ideal temperature can occur any time between mid-November and January, and the winery staff and volunteers must be prepared to spring into action immediately. The frozen grapes are hard as marbles and transform the water they contain into ice, leaving only the rich, concentrated grape nectar to ooze from the wine press. Some of the Icewine Festivals feature every aspect of the process and give the participants the opportunity to do the work as well as enjoy the final product. Such a small volume from so many grapes helps to explain the premium price one must pay to experience the magic of icewine!

CHAPTER SIXTEEN

The Twentieth Century Brought a Revolution to Canadian Tables

THERE WAS A MOOD OF OPTIMISM IN Canada as the twentieth century began. For nearly thirty years, there had been long periods of depression, but now trade was increasing, agriculture and light industries were prospering, and prices were rising as Canadian-made products were in demand. The first Canadian hydroelectric power was produced in 1895, just in time to serve the new industries.

In the first decade of the twentieth century, nearly three million immigrants arrived in Canada from the United States, Great Britain, and eastern and southern Europe. Many of these newcomers were headed for the territories between Manitoba and British Columbia, soon to be known as "The Breadbasket of the World."

A significant number were also headed for the new industries in central Canada and for the Great Clay Belt in Northern Ontario, where a railway construction worker found silver in 1903 near Cobalt. Intensive prospecting in the Precambrian Shield, said by geologists to be the oldest rocks in the world, soon led to the discovery of gold at Porcupine and Kirkland Lake, and these strikes were the catalyst for fresh waves of newcomers.

In 1901 the population of Canada was just over five million and included one of the most diverse groups of people in any country in the world. In settled towns and cities such as Halifax, Fredericton, Montreal, Toronto, and Victoria, lavish dinner parties, elegant luncheons, and bountiful picnic baskets were the norm, while recent arrivals were riding the rails or travelling in ox carts over rutted trails to locate their newly acquired farmland in western Canada, not sure where and when they would find their next meal. Even in well-developed areas there was a great difference between urban and rural Canadians. For decades Canada was basically an agricultural nation, with the focus on owning land and either hunting, fishing, or foraging for food, or farming it to produce a good harvest that would make the owners self-sufficient for the coming year. Hospitality and sharing resources were every-day ways of life. As we have seen, dinner was at noon as the men and boys came in from the fields to eat a substantial meal of potatoes, root vegetables, meat or game, and pies, pudding, or home-preserved fruit for dessert. Visitors were always welcome, and extra places were quickly set at the table for unexpected guests.

As tiny communities grew into towns and cities, we find that an increasing number of men worked in offices, mills, factories, or other industries and carried a lunch pail to work, containing cold sandwiches to eat at noon. Miners were also carrying lunches that had been packed at home to eat underground. This account from Cobalt confirms how the miner's children searched the pail for treats, especially cookies that had not been eaten but had been softened by the dampness in the mine.

> It was a treat for the children to see what Dad had left in his lunch pail after a shift underground. Sandwiches were not palatable having absorbed an unpleasant flavour and being unrefrigerated in the humid and hot atmosphere underground. Apples and oranges were Evelyn's favourites and she does remember that cookies softened after a shift in a mine. Her French-Canadian mother packed a good lunch and there were cookies returned for the kids. Evelyn doesn't think that this practice was restricted to any ethnic group; more likely an industrial group.[1]

The above description is quite a contrast to the routine of miners in Cape Breton a century earlier, as we learn in *A History of the Island of Cape Breton*:

> The working time for an 1827 Cape Breton miner extend-ed from 5:00 a.m. to 7:00 p.m. with a one hour breakfast period at 9:00 a.m. and the same for dinner at 1:00 p.m. Summoned by a bell at 9:00, the workers all rushed to the

store, swallowed a glass of raw rum and went to breakfast.
The same process was repeated at 1:00 before dinner and
again at 7:00 when the day's work was done.[2]

By the twentieth century, dinner was now in the late afternoon or
early evening when the men arrived home from work, and it was prepared
with ingredients that may have come from the gardens but were often supplemented by items purchased from local merchants and nearby markets.

The T. Eaton Company Limited, founded in Toronto in 1869 as a
dry-goods store, became one of the most important suppliers of household
utensils and equipment in Canada because of its booming mail-order business. This success was inspired by the firm's catalogues, which it began
publishing in 1884 and continued until 1976.

Sears Canada Inc.

"Goods satisfactory or money refunded," the guarantee of the T. Eaton Company,
won the loyalty of Canadians from coast to coast for almost a century.

The 1902 spring and summer catalogue was designed to serve and to tempt both rural and urban housewives with advertisements for:

> Leader churns, #1, 9 gals, $4.40; butter ladles 5¢, 8¢; salt boxes 10¢; butter moulds, 1/2 and 1 lb. 20¢; butter spades, 5¢ each; maple bowls, 10¢, 20¢, 35¢, 50¢; as well as chafing dishes, nickel plated, nickel stand, complete, 3-pint size, $5.00, "Marion Harland" coffee pots, well made strong and handsomely nickel plated parts, cannot possibly get out of order, 1 pint size, 85¢.[3]

In 1903 a special settlers' catalogue was issued, recognizing the influx of newcomers and using the chatty and fatherly approach that had evolved by then:

Have You Tried Eaton's Mail Order System?

> Most people have. If you have lived in Canada any length of time in all probability you have and are using it to-day. If you and we are strangers we want to get acquainted with one another, that is why we send you this little catalogue. In compiling this booklet one of the objects kept in view is that of giving useful and accurate information to the new Settler and Home Seekers in the Great Canadian North West. To them the store's usefulness knows no limit. It provides every possible need for furnishing the home from the cellar to the attic; its stocks embrace every Household Help and also include wearing apparel of every reliable kind for man, woman and child. The distance need be no barrier for the Eaton Mail Order System extends to every Town, Village and Post Office in the Dominion of Canada from the Yukon to Nova Scotia.[4]

The January-February 1909 catalogue must have been hard to resist, for it featured:

Our Clyde Shaped Tea Set, 12 Tea Plates, 12 Cups and Saucers, 2 Cake Plates, 1 Slop Bowl, 1 Creamer, $1.85; A Charm Table Set of "Press-Cut" Glass, 1 Butter Dish, 1 Cream Jug, 1 Sugar Bowl, 1 Spoon-holder, 1 8-inch Fruit Nappy, 12 4-inch Nappies, 1 11-inch Celery Tray, 1 5-inch Handled Nappy or Pickle Dish, 1 9-inch Cake Plate, 1 Salt Shaker, 1 Pepper Shaker, 1 Oil or Vinegar Bottle, Complete Set, 23 pieces, $1.58. If you needed to replenish your drinking glasses, a set of 6 Thin Blown Glass Table Tumblers with engraved star and band pattern, packed in a paper box could be yours for 25¢![5]

By 1913 the standard grocery items of Ceylon or China black teas, green teas, coffees (Mocha, Java, Jamaica, or Guatemalan), green coffees, and a wide range of dried fruits were supplemented by canned fruits: "Lombard Plums in syrup, 10¢; Choice Strawberries, Red Raspberries or Pitted Cherries, 20¢; California Apricots or Delicious Pineapple, 30¢."[6]

These prices appear to be ludicrously low; however, we must compare them to earning power in the same period. In 1905 wages were rising and hours of work were dropping. A very few trades were gaining the eight-hour day. Perhaps the greatest advance was made by workers in seven British Columbia smelters, who had their working hours reduced from eighty-four to fifty-four per week. In that year, stonemasons earned 45 cents an hour. Snow-shovellers in Prince Edward Island, after a brief strike, won a raise from $1 to $1.25 per day. Farmhands received $100 to $250 per year, according to experience. The chief of police in Saint John, New Brunswick, had his annual salary increased from $1,200 to $1,500. In Toronto a young lady might earn $3 per week for "light office work," a "smart boy" $2.50 a week for work in a factory. Stenographers started at $8 a week. In Hamilton workers in a canning factory made $2 or more a day peeling tomatoes. Sirloin steak sold for 12 1/2 cents a pound, rib roast for 10 cents, tea for 25 to 60 cents a pound, depending on quality and kind. Bread was up to 4 cents a loaf.

By 1915 some wages were still being raised, but many were dropping as the economy settled down from a period of inflation. Food prices had gone up substantially. Sirloin steak was 23 cents a pound, loin spring lamb was 24 cents a pound, and chicken was 28 cents a pound. Bread was 6 cents a loaf, while butter was 32 cents a pound.[7]

World War I had begun in 1914 and brought honour and recognition to Canada and Canadians on the battlefields of Ypres, Vimy Ridge, and Flanders, but it also brought conscription in 1917, which seriously divided the rural and urban dwellers of Canada. "Food will win the war" was Germany's slogan as its submarines tried to cut Britain off from food supplies in Canada and starve the Mother Country's people into submission. In Canada farmers believed in the same slogan and that their place was at home on the farm and not in the armed forces. They and their families resisted conscription to the contempt and abuse of urban dwellers who were facing problems of their own. Their domestic servants were vanishing into the munitions factories, leaving many a housewife facing a rebellious coal or wood stove with a worn copy of *The Home Cook Book* in her hand.

When the war ended in 1918, Canada faced a short but severe depression and farmers were hard hit, because during the war they had dramatically increased the production of food, investing heavily in machinery. Suddenly, prices were radically reduced, and farmers were facing heavy losses. The farm was also perceived to be a dull, dreary, second-class place to be, and the exodus to the towns and cities that started during the war continued as young single men and women looked to urban centres for work. One of the major complaints of farm women was the shortage of labour to help do the work indoors and outdoors. Another grievance was the total lack of electricity, believed to be the answer to all of their problems. These issues would continue to cause tension between farmers and town dwellers.

The war years and the years immediately following also saw increased pressure from the temperance movement across Canada. In 1918, for the first time, legislation covered all jurisdictions when the federal government finally stepped in to shut down liquor traffic completely.[8] It was unlawful to possess beer or liquor except in one's own home, or to sell liquor as a drink. Taverns, bars, and all liquor outlets except government distilleries were closed. It was possible for a doctor to prescribe alcohol to a patient thought to be in need of it, so liquor as a drink could be legally obtained by simply being "ill" and having it prescribed to you for "fainting fits" or "bites of mad dogs." Illegal stills and outlets, known as "blind tigers" and "blind pigs," flourished to such a degree that bootleggers and rum-runners became very wealthy while ordinary citizens struggled along in relatively hard times. The reality of growing up in a temperance home and signing the pledge usually meant that spirits were available for seasonings and for medicinal purposes only.

When the Great Depression began in 1929, it brought many young single children home to the farms they had abandoned earlier, and in the towns and cities thousands of people were suddenly out of work, dependent for food and clothing on bread lines, soup kitchens, and relief programs provided by governments, and usually referred to by jealous neighbours of the recipients as "pogey." Many families realized for the first time that popcorn went a long way towards filling empty stomachs.[9]

"Make it do, make it over, use it up" became the Canadian slogan. Farm families had the best and worst of the Depression, for they had some degree of self-sufficiency with their gardens and livestock. However, they now had to cope with the sudden return of family members who had left the farms years before for high-paying city jobs and now, having lost those same jobs, were back on the farm to survive. As well, there were the "tramps," that steady stream of men knocking on doors looking for handouts and willing to do anything to pay for it. Tales were told of the marks tramps put on gateposts if they were treated kindly and fed before being sent on their way. Such signs told other homeless men where they could find refuge for a few hours at least.

In Canadian kitchens, cooks learned how to make something out of nothing, or next to nothing. Recipes like "Economy Cake," "Save All Pie," and "Economical Chicken Salad," which used only one cup of chicken to feed a family of ten, were used whenever a family was fortunate enough to have the ingredients to make them. Those still eating three meals a day could expect to have porridge for breakfast, bread fried in lard or drippings at noon, and macaroni for supper, all washed down with strong, hot tea.

Enterprising and innovative cooks developed new recipes for Macaroni and Cheese, Macaroni and Tomatoes, Fried Bread, Bread Pudding, Bread Sauce, casseroles of bread stuffing, and every conceivable form of baked and steamed bread, biscuits, dumplings, and puddings. The skill of using up leftovers by combining them with other leftovers and perhaps adding a new ingredient was honed to a fine art.[10]

From the desperation of the Depression, many positive things emerged — credit unions, buying clubs, cooperative canneries, turkey pools, a revival of beef rings and the barter system, as well as many other enterprises that helped thousands of Canadians to earn their own living through their own efforts.

Soon the motor car, airplane, radio, and a thousand other inventions swept into use and revolutionized ways of doing things in business, factories, farms, and homes. For instance, radio eventually brought the voice of Kate Aitken, food editor of Montreal's *Standard*, director of women's activities at Toronto's Canadian National Exhibition, and director of the Exhibition Cooking School, into every home with her tested recipes and cookbooks dedicated to inexpensive daily living. Her theme was "In the hands of Canadian women lies the health of the people of Canada. *Food is our Business*. It's an intelligent business and its dividends are paid daily in the health and happiness of the members of our family."[11]

World War II was well named the Global War as Canadian men and women served around the globe from 1939 to 1945. The conflict also brought conscription, food rationing, munitions factories, instant towns such as Ajax (which covered some of Ontario's best farmland), shift work, training locations for airmen from the British Commonwealth, and eventually "war brides" coming home with their husbands to make a new life in Canada. In all, 64,451 war brides and their children were transported to Canada across the Atlantic between 1942 and 1948, bringing with them food traditions from all over the world. The postwar years also brought new waves of immigrants who influenced farming, agriculture, and new tastes in food, for the new well-spiced international cuisine they introduced was a great attraction for Canadians after the blandness of wartime foods. These new arrivals made many contributions to Canadian life. For example, the Dutch from Holland bought land in the Holland Marsh area in Ontario, reclaiming it and turning it into one of the best areas in Canada for growing vegetables.

The postwar years also found manufacturers trying to place every sort of tinned, packed, packaged, bottled, and frozen food into the hands of the servantless housewife. Television had had its inauguration in North America at the 1939 world's fair in New York City, but it did not begin to fulfill its function as an advertiser — a function that has almost swamped it today — until 1946. In that year Standard Brands realized the potential of television for food and beverage advertisements and sponsored *Hour Glass*, which advertised the firm's products at regular intervals during the first hour-long entertainment. Television sets became an indoor status symbol in the 1950s, and those tiny black-and-white screens prompted a flurry of new products such as TV dinners by Swanson in 1953, as well as the TV tables that in many homes brought the daily family conference around the dinner table to an end.

Electrical appliances of every conceivable type flooded the market: mixers, blenders, freezers, and new and larger refrigerators, changing forever the Canadian kitchen. The term *barbecue*, from the Spanish and Haitian, meaning "framework of sticks," was in use as early as 1709, but this method of cooking, particularly on backyard barbecues, became very popular in the 1950s and 1960s. The scent of steaks, roasts, fowl, hot dogs, hamburgers, and baked potatoes being roasted over charcoal or fruit woods was the outdoor status symbol in the new subdivisions being built on the edge of every village, town, and city.

Fast-food outlets began to appear along Canada's highways or at busy intersections to serve people who had to eat on the run. Hockey player Tim Horton opened his initial doughnut-and-coffee shop in Hamilton, Ontario, in 1964, starting a trend that appears to have no limits. It was soon followed by the first golden arches of McDonald's outside the United States, which opened in Richmond, British Columbia, in 1967. McDonald's and its competitors welcomed us all, from toddlers to seniors, and we soon learned that a Big Mac was not a high rigger from British Columbia's forest industry but a type of hamburger. Elaborating on this idea of offering a standard menu at a standard price, restaurant chains developed with well-appointed dining rooms where families could have dinner, safe in the knowledge there would be no surprises when the bill came.

Another product that dramatically changed the way we eat had its origins in the mid-1940s. Percy Spencer, a scientist at the Raytheon Company in Massachusetts, had a candy bar in his pocket and found to his horror that it was melting as he tested very short electromagnetic waves. As the candy ran down his leg, he began to suspect that microwaves could be harnessed for cooking and baking food. Canadian housewives were reluctant at first to try this new method of cooking, but

Soon after hockey player Tim Horton opened his first doughnut-and-coffee shop in Hamilton in 1964, this advertisement appeared in Favourite Recipes, *a fundraising cookbook published by the Ladies Loyal Star Lodge No. 134, Hamilton, Ontario.*

today most Canadian kitchens have a microwave oven. We even find them lurking in such unexpected places as bus depots, so that when you order your meal or snack, you receive it on a paper plate cold or even frozen and are waved towards the distant microwave to jiggle the buttons and heat your own selection.

Thanks to the research of many Canadian scientists, the twentieth century brought new plants to our gardens and fields and new products to our pantries and dinner tables. In addition to developing hardy Marquis wheat between 1902 and 1910, which he achieved by crossing Red Fife and Hard Red Calcutta, Sir Charles Saunders watched as it grew in popularity until it accounted for 90 percent of all wheat grown in western Canada by 1920.

Chemist and pharmacist John McLaughlin opened a soda-water-bottling business in Toronto in 1890, and while experimenting with various flavours, tried adding ginger root, a favourite of both First Nations and newcomers. Pale Dry Ginger Ale was introduced in 1904, with its distinctive label showing a beaver sitting on a map of Canada. The drink was an instant success, not only with Canadians but also across North America as new bottling plants opened in Winnipeg, Manitoba, and in Edmonton, Alberta. In 1907 the beverage was patented as "Canada Dry Ginger Ale," the "Champagne of Ginger Ales," and a century later the pop continues to be found everywhere — in homes, hospitals, soda fountains, grocery stores, and restaurants in Canada and ninety other countries on five continents.

Three pediatricians, Doctors Alan Brown, Theodore Drake, and team leader Frederick Tisdall, working at Toronto's Hospital for Sick Children, created a mixture of ground and precooked wheat meal, oatmeal, and cornmeal in 1930. Called Pablum, this new bland and mushy baby food revolutionized the feeding of infants, for it was affordable, nutritious, and easy to prepare. It was also regarded as much tastier than the previously used, rickets-preventing cod liver oil.[12]

Edward Asselbergs invented another bland and mushy food in the form of instant mashed potatoes when he worked for Canada's Department of Agriculture in 1962. The instant spuds never became popular with the general public but are widely used in convenience foods and meals for the military.

Cookbooks proliferated in the twentieth century. This little one from Cow Brand Baking Soda was published in Montreal in 1933. The simple kitchen portrayed on its cover would soon be transformed by major inventions and developments.

179

Nearly two decades later, in 1980, the Yukon gold rush was honoured with the naming of the Yukon Gold potato by researchers at the University of Guelph. It has been hailed as a perfect multi-purpose potato, because its smooth, yellow, waxy skin does well when baked or boiled and mashed. The same team developed the Red Gold, another popular hybrid, while a research team in New Brunswick came up with Rochdale Gold, introduced to the world in the twenty-first century.

Every decade of the twentieth century also brought a wealth of cookbooks, recipes, and ingredients to the Canadian table, a fact that has been elegantly documented and illustrated by Carol Ferguson and Margaret Fraser in *A Century of Canadian Home Cooking*.[13] Despite this rapid pace of change, it is amazing that some foods and beverages appear to have a constant place of honour on our tables. Just one example of this tendency appears in "Cooking Chat," written by Margaret Carr in May 1954, in praise of tea:

> Tea is something to take when you are cold and when you are hot; when you are worried; when your brain doesn't seem to function and when you want to spend a pleasant half-hour talking to a friend in a corner of the garden or before a blazing fire. Did you know that 1954 marks the golden anniversary of the tea bag? In 1904 a New York tea merchant, Thomas Sullivan, ordered silk bags to hold samples of tea to be handed out to customers. The customers soon demanded tea bags as a product and several years later the silk was abandoned for gauze. To-day tea bags hold a blend of 20 to 50 different kinds of tea. Each bag is automatically weighed and filled to hold exactly enough tea to make one cup.[14]

As the twentieth century drew to a close, tea had not lost its allure. "Canada's love affair with tea continues to blossom as 9 out of 10 adults enjoy tea. And while the majority of Canadians choose tea for its great taste and soothing properties, there is a growing awareness of its health benefits."[15] In 1999 tea was named the "Beverage of the Year" by *Eating Well* magazine, and the popularity of hot, cold, black, green, or specially flavoured tea continues to soar.

CHAPTER SEVENTEEN

Anything Baked
by a Man

In MANY COMMUNITIES ACROSS CANADA, THE WEEKLY farmer's market and the annual agricultural fair are anticipated with pleasure, but often for quite different reasons. Actually, these two community events have much in common historically. Markets and fairs date back to the medieval period in Europe, with its walled cities and cathedrals or churches surrounded by stalls that provided a focus for both events. Occasionally, we find the term *fair* being used to describe a larger, special kind of market, where the citizens would assemble to buy, sell, barter, socialize, and (with luck) find good food.

We know that long before the arrival of newcomers to North America there was a well-established trade and barter system up and down the continent. The First Nations may not have called this network or their gatherings "markets," but they served the same purpose of exchanging surplus goods and acquiring exotic items not available in their own home territories. With the arrival of fishermen and fur traders from Scotland, England, and other parts of Europe, the first temporary markets came into existence, with Native trappers and hunters bringing their precious furs to the ships or to the trading posts to barter for guns, powder, shot, ball, tobacco, blankets, beads, ribbons, rum, and high wine (a combination of alcohol and flavoured water).

It is believed that fairs predate the arrival of newcomers, as well. We learn that much from Jean de Brébeuf's account in the *Jesuit Relations* of the First Nations at Ossossane when he compares "the laying down of the bundles of bones at the feast of the Dead to the laying down of earthen pots at the Village Fairs"!

The open, or "plaza," area between longhouse clusters provided an adequate amount of village space for such fairs to take place. They appear to have been an economic event, for food was not served from the pots on the ground, so it was not a feast in the ceremonial sense. As well as the earthen or earthenware pots (a term commonly used in the *Jesuit Relations* to describe the pottery made by the Ontario Iroquoians and the Iroquois), other goods such as painted robes may have also been offered for sale.[1]

Fairs and markets were not only useful bartering opportunities for the First Nations, but for newcomers, as well. As settlers began to arrive and communities developed, the traditions of the markets they had known "at home" were important to them, and markets were established wherever they settled. A market opened in Quebec City in 1676 that was well stocked with livestock, wild game, fish, and fruit. Occasionally, French wines and coveted items such as pickled artichokes or truffles in oil arrived in the colony to tempt the more affluent customers.[2]

A traveller to Lower Canada in 1792–93 gives us a description of availability and prices:

> The markets of Quebec are cheap and abundantly furnished. I never was in any place where there seemed to be such a great quantity of good things at moderate rates. A turkey might be purchased at 15d sterling, and other articles of provision in proportion. Game is brought in, in large quantities. The mutton is very small. I have seen a maidservant returning from market carry a whole one in a basket on her arm.[3]

Another traveller, John Lambert, listed the products available when he visited the Quebec City market in the summer of 1806: "seven types of meat, eight of poultry or game, thirteen of fish, sixteen of vegetables, and ten of fruit, not to mention a variety of grain, sugar, fat, and cheese. Butchers, bakers, caterers, and innkeepers sold food too, as did retail shops, which also dealt in imported seasonings and condiments."[4]

The Halifax Farmers' Market has a long, colourful, and controversial history, beginning in 1750, a year after the founding of the city. By 1799 those market facilities were deteriorating. The preamble to the Market

House Act of 1799 stated "it would greatly tend to benefit both the town and the country if a separate Market House were erected in Halifax for the sole use of persons bringing from the country meat, poultry, butter and other victuals and in which they might expose such articles for sale." A structure was built in 1800, but no convenient place for the sale of vegetables was maintained, so country producers were allowed to sell in the streets and square in front of the market until the middle of the century.

In 1848 the City of Halifax was incorporated, and the original City Charter conveyed the Country Market property to the city "for the public and common benefit and use of the City of Halifax according to the true interest and meaning of the original grant." After much heated debate, and over the objections of local merchants, a new market was built in 1854. However, it never housed the country vendors, because they refused to attend. The *Acadian Recorder* of 1918 recalled the events of 1854:

> All the best stalls being let to the Halifax butchers, the country people from the first refused to use the market as a place for the disposal of their produce and in spite of the fines and threats gathered their teams and wares around the Post Office Block and with coloured people and Mic Macs established the picturesque street market which became the feature of Halifax.

One of the items the Mi'kmaqs were probably bringing to sell were their splint baskets and other containers. Many of the wares were, and are, linked to food, such as baskets for shopping, storage, apples, potatoes, picnics, eggs, and berries. Without doubt a market would have been a fine place to display and sell such merchandise.

Arthur Wentworth Hamilton Eaton writes in *Chapters in the History of Halifax, Nova Scotia*, published around 1915, that

> A highly picturesque feature of Halifax has always been the "Green Market" held on Wednesday and Saturday mornings on the sidewalks near the post office and marine slip. All summer through as regular as these mornings come a mixed company of "Chezzetcookers" and Negroes. The

former, some of the dark-skinned descendants of the old Acadians, have been accustomed to troop into town across the Dartmouth Ferry, their rude wagons laden with farm produce, poultry, flowers, and small domestic wares of various sorts and ranging themselves along the sidewalks unobtrusively offering their goods for sale.

Phyllis R. Blakeley observes in *Glimpses of Halifax from 1867 to 1900* that "Unlike the tourists, the City Fathers were untouched by the picturesque scene in the Market Square because they were besieged by complaints from the merchants of the street surrounding the post office. The crowds and carts on the sidewalk and roadways interrupted their business." This controversy was a topic of public debate until a new market structure was built in 1916 on Market Street.[5]

Many communities held markets long before a building was constructed, as we learn from a New Brunswick diary entry for 1811: "As there is no market in the Province except St. Johns [*sic*], Fredericton is but precariously supplied, and those who did not farm in some degree for themselves must be content to eat but veal in the spring, lamb in the summer, and salt or frozen meat in the winter."[6]

The Old City Market in Saint John, New Brunswick, erected in 1876, has the honour of being Canada's oldest covered marketplace. The market building, with its extremely high dovetailed ceiling created to look like the upturned hull of a boat, is constructed on a downward slope between Charlotte and Germain streets. This market is truly about local food such as dulse, the native seaweed that is picked from rocks in Dark Harbour on Grand Manan Island and dried to a consistency between paper and leather. Dulse is a rich purple and is a plentiful, inexpensive delicacy.[7]

Although Saint John can claim the oldest market building, the residents of Windsor, Nova Scotia, may have hosted the first agricultural fair in Canada in 1765, encouraged and supported by the ladies and gentlemen of Halifax. Prizes were offered for the best cattle, horses, sheep, butter, and cheese exhibits.[8] The group behind this event was the forerunner of several agricultural organizations, including the King and Hants Society in Nova Scotia in 1789, a society in Saint John, New Brunswick, in 1790, and the Agricultural Society of Upper Canada at Newark

(Niagara-on-the-Lake, Ontario) in 1792. The last held an agricultural fair at Queenston the year before, believed to be the first in what is now Ontario. A British traveller to Upper Canada described a meeting of the Agricultural Society of Upper Canada:

> They had monthly meetings at Newark at a house called "Freemason's Hall," where they dined together. It is not supposed that in such an infant settlement, many essays would be produced on the theory of farming or that much time would be taken up with deep deliberation. Every good purpose was answered by the opportunity it offered of chatting in parties after dinner on the state of crop, tillage etc. Two stewards were in rotation, for each meeting, who regulated for the day. The table was abundantly supplied with the produce of their farms and plantations. Many of the merchants and others, unconnected with country business, were also members of this society. All had permission to introduce a visitor. The Governor directed ten guineas to be presented to this body for the purchase of books — a countenance honourable to himself and to the Society.[9]

These agricultural societies usually met on a monthly basis and were preceded by a convivial dinner, hosted on a rotating basis by different society members. Alas, the Upper Canada Society faltered and finally dissolved as the War of 1812 loomed, despite the patronage and financial support in its early years from Upper Canada's first lieutenant-governor, John Graves Simcoe.

Just as each Canadian community has developed in its own unique fashion, so has each of the country's markets. Many have evolved to serve the cultural communities that surround them, while others have grown because of a local specialty or demand. Toronto, for example, has many markets. However, the two largest are quite different. The St. Lawrence Market had its beginning in 1803 when the Town of York established its first public market on five and a half acres of land now bordered by Front, King, Jarvis, and Church streets, where the present St. Lawrence Hall and Upper Market stand. Like markets in many other communities, the St. Lawrence Market was an open-air affair for almost twenty years until 1820 when a simple open shed was constructed on King Street. Three years later a public well and pump were set up there, as well, and a whipping post, stocks, and pillory were built in Market Square. In 1831 the small wooden market structure was torn down and a red brick Market and Town Hall (later used as the City Hall) was erected in a square bounded by King, Jarvis, Front, and West Market streets.

In 1834, when Mayor William Lyon Mackenzie proposed a new tax as the town of York became the City of Toronto, there was so much stamping and uproar in the crowded upper balcony where the townsfolk watched the council meeting that it collapsed, with many serious injuries sustained on the butchers' hooks in the stalls below. In 1837 a free public feast was held at the market to celebrate Queen Victoria's coronation. A whole roast ox, beer, a hundred-pound plum pudding, band music, and fireworks made it the best market day in history. On April 2, 1840, Queen Victoria's recent marriage to Prince Albert was also celebrated there with another "ox roasted whole … brought into the centre of Market Square in procession." Citizens were invited "if clean and if they brought their own eating utensils."[10]

Kensington Market, meanwhile, began almost by accident in the early twentieth century, with homeowners in the area selling their excess garden vegetables from carts and tables in front of their homes. Housewives soon learned that if they travelled to certain streets they would have choice produce on offer, and so the market began to develop like one of its European open-air counterparts, with vendors from many cultural groups — Jewish, Italian, Chinese, Ukrainian, Spanish, Portuguese — bringing the world to the customer. Kensington Market is bounded today by Bathurst, College, and Dundas streets and Spadina Avenue, and several of the gateways to the market are marked by towering sculptures, such as the steel creation at Baldwin Street and Spadina Avenue that shows the market icons of bread, meat, and cheese circling the globe.

> The Market is Toronto at its best: Ferociously independent, enchantingly eclectic, culturally diverse, touristically tolerant, racially inclusive, class sensitive, ever changing.
>
> Maybe you haven't checked it out lately, but a "restaurant row" mixes naturally among the cheese mongers, butchers, fruit-and-vegetable vendors and bakers.

> Breakfast joints, cafes, take-out shops and sit-down spots
> serve fresh market fare: French, Ethiopian, Mexican,
> Persian, Portuguese, Jamaican, West Indian, Chinese,
> Japanese, Taiwanese, Hungarian-Thai, Latin American,
> Middle Eastern …[11]

In the village of Bytown (now the city of Ottawa), when Lieutenant-Colonel John By laid out a street plan in the 1820s, there was no market building, simply an open area on George Street in Lower Town where farmers sold their vegetables and produce from carts and makeshift stands (similar to Kensington Market). In 1857 the newly renamed Ottawa was chosen by Queen Victoria to become the capital of the Province of Canada (Canada West and East). Ten years later, when the four provinces of Nova Scotia, New Brunswick, and the two Canadas, now renamed Ontario and Quebec, were united as the Dominion of Canada, Ottawa became the new country's capital.

Since then Ottawa's ByWard Market has never looked back and has developed into one of the finest markets in Canada. A visit to ByWard is not only a shopping experience but a cultural exchange, because the capital has become the home of so many embassies that a variety of fruits, vegetables, meats, cheeses, breads, fish, and spices are always in demand. Here, too, the brave gourmand can sample a new pastry confection called a Beavertail, deep-fried and dusted with sugar, or spread with a favourite preserve.

Just as fate affected the ByWard Market in Ottawa, so, too, did it transform the nearby market town of Smiths Falls, sending the annual poultry and turkey fair soaring. During the American Civil War in the early 1860s, a buyer from New York State named W.J. Wright is reputed to have come through. He bought up all the available poultry, driving the birds on foot to Brockville, ferrying them across the St. Lawrence River, and then driving them to the place of slaughter and sale. In 1865, William Keith, publisher of the *Review* in Smiths Falls, suggested it would be easier to buy the poultry dead in Smiths Falls, then ship them to their destination in the United States in the cool of winter. Specifications pertaining to the fattening, killing, and dressing of the fowl were published, and the poultry fair was held in December at a time of year when the birds could be transported at sufficiently cold temperatures to ensure the quality and

Harold Nichol Collection

This wide main street in Smiths Falls, Ontario, was the ideal location for the annual turkey fair held in December in the late nineteenth century.

safety of the meat. At the first poultry fair some ten tons of fowl were brought in by the area farmers and all were purchased by Wright, beginning an annual turkey-fair tradition every December.[12]

To drive the poultry on foot from Smiths Falls to Brockville, onto the ferry, and into the northern American states, it would have been necessary to protect the birds' feet with a mixture of sand and tar, a practice common in England when it was necessary to move poultry long distances from farms to city markets. This custom began in Saxon times to supply customers with geese for their Michaelmas celebrations at the end of September. Legend tells us that twenty thousand or more geese, their feet treated with tar and sand, were walked by their owners from farms in Norfolk and Lincolnshire to meet their fate in the Nottingham market.

An agricultural crisis transformed the annual poultry fair in Smiths Falls in the 1880s. The area "was visited with a plague of grasshoppers, which ate up almost every green thing on the farms. Someone suggested the breeding of turkeys as a means of exterminating the plague and in the following summer many broods of turkeys were hatched out. The little fellows in turn fell upon grasshoppers, and it was not long before the latter were visibly thinned out." The large flock of turkeys threatened to glut the Smiths Falls market, but at the annual turkey fair "buyers were on hand from Montreal and two or three American cities." They bought up all the turkeys at good prices, "one or two carloads of dressed poultry were shipped to New York," and the following year "the stock of turkeys was largely increased, and so also were the stock[s] of geese, ducks, and hens."[13]

By 1887 the annual Christmas turkey fair of Smiths Falls, as it came to be called, attracted as many as forty-one registered wholesale buyers, with farmers bringing in turkeys from as far away as Farmersville (later Athens). The event was estimated to be worth some $8,000 in business to town merchants. The turkey fair came to be held on Beckwith Street, with the farmers' sleighs ranged side by side along the length of the wide thoroughfare. But as the fair grew larger, the sleighs also came to fill the length of Main Street. The care of poultry as a particular responsibility and source of income for farm women was evident in their presence at the turkey fair, pitching the merits of their fowls to buyers. The *Rideau Record* in December 1887, watching one buyer "hesitating somewhat before taking the lot," overheard one farm woman "by way of helping him to a decision [say] 'they're just as good at the top as they are at the bottom, root 'em over.'"[14]

Many of the surrounding communities in eastern Ontario attempted to host their own poultry fairs and markets. However, none of them could match the "Original and Largest Poultry Market in the Dominion," as it was proclaimed in the *Rideau Record* on Christmas Eve in 1887.

By the middle of the nineteenth century, agricultural societies and the fairs they sponsored appeared to be gaining in popularity, a trend that a small sampling from Canada West (Ontario) confirms. In 1855, Markham Village became the home of the famous Markham Fair. Many Markham men had been active in the Home District Agricultural Society for at least twenty-five years. In 1856 a rural fair was held in Unionville; in 1857 an expanded fair was held in Markham, and reported thus: "The day was as pleasant as could be desired and a greater number of respectable persons we have never seen on any similar occasion." The Markham Band "discoursed sweet music" for the "respectable" visitors. At all events, 1855 is the accepted starting date, and in 1955 the fair celebrated its centennial, proudly calling itself "Canada's Greatest County Exhibition," under the auspices of the Markham and East York Agricultural Society. Early records of the society are hazy, but minutes were kept, beginning in 1855, and we have a description of prizes and attendance:

> The prize list of 1855 offered for horses, cattle, sheep and swine, prizes of 15s. and 10s.; poultry 5s. and 2s.; cereal grains, 15s. and 10s.; dairy products, 5s. and 2s.; and agricultural implements, 10s. and 5s. There were displays of quilts and ornamental needlework, and a pair of fine boots, pegged, won 2s.6d.
>
> In 1855, it was reported that "many ladies were present, a circumstance that should not be lost sight of, for the presence of the fair sex in a gathering suited and conducted in a manner agreeable to their refined tastes has a decidedly humanizing tendency on the lords of creation."[15]

In the Haldimand-Norfolk area of today's Ontario, with fine farmland under cultivation, the traditions of agricultural societies and fairs flourished.

> April 19, 1856: Walpole Spring Agricultural Show held in Jarvis.
>
> October 4, 1856: Oneida and Caledonia Agricultural Society Fall Show held at Caledonia.
>
> October 8, 1856: Walpole Agricultural Society Fair held at Mr. Graham's tavern, Stage Road, Walpole.
>
> November 18, 1856: The *Caledonia Advertiser* reported that competition was stiff at the York Plowing Match for the prizes totalling £8.5s.
>
> April 25, 1857: Haldimand County Agricultural Society held its spring show.
>
> October 17, 1857: Agricultural Society of the Upper Part of Haldimand County held a fair in Mount Healy.[16]

We learn from Charles Forbes, a Royal Navy surgeon, that farmers in British Columbia, whether First Nations or newcomers, were part of this growing movement by 1862:

Nowhere does the potato flourish more, or attain a better flavour; it is grown in great quantities by the natives on all parts of the coast. The Hydah [Haida] Indians of Queen Charlotte's Island hold an annual potato fair, customers reaching them from Fort Simpson on the mainland....

An Agricultural and Horticultural Society has been formed, and was very successfully inaugurated in the autumn of the present year. The first exhibition was held in October, prizes being awarded to the exhibitors of the best horned cattle, sheep, stallions, and brood mares (thoroughbred and for farming purposes) and also for pigs.... Large herds of cattle exist in the mountains in a wild state, having strayed from the different farms and settlements.[17]

In larger communities such as London, Ontario, which inaugurated an agricultural fair in 1861, or Toronto, which held one in 1846, these shows were often called provincial exhibitions or industrial exhibitions, with exhibits featuring "new inventions" of farm machinery and equipment, stoves, iceboxes, kitchen cabinets, and the latest household furnishings and equipment.

The popularity of markets has waxed and waned in Canada over the centuries. By the middle of the nineteenth century in eastern and central Canada, hundreds of communities had established them as a way for their farmers, market gardeners, and fishermen to sell surplus produce, animals, and fish. The fairs also provided local housewives with a means to procure fresh ingredients at modest prices and gave them opportunities to meet, greet, and gossip with their neighbours.

In 1877, Hector Fabre gave a lively description of a market in Quebec City. What follows is his account reprinted in *A Taste of History*, published by Environment Canada:

At the market, Quebec City, May 20, 1866: Last Saturday, there was a dense crowd at the market in the Upper Town. The sellers could hardly keep up with the buyers. Busy housewives, honest stewards, bargaining over every item;

demanding gourmets, rejecting and discrediting the produce, examining the carts from top to bottom to find the
gem they were searching for; fathers of families, trailing
after them two or three porters; old bachelors, ferreting out
the succulent chop for their dinner, meeting, pushing and
shoving, filling the market and overflowing from the sidewalks. Almost everyone looked happy and seemed to be
smiling in anticipation, thinking of the good dinners they
would prepare.[18]

Quebec City is still renowned for its open-air markets, while the rest
of the province excels in cottage and farm-gate businesses or produce
stands in the country. Loyal city dwellers are willing to drive several miles
to buy their favourite loaves of bread, fine maple syrup, and fresh herbs.
With close to a thousand apple orchards, Quebec is also famous for its
cider-making industry, and if you want either a sparkling cider or a still
cider, you must seek out one of these roadside stands.

The Nova Scotia Fruit Growers Association (NSFGA) was incorporated in 1864 and staged exhibitions in temporary quarters beside the
Kentville Court House until the Halifax Exhibition opened permanent
facilities in 1897. In 1874 "the elite and beauty of the Town ... were busily examining and admiring the different Fruits, Flowers and Vegetables,
arranged on the tables and stands prepared for that purpose." The display
included such cherries as Belle de Choisy, Bigarreau, and Starr's Prolific.
Strawberries were represented in dishes of Triomphe de Gana, Jucunda,
and Wilson's Albany. Currants were "shown in great perfection."

Apples were not shown until the September Exhibition at Wolfville,
with many varieties of plums, pears, apples, and crabs. The association's
broad interests were further reflected in the inclusion of peaches, grapes,
and flowers, as well as "Sewing Machines and Musical Instruments, etc."[19]

These agricultural societies and the fairs and markets they hosted may
be among the oldest continuing organizations in Canada, and we know that
they had a profound effect on our food traditions. Their primary goal was
to encourage agricultural progress by acquiring and maintaining higher-
quality livestock, crops, fruits, and vegetables; purchasing books and making
them available to the public; and holding agricultural fairs. Long before

provincial ministries of agriculture were established in Canada, the agricultural societies were promoting livestock-breeding practices, dairymen's and fruit-growers' organizations, plowing matches, regional fairs, and many other activities.

The fairs were, and are, a combination of educational exhibits, competition, displays, livestock shows, horseracing, plowing matches, parades, band concerts, and stage shows. After Chicago's World's Columbian Exposition of 1893, and spurred by the introduction of carnivals and midways, these additional features began spreading across Canada, and so began a tug-of-war between education and entertainment.

One aspect of the fairs that has remained constant is the competition that involves food preparation and presentation, and the ribbons awarded to the winners. *Best of the Fairs*, containing prize-winning recipes from Canadian fairs, was published in 1968 by the Canadian Association of Exhibitions and Robin Hood Multifoods. The book gives us some tips on what the judges were, and are, looking for when awarding marks (maximum one hundred) and ribbons: external appearance, internal appearance, texture, flavour, shape, colour, crust (for bread), size, thickness (for cookies), filling (for pies and tarts), container, seal and label (for preserves).[20]

Many agricultural societies and/or fairs published their own cookbooks. Just one example is *Sharing Treasured Recipes*, a centennial project of the Ladies' Division of the Norwood, Ontario, Agricultural Fair, 1878–1978. It contains thirty-nine pages of recipes, some of them historic:

YE OLD CURRANT SAUCE FOR VENISON
Boil an ounce of dried currants in half a pint of water a
few minutes; then add a small teacupful of breadcrumbs,
6 cloves, a glass of port wine and a bit of butter. Stir until
the whole is smooth. 1836. Donalda Williamson[21]

A logical outcome of the success of the spring and fall fairs in rural Canada was the introduction of rural school fairs. In 1909 the Ontario Department of Agriculture launched this new and ambitious program of fairs to be held annually throughout the province. The rural school fairs became very popular, for they were free, they were held on a school day, and they were enthusiastically endorsed and supported by adult

As Canadian communities and shoppers have become more culturally diverse, local vendors and markets have offered increasingly exotic ingredients to tempt buyers.

organizations and institutions — the Agricultural Societies, Women's Institutes, and Farmers' Institutes.

The class that girls were particularly encouraged to enter was, of course, called "Cooking." On the prize lists, recipes were often given for such favourites as Baked Custard, Date Loaf, Chocolate Layer Cake, Cup Cakes, Apple Pie, or School Fair Cookies.[22]

New Canadians have maintained their love affair with rural fairs for hundreds of years. However, in the twenty-first century roles are changing, and so are the classes and entries exhibited. Mark Kearney, in his article "Everyone Can Win a Ribbon … in the Right Category," points out that when he competed at the Western Fair in London, Ontario, in 2005 in the category "Anything Baked by a Man," he "lost to a guy from Bundaberg, Australia," despite the brandy with which he laced his pumpkin pie.[23]

So, we as Canadians are now taking on the world in preserving a tradition started by our First Nations.

CHAPTER EIGHTEEN

The Bountiful Harvest with Which Canada Has Been Blessed

For thousands of years, the First Nations have recognized and celebrated the changing seasons, harvests, and the gifts of food from the Great Spirit. The First Nations did not have a calendar for their customs, ceremonies, and celebrations but were guided by the sun and moon in the cycle of the seasons and the cycle of life.

As newcomers arrived, bringing with them their memories of celebrations in their homelands, they often found that their neighbours were celebrating on different days and in very different ways. Within each community, there could be differing cultural traditions, events to be remembered, and times of cleansing or renewal marked by the calendar. There were goals achieved, victories won, times of rejoicing, sorrow, or thanksgiving, which the community or cultural group recognized with food and fellowship. These were not just reunions or old habits transported to a new land, but a recognition that it was, and is, important to remember and to celebrate with family, friends, and food the small, everyday pleasures as well as the large, momentous events that affect our lives.

For the newcomers, New Year's Day, January 1 by the Gregorian calendar, was — and, of course, still is — a time to celebrate the blessings of the past year, to make resolutions about good behaviour for the months ahead, and for family and friends to gather together. Foods and traditions have varied across Canada. However, French, English and Scottish gentlemen observed the well-known custom of paying New Year's calls on the ladies in the community, where wine and cake was laid out for the visitors, or sometimes sherry and Christmas cake.

New Year's Day was also a time for visits to friends, clergy, heads of government and, in many communities, the hosting of levees by mayors, reeves, and heads of state. Lieutenant-Colonel R.B. McCrea (Robert Barlow) of the Royal Artillery gives us a colourful account of this custom on New Year's Day in St. John's, Newfoundland (Fish-and-fog land to the author) in 1869:

> "Glory to God in the highest, peace on earth, good will towards men," so rung out clear, musical, and pleasant, the bells of the Catholic Cathedral, on a New Year's morn, so many of us interpreted the distant harmony, as we made ready to give that greeting to friends and neighbours after the good old French custom, possibly introduced from Canadian sources here. Yet there were still the official visits of ceremony, which we, as in duty bound to our elders and supervisors, prepared to pay. Crossing too over the chequered marble in the hall of Government House, in our visits of respect to the venerable chieftain who, in his red morocco chair of state, looked like one of the Northern Vikings, a tower of strength and power, come back in the form of rare old British gentleman.
>
> "Thank ye, thank ye, gentlemen," said he, as we offered our congratulations; "I'm pretty weel for an auld man; but I'll throw a line with ye, Maister Wolfe, after the trout at Cape Race, if this confounded cough will leave me strength enough in May. Ye see, I'm just treating it myself with a little plain water, and a squeeze of orange in it. Have you seen her ladyship? Wheel then go and see her, and ye'll find a glass of something better to drink our gude Queen's health."
>
> Our own good Bishop gave us next his word of goodwill, and we soon found ourselves under the portico of his honour the Chief-Justice, Like his best friend the Governor, Sir Francis sat in his big morocco chair, doing full dignity to the ermine, spite of the merry twinkle of his eye, when he whispered.

"Be off now with your blarney, and get a glass of something with Lady Brady. You see," he continued, "I've a bad cough, and I'm just after moistening my throat with a little water, with a squeeze of orange in it."

Singular identity of beverage! Fragrant too with a delicate aroma; but I fancied rather that of the lemon than the orange, and the light colouring due to the distilled juice of the cane. A mistake on our parts, no doubt.

And yet it was singular again — very singular, it must be confessed — when we stood in the parlour of the jolly old President of the Council, that he, with his gouty feet swarthed in flannel, should remark —

"And what will ye be taken, mee dear fellows? Is it poort? Ypi're right, there is worse than that in the world, You see I'm just moistening mee lips with a drop of water, with a squeezed of orange in it; help yourselves."

Our last visit — last but not least — was to *the* great man of Fish-and-fog-land … at his palace under the shadow of his great cathedral, on the heights commanding the city. As it happened, we were just in the nick of time to see him in all his glory. Yes there on the steps of his front door, in long, black robes, adorned with the massive gold cross and chain; with attendant priests around, the Bishop stood — a fine, genial, well-favoured man — about to receive the address of congratulation from the "Sons of Fishermen" or the Irish Society.

Then to his Lordship (John Thomas) we paid our respects and congratulations as was right and proper. A hearty reciprocation and a glass of champagne were his return for the compliment.[1]

Traditionally, Canadian families have gathered on New Year's Day for a hearty meal. Depending on the cultural group, the food has varied, but usually a favourite dish appears. Those favourite dishes can differ dramatically, as just two examples illustrate. The Acadians, who began settling in eastern Canada in the late seventeenth century, favour *Poutines Râpées*

Guests in the dining room of Thomas Montgomery's Inn could anticipate some Irish favourites prepared by Margaret Montgomery such as cakes and puddings flavoured with spirits on special occasions.

made from raw and cooked potatoes, onions, and either fresh lean pork or salted fat pork, while Greek settlers who arrived in Manitoba in the late nineteenth century baked *Vasilopeta*, or *Basilopita*, their New Year's Bread in honour of St. Basil's Day. A coin is baked in it, and whoever receives that slice will have good luck in the New Year.

The Lunar New Year for Canadians of Chinese ancestry is their biggest celebration and can fall between January 21 and February 20. This occasion is a universal day of new beginnings, and everyone wants to recognize and rejoice, settle debts, ask forgiveness for past sins and misunderstandings, clean the house, have a haircut, and prepare for a celebration with family and friends on New Year's Eve. Many fundraising dinners are held at this time, with colourful and symbolic food. Tangerines and oranges depict ingots of gold and represent abundant happiness. A fish served whole is a sign of plenty, and if the fish's head points at you, it is considered exceedingly lucky. Vivid green vegetables represent jade, while peaches are a sign of immortality or long life and are found on figurines and decorations.

A vegetarian dish, *Jhi*, is always served, and it includes *fat choy (fa cai)*, a black hair-like substance resembling the hair on corn. By itself it does not have much flavour, but it takes on the taste of the dish. Since the ingredient's name means prosperity, everyone tries to make sure they have *fat choy*. Lotus seeds are a sign of fertility and an abundance of sons. Chicken stands for liveliness and is almost always served.

While sharing a Chinese meal, the host takes great care in placing the teapot on the table to avoid pointing the spout at a guest. In olden days, if the host wanted to indicate to a guest in attendance that he was on the "hit" list of the host, the pot would deliberately be placed with the spout facing the intended victim as a form of warning.[2]

As spring approaches, all Canadians give thanks for the longer days and brighter sunlight, knowing that the growing season has returned. It would have been when the Sugar Moon appeared in late winter that the First Nations in eastern and central Canada moved to the stands of maple trees to camp and to prepare for the harvest of sweet sap. They began with a ceremony of thanksgiving for the trees and for the first container of sap. Dancing and feasting followed, with traditional foods such as corn soup, beans, and squash being served.

At almost the same time the Maliseet Nation in eastern Canada was giving thanks and celebrating the fiddleheads peeping through the riverbeds and stream banks. These curled fronds of the ostrich fern were a welcome sign of spring and a confirmation that the Great Spirit was again looking after their needs. Feasting with salmon, game, and fiddleheads was a tradition at the spring powwow.

Many tribes and nations attribute special powers, particularly healing ones, to the wild fruits in their area. During winter, the Natives would ask the Great Spirit to renew these life-giving plants, and when they appeared, there were thanksgiving ceremonies and a feast as they ripened. The Iroquois still hold a three-day thanksgiving festival each year before the beginning of the corn harvest. The last full moon in August, known as the Rice Moon, has always signalled some members of the First Nations (Algonquin, Ojibwa, and Northern Cree) to move to their camps near the shallow waters of the northern Great Lakes and the lakes in Manitoba and Saskatchewan to give thanks and to prepare for the wild-rice harvest.

The First Nations were already celebrating the many blessings of the land and the waters and giving thanks as the years unrolled when an explorer/adventurer introduced another thanksgiving celebration in the late sixteenth century. In the summer of 1578, Martin Frobisher attempted for the third time to find the Northwest Passage to Cathay. Sailing under the English flag of Queen Elizabeth I and commanding fifteen vessels with over a hundred colonists and workers, he must have been optimistic about the outcome of his proposed exploration and settlement.

Alas, in the storms, ice, and fog of the northeast Arctic, the vessels were lost for a time and the expedition appeared doomed. Suddenly, by the greatest good fortune, the explorers were reunited and gave thanks for their good fortune:

> Here euery man greatly rejoyced of their happie meeting, and welcommed one another, after the Sea manner with their great Ordinance, and when each partie had ripped vp their sundry fortunes and perils past, they highly praysed God, and altogither vpon their knees gaue him due, humble and heartie thankes, and Maister Wolfall a learned man, appointed by her Maiesties Councell to be their Minister and Preacher made vnto them a godly sermon, exhorting them especially to be thankfull to God for their strange and miraculous deliuerancce in those dangerous places, and putting them in mind of the vncertintie of mans life, willed them to make themselues always readie as resolute men to enjoy and accept thankefully whatsoeuer aduenture his diuine Prouidence should appoint.[3]

The Canadian Encyclopedia tells us that Frobisher and his men then tucked into plates of salt beef, sea biscuits, and peas. These would have been standard rations in the sixteenth century on British ships, and the sailors had eaten them many times before, but not with such enthusiasm as they did when giving thanks for their survival. Thus began a long and honourable tradition of giving thanks for one's blessings throughout the year, a custom that is now practised by almost every cultural group and which today has become an established holiday in many countries.

In 1710 when Port Royal passed into English hands for the last time, the townsfolk and the military held a Day of Thanksgiving. In 1763 the citizens of Halifax commemorated the treaty known as the Peace of Paris that brought an end to the wide-ranging struggles between nations known as the Seven Years' War or the French and Indian War. In Lower Canada (Quebec), the first thanksgiving was proclaimed on December 22, 1798, and celebrated on January 10, 1799. In Upper Canada (Ontario), the first thanksgiving was proclaimed on May 17, 1816, and celebrated on June 18 to commemorate the end of the war between Great Britain and France. Queen Victoria declared June 4, 1856, a day of thanksgiving in recognition of Britain's victory in the Crimean War.

The government of the Provinces of Canada created the nation's first Thanksgiving Day in 1859, with a declaration that asked all Canadians to spend the holiday in "public and solemn" recognition of God's mercies. On October 9, 1879, the marquis of Lorne, then Canada's governor general, proclaimed a statutory holiday on November 6 and "a day of General Thanksgiving to Almighty God for the bountiful harvest with which Canada has been blessed."

For several years, thanksgiving celebrations in Canada were held in October, November, or December, for a time combined with Remembrance Day, and at another time merged with the late November Thanksgiving date in the United States. None of these were satisfactory, and finally in 1957 Canada's House of Commons passed legislation making Thanksgiving Day an annual holiday to be celebrated on the second Monday of October, rendering annual proclamations unnecessary.

A combination of factors appears to have shaped and influenced those early thanksgiving celebrations in Canada, including the established traditions of the First Nations of recognizing the changing seasons and the annual cycle of plenty and harvest, thus ensuring food for the long winter ahead. In addition, immigrants from Europe brought with them well-established memories of Harvest Home Festivals in their rural homelands, and no doubt they were impressed by the incredible bounty of fields, forest, and water they found in Canada.

What of the well-known thanksgiving festival ordered by Governor William Bradford in the autumn of 1621 in Massachusetts's Plymouth Colony? What of the wild turkey, geese, ducks, venison, pumpkins, and corn? What of Chief Massasoit and his ninety braves who were the guests at the feast? Did this event affect the Canadian celebrations of thanksgiving?

According to Andrew Smith, a writer and lecturer and the editor-in-chief of the *Oxford Encyclopedia of Food and Drink in America*, that celebration is an origin myth and an invented holiday created in the nineteenth century and promoted by Mrs. Sarah Hale, editor of *Godey's Lady's Book*. Through her letters, speeches, and magazine articles, she urged a Thanksgiving Day when everyone would celebrate together. As the U.S. Civil War loomed, she believed such a day would hold the country together and managed to convince a nation that the Pilgrim Thanksgiving had actually happened.[4] At the end of the Civil War, President Abraham Lincoln proclaimed the last Thursday of November as Thanksgiving Day in the United States.

Meanwhile, in Canada, clergymen, politicians, and merchants all appear to have tried to shape the tradition and the way in which the day should be celebrated — attending church, travelling for the holiday on trains offering Thanksgiving tickets with reduced rates, enjoying ceremonial amusements, buying "Thanksgiving goods," or sitting down with family and friends to a Thanksgiving dinner. Church and state were obviously both struggling to control the holiday.

We have very few menus or details to help us reconstruct those early Thanksgiving meals. However, by the middle to late Victorian period, Canadian families seem to have compromised and combined their options in many areas. In 1891 at Woodside, the boyhood home of William Lyon Mackenzie King, future prime minister of Canada, we learn that:

> When Woodside was the Kings' home, Thanksgiving was a special occasion, shared with relatives and friends, to give thanks for the past year's blessings. As a devout Presbyterian family, the celebration involved church services in Berlin (now Kitchener), a beautiful dinner prepared by Isabel and her daughters, and an evening of fun to top it off perfectly.
>
> The religious service occupied a central part of the Thanksgiving holiday. In Berlin, at St. Andrew's Presbyterian Church where the Kings attended, the halls

were decorated with fruits and vegetables instead of the standard flowers. The altars, columns, and archways were decked out with a bounty of agricultural produce and samples of the best local baking.

After church services, a hearty dinner was shared with a few close friends and relatives. The Canadian Thanksgiving was greatly influenced by its American counterpart. Women's magazines of the time offered suggestions on every aspect of the occasion, from decorating to menus. A separate table, as always in Victorian tradition, was set up for the children. Tables were decorated with vases of wheat sheaves, and centerpieces created from autumn fruits and vegetables.

After dinner came fun and socializing. The adults and older King children would dance. At the 1892 Thanksgiving, Jennie learned the minuet, an old-fashioned and therefore novel dance. The children partook in the much-loved activity of taffy pulling.[5]

The Woodside Chronicler suggests the Kings may have enjoyed:

A TRADITIONAL VICTORIAN MENU FOR THANKSGIVING
(As it appeared in *The Delineator*, late 1800s)
Tomato Soup with Macaroni, Celery
Roast Turkey with Stuffing & Cranberries
Mashed Potatoes, Squash
Onions, Olives
Chicken Pie, Lettuce Salad and Dressing
Pumpkin Pie, Minced Pie, Nuts, Raisins
Coffee[6]

As publishing of cookbooks increased in the twentieth century, we can trace those dishes that were favourites at the Thanksgiving table. In 1931, Katherine Lewis Flynn of Prince Edward Island recommends the following menu:

THANKSGIVING DINNER
Oyster Soup, Crisp Crackers
Celery
Roast Turkey Giblet Stuffing
Brown Gravy
Mashed Potatoes Turnip Cones
Creamed Onions Spiced Cranberry Jelly
Fruit Salad
Thanksgiving Pudding with Sauce
Squash Pie Mince Pie
Assorted Nuts and Raisins
Coffee[7]

In 1941, Nellie Lyle Pattinson in the *Canadian Cook Book* recommends:

THANKSGIVING DINNER
Colour Scheme — bronze and yellow. Flower Suggestions —
Chrysanthemums, autumn leaves
Crabmeat Cocktail
Celery Gherkins Pickled Pears
Julienne Soup Dinner Rolls
Roast Turkey Cranberry Relish
Fried Egg Plant
Cauliflower Au Gratin Green Beans
Avocado Pear Salad
Bombe Glace Petits Fours
Bonbons Nuts Grapes
Coffee[8]

In 1957, Queen Elizabeth II and Prince Philip were entertained at Rideau Hall by Governor General Sir Vincent Massey and Lady Massey on Thanksgiving Day, Monday, October 14. The meal was served by thirty-five footmen on a banquet table laid with the finest crystal, china, and silver in the land. The menus (bearing a gold crown) detailed the feast:

First on the menu was consommé Flavigny, a delicate chicken broth flavored with curry and enhanced with mushrooms. This was followed by homard à la crème le riz pilaw or lobster with rice sauce.

The third and main course was duckling from Brome Lake, Quebec, and this was prepared with oranges and served with small fried potato waffles.

The fourth course consisted of the hearts of "princess" artichokes with asparagus tips and Hollandaise sauce. For dessert there was "pompadour" ice cream served in drum-like shapes, with dry fancy cookies in gaily decorated baskets.[9]

In 1979, when the Canadian Home Economics Association published *A Collage of Canadian Cooking*, we were told that

Nova Scotians celebrate the Thanksgiving harvest with bounty from the sea and soil and recommend a Maritime Thanksgiving Dinner. In the early days if fowl was not available, salt herring was substituted, earning it the tongue in cheek name, "Digby Chicks."

Maritime Clam Chowder
Roast Turkey with Oyster Stuffing
Cranberry Orange Relish   Giblet Gravy
Whipped Potatoes
Maple Syrup Squash   Corn Casserole
Mincemeat Pie   Creamy Apple Pie[10]

Oh, Canada! A Celebration of Great Canadian Cooking by Bunny Barss suggests that in Alberta "The pioneers celebrated Thanksgiving with venison, duck, wild turkey, goose, seafood, cornbread, vegetables and desserts made from wild fruits." She goes on to recommend a modern Thanksgiving dinner suitable for 1987:

Traditional Roast Turkey
Cornbread Stuffing
Cranberry Sauce
Mashed Potato Casserole
Succotash
Broccoli Spears
Pumpkin Pie with Sweetened Whipped Cream OR
Maple Mousse[11]

In 2002, Her Majesty Queen Elizabeth II and the Duke of Edinburgh were again guests on Thanksgiving Day at Rideau Hall. This time they were hosted by Governor General Adrienne Clarkson, who oversaw much of the planning, including the gold tablecloths, gold-rimmed Limoges plates, silverware engraved with a vice-regal lion, the crest of the governor general of Canada, Portuguese cut-crystal ware, handwritten place cards, menus bound with silken tassels, and daring centrepieces of sunflower and bittersweet.

Their Thanksgiving Day luncheon menu on Monday, October 14, included

grilled red chard–wrapped Cortland apple and Quebec foie gras with Bella Coola pine mushroom rillettes; roulade of Southern Haida Gwaii spotted prawns and Nunavut Arctic cod, served with fricassee of fall vegetables and Miramichi Bay lobster; butternut squash cannelloni filled with a tarragon-scented polenta; bosc pear and dried fig pudding Napoleon; candied Saskatchewan High Bush cranberry and Rideau Hall Garden pumpkin ice cream. Potables: Stoney Ridge Cellars Cuesta Estates Old Vines Chardonnay 1997 from the Niagara Peninsula and Summerhill Cipes Brut from the Okanagan Valley in British Columbia.

Not your typical Thanksgiving repast, but yummy, from all accounts.[12]

As October 31 approaches, many Canadians prepare for a modern Halloween when young people, and the young at heart, knock on neighbours' doors. Finding a suitable pumpkin to carve into a smiling face, preparing treats to give out at the door, helping younger members of the family to prepare a costume are all part of the annual ritual. As darkness falls, the children, dressed in an array of costumes ranging from traditional witches, devils, and other spirits to space creatures, start knocking on doors and chant, "Trick or treat," thus continuing a celebration that is more than two thousand years old and which is steeped in more tradition, controversy, and folklore than any other.

The origins of Halloween may go back to the ancient Romans, who at a similar time of year held a feast in honour of Pomona, the Goddess of Tree Fruit, such as apples and cherries, with much feasting and merrymaking and giving thanks for a bountiful harvest. The Celts and their priests, the Druids, believed there were only two seasons in the year, summer and winter, and that summer ended on October 31, as did the year, so that November 1 was New Year's Day and also the first day of winter.

By October 31, the herds should have been safely stabled in barns, having been brought from their summer pastures, so households could gather to celebrate. Storehouses would be opened to start using the grain and other produce that had been harvested for the winter. This occasion was called the Festival of Summer's End, or Samhain, and it was believed that the Lord of Death allowed those who had died in the previous year and had taken on the bodies of animals to return to their old homes. Fires were set on the hillsides, as it was believed the flames welcomed good spirits and prevented evil ones from coming near. Special foods were prepared to welcome good spirits when they arrived at the door.

In addition to lighting fires and preparing food for the return of departed loved ones, All Hallow's Eve began to develop new traditions as various cultural groups observed the festival. The Irish are credited with the jack-o'-lantern, made from carving a turnip or a potato to look like a human head. Then a candle was placed inside so that the lantern could be carried around to ward off evil. The "lamp" was named after an Irish tailor called Jack, who angered both God and the devil and was not allowed to enter either heaven or Hades but was forced to wander the earth until Judgment Day, carrying his lighted turnip to find his way.

The Scots contributed many traditions to All Hallow's Eve, centred around food, beverages, and foretelling the future. Bobbing for apples was a favourite that was practised by courting couples. Each apple would be given the name of a desired mate. If the bobber succeeded in biting the apple on the first try, then the love would thrive. If the apple was caught on the second bite, the love would exist only briefly. Success on the third chance meant hate, not love. Another custom involved peeling apples with a small knife. The long spiral of apple peel was thrown over the left shoulder, and when it landed, it resembled the first letter of a sweetheart's name.

New arrivals to North America brought their memories surrounding Halloween with them, as Captain James Alexander noted in his *Transatlantic Sketches*. In 1833 he was travelling on the Rideau Canal between Bytown (later Ottawa) and Kingston with Colonel and Mrs. John By and their two daughters. Several officers made up the party, which was paddled in birchbark canoes by Canadian voyageurs:

> We spent the evening of Halloween among drowned woods and swamps, and a deluge of rain, whilst we recounted the legends and ghost stories, with which the Scottish crones are wont to affright their juvenile audience on that dreadful night, and then had a round of music.

> The night drove on wi' sangs and clatter,
> And aye the ale was growing better!
> The storm without might rair and rustle;
> We didna mind the storm a whistle![13]

Canadians have seen many changes transform Halloween. Pumpkins, which were plentiful in Canada, were quickly substituted for potatoes and turnips in fashioning a jack-o'-lantern. In 1890 in Halifax when apple bobbing was on the program at the Queen's Hotel, it was the bellboys who bobbed, not the guests, and they were looking for coins, not for their true loves! Canadian newspapers printed stories of young people in Prince Edward Island carrying lighted cattails that had been soaked in kerosene for several days as they went around in old clothes looking for treats. Tricks were played on those who did not give a treat, and one of the most popular was to remove and hide the gates that hung at the entrance to farm homes.[14] In Toronto an Anti-Treating Society was formed, and in 1876 the *Daily Globe* published an article describing a free concert held the night before in a schoolhouse in order to keep trick-or-treaters off the street. The church minister gave readings, the church choir sang, and piano solos were performed. In Canada's modern communities, there are many evangelical Christians, observant Muslims, and Orthodox Jews who forbid their children from taking part in Halloween because of its connections with witchcraft and the occult.

Today many communities organize a party for the children and young people to discourage door-to-door solicitation because of concerns about its pagan overtones or about the safety of the children and the contents of the treats they might be given. Most of us, however, will continue to gear up for the annual visitation and prepare treats that carry with them much of the symbolism of this centuries-old celebration.

The Festival of Lights, or Diwali (Diwali/Dipavali), is celebrated in October or November. It is the most popular Hindu festival of the year, for it marks the beginning of winter and culminates on the night of the new moon. Oil lamps called *dipas* are lighted in honour of the goddess Lashmi, mantras are sung, and prayers and fresh fruit are offered for prosperity and unity with one another. Traditions include the paying of all debts, cleaning the house, and dressing in one's best — all familiar to those Canadians of Scottish ancestry who celebrate Hogmanay. Canadians of Chinese ancestry will also recognize many of these traditions during the celebration of the Chinese New Year.

The origin of the term *Hogmanay* is lost in the mists of time. Some historians think it may derive from the old Norman French *hoguignane,* or the Old French phrase *aguil' anneuf,* meaning "To the New Year." Others claim that both Hogmanay and *guignotee* (the old custom by which French Canadians visit houses on New Year's Eve) came from a French phrase meaning "To the mistletoe, the New Year."

For Scottish Canadians, the celebration of Hogmanay on New Year's Eve is the highlight of their year. The feast is centuries old and is steeped in tradition, folklore, superstition, and symbolism, all reflecting the history of the Scots, both in their homeland and around the world. Many of the customs revolve around food and ingredients — the preparation, the decoration, and finally the presentation of victuals to friends and family on New Year's Eve as midnight approaches.

As the old year draws to a close, the Scots believe (as do many other cultural groups) that it is time to pay the bills, clean the house and outbuildings, mend the clothes, return borrowed items, and make peace with enemies. An abundance of good food must also be prepared in preparation for the New Year's Eve visitors, all of whom will receive a warm welcome, whether expected or unexpected.

Weeks in advance of Hogmanay, traditional dishes such as Black Bun (also called Scotch Currant Bun, Rich Bun, or Scotch Xmas Bun) are prepared. In the old Scottish dialect *bun* meant "plum cake," and this is truly a surprise cake for those trying it for the first time. It is believed to have originated in Scottish bakeries when they were only allowed to make cake for special holidays. Bakers set aside a lump of bread dough to which fruit and spice were added. This rich, spicy mixture would not stay together, so it was enclosed in a thin casing of bread dough, which through the years has become a casing of short, rich pastry.

Hogmanay Shortbread is often made in a large circle, with the edges notched with thumb and finger to symbolize the sun's rays in the coming year, a custom that originated in the ancient days of sun worship. The large Shortbread is cut into wedges while still warm. In Nova Scotia small cookies called Scotch Cakes are often cut into fancy shapes before they are baked.

Whenever or wherever Canadians of Scottish ancestry gather for a celebration, the crisp, crumbly buttery biscuit known as Shortbread is part of the festive table.

In pagan times, the Greeks and Romans cut crosses on buns and cakes to symbolize the four seasons of the year. Christians continued this practice as a symbol of their faith. Hence the cross on Oatcakes, which in Canada are also called Bannock. They are a combination of oatmeal, salt, fat, and water. Oatcakes or Bannock came to Canada with the Scots, and the First Nations adopted or adapted them to their own ingredients and needs. Many Canadians think of Bannock as their national food. Oatcakes were originally cooked on a griddle (one of the oldest cooking utensils common to all Celtic countries). However, they are often made in a heavy frying pan or baked in the oven.

Scots Eggs, or Scotch Eggs, are a great favourite during the celebration of poet Robert Burns's birthday and St. Andrew's Day (November 30) as well as on Hogmanay. They are served for breakfast, presented as a savoury on special occasions and, during the summer months, are taken on picnics and other outings. Scotch Eggs are made with hard-boiled eggs, peeled and wrapped in sausage meat, then rolled in crumbs and deep-fried.

Haggis is known as "the great Chieftain o' the pudding race," and a Hogmanay table would not be complete without this famous dish (also immortalized by Robert Burns). When Haggis is made in a sheep's stomach, a cross is cut in it when it is ready to be served. On many occasions, Haggis is served with "clapshot" or "tatties 'n neeps," which are equal amounts of potatoes and turnip, boiled, mashed together, and served with generous portions of butter, salt, and pepper.

For those people who don't want to search for a sheep's stomach to make Haggis in the traditional way, a modern version called Pan Haggis is becoming popular with Scots around the world. This concoction is a combination of boiled grated liver and onion, suet, oatmeal, salt, pepper, and herbs simmered or steamed until the flavours are well blended.

Traditionally in Scotland, New Year's Eve began with the children swaddled in white sheets going house to house, calling for treats:

Hogmanmay,
Trollolay!
Get up, good housewife, and shake your feathers,
And dinna think that we are beggars,
For we are bairns come out to play,

211

Get up and gie's our hogmanay.
My feet's cauld, my shoon's thin;
Gie's my cakes, and let me rin.

The favourite treat for the children was, and is, an Oatcake, sometimes accompanied by soft cheese, unsalted butter, honey, preserves, or marmalade.

It is believed that descendants of Scottish families who settled in Northern Ireland took the traditions of Hogmanay with them, and in Clogher Valley mummers (neighbours who wore sheets, costumes, and masks) went door-to-door singing, dancing, and asking for a treat of cakes. Mummers of all ages wearing masks and costumes still sing and dance their way into their neighbours' hearts and homes in Newfoundland, any time from Christmas to January 6, Old Christmas Day on the Julian calendar.

Hogmanay is a communal celebration, and all visitors are welcome in a Scottish home, but anticipation mounts as midnight approaches to see who will be the "first-footer," the first person, other than a member of the family, who crosses the threshold after the clock strikes midnight. Everyone believes this person will determine the fortune of the family and household for the coming year. The custom of first-footing derives from the good fairy of Norse folklore. A dark-haired man bodes well for the coming year, while a redhead or a woman is considered unlucky. As a result, first-footers are usually dark-haired men who carry gifts, including whisky, tea, coal, or salt, each symbolizing something different — good health, good fortune, good luck, a warm home, a full larder, or a healthy year, depending on the community or the geographical area of Canada.

The first-footer is offered refreshments from the Hogmanay table, including two favourite beverages, Het Pint and Atholl Brose. The first is a combination of ale, Scotch whisky, sugar, eggs, and nutmeg, which is slowly warmed while being constantly stirred and poured between pan and mugs or tankards until it froths. The initial mention of Atholl Brose was in 1475 when the Earl of Atholl filled a small well in a rock with this delicious beverage so that he could capture a foe he knew would linger to drink the irresistible brew. From the legend developed the tradition of offering Atholl Brose to guests on Hogmanay to bring them good luck in the coming year. And it is indeed an irresistible brew — a combination of Scotch whisky, honey, oatmeal, hot water, and whipped cream, the last being a modern addition.

In the wee small hours of the morning before the guests retire to bed or leave for home, they still join hands, form a circle, and sing "Auld Lang Syne." This salute to friends and loved ones is attributed to Robert Burns (1759–1796), the national poet of Scotland. Burns claimed he did write the words, but the melody of this widely sung song was based on fragments of an old Scottish folk tune:

> Should auld acquaintance be forgot,
> And never brought to mind?
> Should auld acquaintance be forgot,
> And days o auld lang syne?
> For auld lang syne my Dear,
> For auld lang syne,
> We'll take a cup o kindness yet,
> For auld lang syne.

CHAPTER NINETEEN

Have We Come Full Circle?

As the twenty-first century unfolds and we consider our food traditions, Canada continues to be a very diverse nation. This long history of diversity began with the First Nations, continued with the early settlements by the newcomers, and develops unabated with every passing day and every new arrival.

There have been several periods in Canada's history when one cultural group has thought another's food traditions were quaint, old-fashioned, or even eccentric. The use of trees, plants, herbs, and animals to cure the ills of body, mind, and spirit by the First Nations and the early settlers often fell into that category. Many groups such as the Pennsylvania Germans, the Chinese, the Italians, and others believed in the curative powers of everyday vegetables, fruits, herbs, roots, bark, and leaves to prevent or to alleviate suffering. Again, their neighbours often regarded these communities with something that bordered on disdain and disbelief. One example of this reaction was that at one point in Canada's history garlic was dubbed "the stinking rose," while today it is often referred to as "the magic healer." Most Canadians in the past considered ginger nothing more than an exotic and expensive seasoning. Only in the twentieth century did it finally receive recognition by the scientific community. There are hundreds of other examples, for we have attempted over the years to ignore some of the simple solutions to our culinary and medicinal needs.

In the late twentieth century, however, there was a renewed concern by Canadians of all cultural groups and walks of life about their increasingly hectic lifestyles and their willingness to embrace quick and easy solutions to their food and beverage needs. Canadians realized they could have any food they wanted, from anywhere in the world, at any time of the year, as long as they did not care how it tasted or how much it cost! There was also a growing dependency on modern medicines and drugs that sometimes triggered allergic reactions that were far worse than the original ailment. And there were worries about the substances that were being added to our foods by manufacturers for a variety of reasons — freshness, colour, taste, or consistency of texture — either directly or even indirectly through animals' diets, pesticides used on or near growing plants, and the chemicals from wrapping materials. Furthermore, our interest in, and growing attraction to, eating out, whether it was in a fast-food restaurant or in the most elegant dining room, raised the questions of where those ingredients and prepared foods had come from and what had been added to them.

These concerns and others have prompted a surge in the popularity of local farmers' markets and spurred the rapid growth of organic farms, butchers, and markets and the emergence of organic sections in supermarkets. The Organic Trade Association in Ottawa is working on Canadian organic standards and regulations and is compiling organic farm and trade statistics while responding to members' needs and requirements. The attractiveness of health foods such as goat's milk, tofu, oat bran, whole grains, free-range

Concern about food additives, pesticides, and chemicals in our diets have led to the growing number of organic farms and markets across Canada.

chickens and hogs, wild foods, honey, maple syrup, seaweed, kelp, and herbs is on the rise. "Reduce, reuse, recycle" has become fashionable again, and some Canadians wonder if the burgeoning interest in environmental concerns explains why garage sales are so popular in our communities.

The Slow Food Movement that began in Italy has now spread around the world. Members include farmers, researchers, educators, chefs, professional associations, and anyone dedicated to stopping or slowing down the loss or impoverishment of the local heritage of grains, vegetables, fruits, and animals that is so important to every community's food culture. Educational programs include publications, workshops, markets, food fairs, awards, and local, national, and international conferences that have inspired a great many interested individuals, along with the media, to learn more about this concept. The Slow Food Movement has many Canadian members, many of whom believe this is a modern name for the way of life of our ancestors — plant it, grow it, harvest it, preserve it, eat it!

Canadian newspapers and magazines publish articles on a regular basis describing the latest scientific research, and we are constantly learning that old-fashioned favourites such as blueberries, cranberries, garlic, and a host of common foods will save our lives, or at least lengthen them, if we will only let them! There is a renewed interest in "comfort foods," those everyday staples of our

ancestors' tables — bread, muffins, soups, stews, casseroles, puddings, pies, cakes, cookies. Authors of cookbooks, food editors, lecturers, and teachers have all risen to the challenge, and we have seen a multitude of articles, speeches, and publications that praise the presence of "comfort" on our tables and in our lives.

Young people love to cook and bake, whether at home, at the cottage, at camp, or out of doors on an open fire. If they are encouraged, Canada will soon lead the culinary Olympics around the world!

At present Canadians are being challenged to prepare their meals with fruit, vegetables, fish, meat, and other ingredients that have come from within a hundred-mile radius of their homes. This trend is called the One-Hundred-Mile Diet, and although it originated in British Columbia, hosts and hostesses across Canada have succeeded in their searches and have proven that it can be done.

This concern for our diet and our environment brings us in a complete circle to the First Nations. They were the original custodians and guardians of this land and its riches, and whenever we, the newcomers, sound the cry for restraint and for the wise use of our resources, we pay them tribute.

NOTES

Chapter 1: In the Beginning

1. Peter L. Storck, *Journey to the Ice Age: Discovering an Ancient World* (Vancouver: UBC Press in association with the Royal Ontario Museum, 2004), 8.
2. Brian M. Fagan, *People of the Earth: An Introduction to World Prehistory* (New York: HarperCollins, 1995), 189.
3. *Ibid.*, 183.
4. *Ibid.*, 191.
5. J.V. Wright, *Ontario Prehistory* (Toronto: National Museum of Man/Van Nostrand Reinhold, 1972), 27–32.
6. *Ibid.*, 44.
7. Stanley Holling, *Medicine for Heroes*, quoted in "Dried Blueberry Flowers a Cure for 'Craziness,'" *Lake of the Woods Historical Society Newsletter*, Vol. 16, No. 1 (April 1997), 6.
8. Thomas Vennum, Jr., *Wild Rice and the Ojibway People* (St. Paul: Minnesota Historical Society Press, 1988), 171.
9. Shauna McCabe, *Destination Prince Edward Island* (Halifax: Nimbus, 2000), ii.
10. *People of the Earth*, 195.
11. *Cross Currents: 500 Generations of Aboriginal Fishing in Atlantic Canada* (Montreal: McCord Museum), exhibition and press release, May 2005– April 2006.
12. Sarain Stump, *Two Forms of Art* (Saskatoon: Saskatchewan Indian Cultural College, 1973; reprinted 1981), 15 and 17.

Chapter 2: They Had Never Known Anything to Taste So Sweet

1. Helge Ingstad, *Westward to Vinland* (New York: St. Martin's Press, 1966), 20.
2. *Ibid.*, 16.
3. William Benton entry in *Encyclopaedia Britannica*, 14th ed. (Chicago, 1967), Vol. 16, 597.
4. *Westward to Vinland*, 17.
5. *Ibid.*, 17.

6. Helge Ingstad, *Land Under the Pole Star* (New York: St. Martin's Press, 1966), and *Westward to Vinland*, various pages, particularly page 149 in *Land Under the Pole Star*, and page 140 in *Westward to Vinland*.

7. *Land Under the Pole Star*, 135.

8. "A Guided Tour Around the Archaeological Site," L'Anse aux Meadows National Historic Site booklet (2002), 6.

9. *Westward to Vinland*, 134–35.

10. *Ibid.*, 141.

11. "A Guided Tour Around the Archaeological Site," 4.

12. *Land Under the Pole Star*, 146.

13. Extensive archaeological and historical research has resulted in many of the buildings being reconstructed at L'Anse aux Meadows National Historic Site by Parks Canada, with costumed interpreters carrying out the daily tasks of the inhabitants a thousand years ago.

Chapter 3: The Sea Was Covered with Fish

1. *Encyclopaedia Britannica* (Chicago, 1967), Vol. 4, 557.

2. D.W. Meinig, *The Shaping of America*, Vol. 1 (New Haven and London: Yale University Press, 1986), 57.

3. Richard Whitbourne, "A Discourse and Discovery of Newfoundland," quoted in Dave McIntosh, *When the Work's All Done This Fall* (Toronto: Stoddart Publishing, 1989), 10.

4. Joseph Hatton, *Newfoundland, the Oldest British Colony: Its History, Its Present Condition, and Its Prospects in the Future* (London: Chapman and Hall, 1883), 205.

5. James Asperne, *An Account of the Island of Prince Edward with Practical Advice to Those Intending to Emigrate* (London: James Asperne, 1819), 14.

6. J. Long, *Voyages and Travels of an Indian Interpreter and Trader* (London: J. Long, 1791), 43.

7. *Ibid.*, 57.

8. Grace Helen Mowat, *The Diverting History of a Loyalist Town: A Portrait of St. Andrews, New Brunswick* (Fredericton, NB: Brunswick Press, 1976), 27.

9. Richard Lewes Dashwood, *Chiploquorgan, or Life by the Camp Fire in Dominion of Canada and Newfoundland* (Dublin: R.T. White, 1871), 22.

10. J. Ross Robertson, *Diary of Mrs. John Graves Simcoe* (Toronto: William Briggs, 1911), 158.

11. John Rowan, *The Emigrant Sportsman in Canada* (London: E. Stanford, 1876), 377.

12. Ivan F. Jesperson, ed., *Fat-Back and Molasses: A Collection of Favourite Old Recipes from Newfoundland and Labrador* (St. John's: Jesperson Press, 1980), various pages.

Chapter 4: "Come Then, Chefs, Cooks, and Boys ..."

1. Leslie F. Hannon, *Forts of Canada* (Toronto: Maclean-Hunter Ltd., 1969), 13.
2. *Ibid.*, 15.
3. George Brown, *Building the Canadian Nation* (Toronto: J.M. Dent & Sons, 1958), 50–51.
4. Michael Weiner, *Earth Medicines and Earth Foods* (London: Collier Macmillan, 1972), various pages.
5. Marc Lescarbot, *The Theatre of Neptune in New France, 1609.* Translated by P. Erondelle (New York and London: Harper and Brothers, 1928), 27.
6. Jo Marie Powers, "*L'Ordre de Bon Temps*: Good Cheer as the Answer," *Proceedings, Oxford Symposium on Food and Cooking, 1990* (London: Prospect Books), 168–69.
7. *The Theatre of Neptune*, 118.
8. *Ibid.*, 118.
9. *Forts of Canada*, 14.
10. *Building the Canadian Nation*, 78.
11. André Pelchat, "Ginseng Rush," *The Beaver*, Vol. 83, No.1 (December 2003/January 2004), 14–17.
12. This priceless record survives in the publications of the Champlain Society.

Chapter 5: A Chain of Men Stretched Across the Continent

1. E.E. Rich, "Pro Pelle Cutem," *The Beaver* (Spring 1958), 12.
2. Florida Town, *The North West Company: Frontier Merchants* (Toronto: Umbrella Press, 1999), 12.
3. Alexander Henry, *Travels and Adventures in Canada and the Indian Territories Between the Years 1760 and 1766* (New York, 1809), *passim.*
4. W.S. Wallace, "Fort William of the Fur Trade," *The Beaver* (December 1949), 16, and *Fort William: Hinge of a Nation*, feasibility study prepared by National Heritage Limited for the Province of Ontario (author's collection), 36.
5. *Forts of Canada*, 209.
6. *Ibid.*, 209.
7. "Scheme for the North West Outfit," North West Company Correspondence, 1791–99, Hudson's Bay Company Archives, Archives of Canada.
8. Ross Cox, *Adventures on the Columbia River* (London: H. Colburn and R. Bentley, 1831), 279.
9. Grace Lee Nute, *The Voyageur's Highway* (St. Paul, MN: Minnesota Historical Society, 1951), 54.
10. Gabriel Franchere, *A Voyage to the Northwest Coast of America* (Chicago, 1954), 266.
11. *Adventures on the Columbia River*, 289.
12. "The Oregon Territory," *The Builder*, Vol. 2 (1844), 9.
13. *Forts of Canada*, 205.

14. *Ibid.*, 205.
15. See *The North West Company from Lachine to Grand Portage: The North West Indian Trade* (Cornwall, ON: Inverarden Regency Cottage Museum, 1993).
16. L.V. Burpee, "The Beaver Club," *Canadian History Association Report* (1924), 73–92.
17. Marjorie Wilkins Campbell, *McGillivray, Lord of the Northwest* (Toronto: Clarke, 1962), 93, and L.V. Burpee, "The Beaver Club," *Canadian History Association Report* (1924), 73–92.
18. Town, *The North West Company*, 109 and 114.

Chapter 6: Bread Was the Foundation of Every Meal

1. Dorothy Duncan, "Victuals and Viands in the New Province of Upper Canada" in *The Capital Years: Niagara-on-the-Lake 1792–1796* (Toronto: Dundurn Press, 1991), 160.
2. John Oldmixon, *The British Empire in America*, 2nd ed., 2 vols. (London, 1741), cited in *When the Work's All Done This Fall* (Toronto: Stoddart Publishing, 1989), 11.
3. James J. Sharp, *Flavours of Newfoundland and Labrador* (St. John's, NF: Breakwater Books, 1981), iii–iv.
4. Marie Nightingale, *Out of Old Nova Scotia Kitchens* (Baddeck, NS: Petheric Press, 1978), 5.
5. *Ibid.*, 7.
6. *Ibid.*, 20.
7. B.A. Balcom, *History of the Lunenburg Fishing Industry* (Lunenburg, NS: Lunenburg Marine Museum Society, 1977), 2.
8. Julie Watson, *Favourite Recipes from Old Prince Edward Island Kitchens* (Willowdale, ON: Hounslow Press, 1989), 12.
9. *Ibid.*, 13.
10. John Cambridge, *A Description of Prince Edward Island in the Gulph of Saint Laurence, North America* (Bristol, 1818), 6–7.
11. Mary Quayle Innis, ed., *Mrs. Simcoe's Diary* (Toronto: Macmillan of Canada, 1965), various pages, particularly 78, 79, 81, 88, and 109.
12. *Ibid.*, 97.
13. *Ibid.*, 109.
14. Dorothy Duncan, "Victuals and Viands," 150.
15. Elizabeth Russell Papers, February 24, 1794, Metropolitan Toronto Library, Baldwin Room.
16. Peter Kalm, *Travels into North America, 1753–61*, cited by Mary Alice Downie and Mary Hamilton in *and some brought flowers: Plants in a New World* (Toronto: University of Toronto Press, 1980), 54.
17. René de Bréhant de Galinée, *The Journey of Dollier and Galinée, 1669–70*, cited in *and some brought flowers*, 54.
18. Dorothy Duncan, "Victuals and Viands," 160–61.
19. *Mrs. Simcoe's Diary*, various pages.

20. *Upper Canada Gazette,* Newark (Niagara-on-the-Lake, Ontario), June 10, 1794, and December 10, 1794.
21. Servos Mill Records, 1794–95, Niagara Historical Resource Centre, Niagara-on-the-Lake Public Library.
22. *Mrs. Simcoe's Diary,* various pages.

Chapter 7: "We Greatly Missed Our Tea"

1. Jamie Shalleck, *Tea* (New York: Viking Press, 1972), 1.
2. See Christopher Moore, *The Loyalists* (Toronto: Macmillan of Canada, 1984).
3. Wallace Brown, "The Loyalists and the Maritime Provinces," *Loyalist Gazette,* Vol. 21, No. 1 (Spring 1983), 8.
4. *The Loyalists,* 115.
5. Brown, "The Loyalists and the Maritime Provinces," 9.
6. William H. Tippett, "The Hannah Ingraham Story," *Annual Transactions* (Toronto: United Empire Loyalists Association, 1904–1913), 115–121.
7. Peter Fisher, "The Grandmother's Story," in *Sketches of New Brunswick* (Saint John, NB: Chubb and Sears, 1825), 127. Reprinted by the New Brunswick Historical Society in 1921.
8. Thomas Earle, "Winter of Discontent: The Loyalists' First Winter in Fredericton," *Loyalist Gazette,* Vol. 21, No. 1 (Spring 1983), 11.
9. "The Grandmother's Story," 128.
10, *Ibid.,* 129.
11. George Leard, "Rum 'n Ribbons," *Loyalist Gazette,* Vol. 21, No. 1 (Spring 1983), 23.
12. Joy Ormsby, "Building a Town," in *The Capital Years* (Toronto: Dundurn Press, 1991), 17–18.
13. A.H. Young, "Letters from the Secretary of Upper Canada and Mrs. Jarvis to Her Father, the Reverend Samuel Peters, DD," *Annual Report and Transactions,* No. 23, (Toronto: Women's Canadian Historical Society of Toronto, 1922–23), 32–33.
14. Mrs. Burritt, "The Settlement of the County of Grenville," *Papers and Records,* Ontario Historical Society, Vol. 3 (1901), 106.
15. L.H Tasker, "The United Empire Loyalist Settlement at Long Point, Lake Erie," *Papers and Records,* Ontario Historical Society, Vol. 2 (1900), 54–55.
16. See various issues of the *Telegraph-Journal,* Saint John, New Brunswick, 1983, and Eleanor Robertson Smith, *Loyalist Foods in Today's Recipes* (Hantsport, NS: Lancelot Press, 1983).

Chapter 8: Victorians at Table: I Looked Forward to Every Meal

1. John Howison, *Sketches of Upper Canada* (Edinburgh: Oliver, 1821), 39 and 118. Reprinted by S.R. Publishers, Johnson Reprint Company, in 1965.
2. Craig Heron, *BOOZE* (Toronto: Between the Lines, 2003), 28.

3. Jo Marie Powers and Dorothy Duncan, "Those Damned Cold Water Drinking Societies," *Public Eating: Oxford Symposium on Food and Cookery Proceedings* (London: Prospect Books, 1991), 240.

4. Harry Bruce, "Confederation," in *Canada 1812–1871: The Formative Years* (Toronto: Imperial Oil Limited, 1967), 65.

5. *Ibid.*, 66.

6. Louis Tivy, *your loving Anna* (Toronto: University of Toronto Press, 1972), 38, 46, 51–52.

7. *Ibid.*, 99.

8. *Daily Telegraph*, Saint John, New Brunswick, December 21, 1878.

9. Frances McNaught and Margaret Taylor, *Galt Cook Book* (Toronto: William Briggs, 1898, reprinted 1980), 441.

10. Author's collection.

11. Pierre and Janet Berton, *Pierre and Janet Berton's Canadian Food Guide* (Toronto: McClelland & Stewart, 1974), 31.

12. Author's collection.

13. Vilhjalmur Stefansson, "Food and Food Habits in Alaska and Northern Canada," reprinted in *Human Nutrition Historic and Scientific, Monograph III* (New York: International Universities Press, 1957), 26–27.

Chapter 9: Rupert's Land Became the Breadbasket of the World

1. Elliott Coues, ed., *New Light on the Early History of the Greater Northwest*, Vol. 1 (New York: F.P. Harper, 1897), *passim*.

2. *Building the Canadian Nation*, 299–302.

3. See *Manitoba's Heritage Cookery* (Winnipeg: Manitoba Historical Society, 1992), various pages for detailed accounts.

4. Jean Murray Cole, *David Fife and Red Fife Wheat* (Peterborough, ON: Lang Pioneer Village, County of Peterborough, 1992), various pages.

5. See *From Saskatchewan Homemakers' Kitchens* (Saskatoon: Modern Press, 1955), various pages for detailed accounts.

6. Beulah (Bunny) Barss, *Oh, Canada!* (Calgary: Deadwood Publishing, 1987), 132.

7. *From Saskatchewan Homemakers' Kitchens*, vii.

8. Beulah (Bunny) Barss, *Alberta Pictorial Cookbook* (Halifax: Nimbus, 1988), introduction.

9. Elizabeth Bird, *The Englishwoman in America*, quoted in *Canadian Farmer* (October 15, 1873), 356.

10. Beulah (Bunny) Barss, "The Chuckwagon Tradition in Prairie Culture," in *Northern Bounty* (Toronto: Random House of Canada, 1995), 48–49.

11. *A Concise Dictionary of Canadianisms* (Victoria, BC: Gage, 1973), 51.

12. *A Collage of Canadian Cooking* (Ottawa: Canadian Home Economics Association, 1979), 163.

Chapter 10: All Aboard!

1. G.R. Stevens, *History of the Canadian National Railways* (New York: Macmillan, 1973), 10.
2. *Ibid.*, 11.
3. *Ibid.*, 17.
4. Robert Surtees, *Northern Connection: Ontario Northland Since 1902* (New York: Captus Press, 1992), 229.
5. *History of the Canadian National Railways*, 211.
6. Moose River Basin Book #1, Ells, 1911, Gross Section Book, Box 107, Ontario Northland Archives.
7. *History of the Canadian National Railways*, 43.
8. Omer Lavalee, *Van Horne's Road* (Montreal: Railfare Enterprises, 1974), 218.
9. *Ibid.*, 272.
10. *Ibid.*, 44.
11. Edmund W. Bradwin, *The Bunkhouse Man: A Study of Work and Pay in the Camps of Canada 1903–1914* (Toronto: University of Toronto Press, 1972), 134.
12. *The Skillet*, Vol. 1 (Montreal: Crawley & McCracken Limited, 1934), 1.
13. *Ibid.*, 1.
14. Private collection of Pamela and Peter Handley, North Bay, Ontario.
15. Miscellaneous correspondence, J.E. Cahoon, vice-president and general manager, Crawley & McCracken Limited, to Mr. A.H. Cavanaugh, general manager, October 16, 1945, Ontario Northland Archives (ONA), North Bay, Ontario.
16. Miscellaneous correspondence, H. Mudrick, Extra Gang #5, to T.D. Saunders, chief engineer; H. Mudrick to A. Jardine, Superintendent Englehart; C.M. Sewell to T.D. Saunders; A. Jardine to T.D. Saunders; L.W. Edwards, foreman, to A. Jardine, ONA.
17. Miscellaneous correspondence, A.H. Cavanaugh, general manager, T&NOR, to R.G. Lee, superintendent, Crawley & McCracken Limited, April 28, 1942, ONA.
18. Interview with Duncan Smith, Palmerston, Ontario, December 20, 1993.
19. Ron Brown, "At the (Railway) YMCA," *The Beaver* (February/March 1999), 34.
20. *Ibid.*, 36–37.
21. E.J. Hart, *The Selling of Canada* (Banff, AB: Altitude Publishers, 1983), 12–13.
22. Menu and price list, Canadian National Railways, August 28, 1940, author's collection.
23. Menu and price list, Canadian Pacific Railway Dining Car Service, 1941, author's collection.
24. Ted Ferguson, *Sentimental Journey* (Toronto: Doubleday Canada, 1985), 46.
25. *The Selling of Canada*, 14.
26. *North Bay Nugget* (August 6, 1982), 1.
27. Michael Barnes, ed., *The Best of Hartley Trussler's North Bay* (North Bay, ON: North Bay Nugget, 1982), 30.

28. Menus and price lists, Ontario Northland Archives Collection, North Bay, Ontario.

Chapter 11: From Sea to Shining Sea

1. *The Journals of Captain James Cook on his Voyages of Discovery*, Vol. 3, Part 2, page 1328, quoted in *Sailors and Sauerkraut* by Barbara Burkhardt, Barrie Angus McLean, and Doris Kochanek (Burnaby, BC: Hemlock Printers, 1978), 146.
2. Anita Stewart, *The Flavours of Canada* (Vancouver: Raincoast Books, 2000), 17.
3. Royal B. Hassrick, *The Colourful Story of North American Indians* (Octopus Books, 1974), 108 and 111.
4. Joseph Despard Pemberton, *Facts and Figures Relating to Vancouver Island and British Columbia* (London: Longman, Green, 1860), quoted in McIntosh, *When the Work's All Done This Fall*, 277.
5. Dorothy Duncan, "Chinese Food and the Canadian Experience," in *Chinese Cuisine American Palate: An Anthology*, Jacqueline Newman and Roberta Halporn, eds. (Brooklyn, NY: Center for Thanatology Research and Education Incorporated, 2004), 72.
6. *Building the Canadian Nation*, 377.
7. *Pierre and Janet Berton's Canadian Food Guide*, 31.
8. *Oh, Canada!* 145–46.
9. *When the Work's All Done This Fall*, 279.
10. *Pierre and Janet Berton's Canadian Food Guide*, 36.
11. Judy Bidgood, *Tea-Time Victoria* (Victoria: Monk Publications, 1983), 9.
12. Susan Mendelson, *The Expo 86 Cookbook* (North Vancouver: Whitecap Books, 1986), 9.

Chapter 12: "You Feed Your Pigs and Cattle ..."

1. Adelaide Hoodless, quoted in *Ontario Women's Institute Story: In Commemoration of the 75th Anniversary of Women's Institutes in Ontario* (Guelph, ON: Federated Women's Institutes of Ontario, 1972), 6.
2. Peggy Knapp, Federated Women's Institutes of Ontario president, 1989–1991, quoted in foreword, Linda M. Ambrose, *For Home and Country: The Centennial History of the Women's Institutes of Ontario* (Guelph, ON: Federated Women's Institutes of Ontario, 1996), 9.
3. *Ibid.*, 41.
4. Lillian White, *Tweedsmuir History of Corinth and North Bayham* (Corinth, ON: Corinth Women's Institute, 1973).
5. For further reading, see Tara Junior Women's Institute, *Cook Book* (Tara, ON, 1932); Tara Women's Institute, *Cook Book* (Tara, ON, 1951); Corinth Women's Institute, *Tweedsmuir History of Corinth and North Bayham* (Corinth, ON, 1973); Quebec Women's Institutes, *Out of Country Kitchens* (Ste. Anne de Bellevue, QC, 1991); National Federation of Women's Institutes, *The WI Book of Party Recipes* (London, Eng., 1969); Women's Institutes of Northern Ireland,

Golden Jubilee Cookery Book, 1932–1982 (Belfast, 1982); IW County Federation of Women's Institutes, *Isle of Wight Cookery Book* (Newport, Eng., reprint 1969); Burriss Women's Institute, *Burriss Family Treasures* (Burriss, ON, 1995); Ontario Women's Institutes, *Environmentally Friendly Hints* (Winnipeg, 1994); North and South Brant Women's Institute, *Cook Book* (St. George, ON, 1967); Burwick Women's Institute, *Cooking Craft* (Woodbridge, ON, 1963); Women's Institutes of Brantford, St. George, Echo Place, Cainsville, Paris, Princeton, Drumbo, and Onondaga, *Community Cook Book*; Auburn Women's Institute, *From Our Kitchen to Yours* (Auburn, Ontario); Pickardville Women's Institute, *Favourite Recipes* (Westlock, AB, 1972); Barkway Women's Institute, *Cooking Favourites of Barkway Women's Institute* (Gravenhurst, ON, 1976); Elders Mills Women's Institute, *Cooking Favourites of Woodbridge* (Woodbridge, ON, 1970); Tec-We-Gwill Women's Institute, *Favourite Recipes* (Newton Robinson, ON, 1979); Women's Institutes of Prince Edward Island, *Popular Recipes* (Charlottetown, 1976); Lyons Brook Women's Institute, *Favourite Recipes* (Pictou, NS); Zion Women's Institute, *Country Cooking 300 Recipes* (Zion, ON, 1976).

Chapter 13: Edith Had Got the Nutmeg!

1. Ruth Holmes Whitehead, *Elitekey: Micmac Material Culture from 1600 AD to the Present* (Halifax: Nova Scotia Museum, 1980), 33–34.
2. Audrey Saunders Miller, ed., *The Journals of Mary O'Brien, 1828–1838* (Toronto: Macmillan of Canada, 1968), 77.
3. *Ibid.*, 109.
4. *Ibid.*, 26.
5. *Voyages and Travels of an Indian Interpreter and Trader*, 35.
6. B.M. Barss and Sheila Kerr, *Canadian Prairie Homesteaders* (Calgary, 1985), 41.
7. Robert Cliff and Derek Wilton, eds., *Jukes' Excursions, Being a Revised Edition of Joseph Beete Jukes' Excursions in and About Newfoundland in the Years 1839 and 1840*, (St. John's, NF: H. Cuff, 1993), 154–55.
8. Marie Nightingale, *Out of Old Nova Scotia Kitchens* (New York: Charles Scribner's Sons, 1971), 11.
9. *Manitoba's Heritage Cookery* (Winnipeg: Manitoba Historical Society, 1992), 242.
10. Beth Boegh, ed., "Homesteading at Pass Lake, 1924–1934: A Memoir by Karl (Charles) Hansen," *Papers and Records*, Thunder Bay Historical Museum Society, Vol. 30 (2002), 32–33.
11. Nellie Lyle Pattinson, *Canadian Cook Book* (Toronto: Ryerson Press, 1923), 385–86.
12. Nellie Lyle Pattinson, *Canadian Cook Book* (Toronto: Ryerson Press, 1941), 28–29.
13. *Pioneer Recipes and Memories* (Mindemoya, ON: Central Manitoulin Historical Society, 2004), 102.
14. *Manitoba's Heritage Cookery*, 154.

15. Marie Nightingale, *Out of Old Nova Scotia Kitchens* (New York: Charles Scribner's Sons, 1971), 11.

16. Carol Petch, *Old Hemmingford Recipes* (Hemmingford, QC: Imprimie Cyan Printing, 1977), 73.

17. *Manitoba's Heritage Cookery*, 167.

18. Valerie Mah, "Chinese Food Traditions," in *From Cathay to Canada: Chinese Food Traditions* (Willowdale, ON: Ontario Historical Society, 1998), 8.

Chapter 14: "I'd Rather Work for a Dollar Less ..."

1. Dennis Carter-Edwards, "Supplying Military Posts in Upper Canada," in *Consuming Passions* (Willowdale, ON: Ontario Historical Society, 1990), 45–46.

2. Letter from Surveyor General's Office to Mahlon Burwell, March 24, 1809, re Road through Middleton (Toronto: Maps and Surveys Office, Ontario Department of Lands and Forests).

3. *Pierre and Janet Berton's Canadian Food Guide*, 19.

4. *Ibid.*, 19.

5. Elinor Thomas, *A Loving Legacy: Recipes and Memories from Yesterday and Today, for Tomorrow* (Westport, ON: Butternut Press, 1987), 40.

6. *Ibid.*, 42.

7. John Macfie, *Now and Then: More Footnotes to Parry Sound History* (Parry Sound, ON: John Macfie, 1985), 41.

8. Joseph Conlin, "Old Boy, Did You Get Enough of Pie?" *Journal of Forest History*, Vol. 23, No. 4 (Santa Cruz, CA: Forest History Society, October 1979), 172.

9. *Ibid.*, 175.

10. Andrew Hacquoil, "Bunkhouses, Hauling Roads, and Finnish Beer: The Logging Camps of Oscar Styffe Limited," *Papers and Records*, Vol. 23 (Thunder Bay, ON: Thunder Bay Historical Museum Society, 1995), 19.

11. Edith Fowke, *Lumbering Songs from the Northern Woods* (Austin, TX: University of Texas Press, 1970), 60.

12. Emil Engstrom, *The Vanishing Logger* (New York: Vantage Press, 1956), 38.

13. *Cookee Book* (International Falls, MN: Koochiching County Historical Society, 1985), 1. As International Falls is on the United States–Canada border, this recipe could have been used in Canadian camps.

Chapter 15: Ladies Please Provide Versus Men Serve Oysters!

1. Elizabeth Hulse, "The Hunter Rose Company: A Brief History," *Devil's Artisan*, Vol. 18 (1986), 6.

2. Sparta WTA, *The Spartan Cook Book* (London, 1908), 4.

3. *St. Luke's Cook Book* (Winnipeg: Stovel Company Printers, 1910), 1.

4. *The Home Cook Book* (North Vancouver: Whitecap Books, 2002), 34. Reprint of 1878 edition published by Rose-Belford Publishing in Toronto.

5. Interview with Marion Leithead, Toronto, December 2005.

6. Jean Barkey, *Stouffville, 1877–1977* (Stouffville, ON: Stouffville Historical Committee, 1977).

7. *Tweed News*, March 2, 1899.

8. *Ibid.*, March 9, 1899.

9. Bruce McGraw, *See You Next Summer: Postcard Memories of Sparrow Lake Resort* (Toronto: Natural Heritage/ Natural History, 1998), 69.

10. Interviews with Egerton Pegg, Donald Goodwin, Kenneth McTaggart, Alfred Pegg, Kenneth Brooks, and Douglas Morden, Greenwood, Ontario, July 8, 2001.

11. *Stouffville Tribune*, Stouffville, Ontario, April 2, 1969.

12. *Ibid.*, March 27, 1967.

13. Interview with Bill Brown, Jr., Greenwood, Ontario, July 15, 2001. Bill Junior often helped his father with this task.

14. Interview with Jean Murray Cole, Indian River, Ontario, July 12, 2001.

15. Marie Nightingale, *Out of Old Nova Scotia Kitchens* (Baddeck, NS: Petheric Press, 1978), 113 and 121.

16. *Aurora Banner*, Aurora, Ontario, September 27, 1872.

17. See Caroline Parry, *Let's Celebrate!* (Toronto: Kids Can Press, 1984) for a comprehensive listing of festivals and special days.

18. Shel Zolkewich, "Furbearers, Beer Bellies, and a Big Ball of Bannock," *National Post* (Toronto), February 28, 2004, SP8.

19. *Ibid.*

Chapter 16: The Twentieth Century Brought a Revolution to Canadian Tables

1. Interviews and correspondence with Helen Devereaux of Sudbury and Toronto; Eva Buchanan and Evelyn Hedman Farrell (daughter of a Cobalt miner) of Sudbury; and Mike Farrell, historian for the Mine Mill Union in Sudbury, May 30, 1997.

2. Richard Brown, *A History of the Island of Cape Breton* (London, 1869), quoted in, Susan MacKenzie and Maureen Freeman, *Welcome to Our House* (Sydney, NS: Sydney Bicentennial Commission, 1984), 39.

3. G. de T. Glazebrook, Katharine Brett, and Judith McErvel, *A Shopper's View of Canada's Past* (Toronto: University of Toronto Press, 1969), 87 and 89.

4. *Ibid.*, vii.

5. *Ibid.*, 131.

6. *Ibid.*, 164.

7. *Ibid.*, xv.

8. Heron, *BOOZE*, 182.

9. Dorothy Duncan, "The 20th Century Brought a Revolution to the Dinner Table," in *Consuming Passions* (Willowdale, ON: Ontario Historical Society,1990), various pages, particularly 243, 244, and 245.

10. Dorothy Duncan, "Make It Do, Make It Over, Use It Up," in *Century Home* (Port Hope, ON: Bluestone House, April-May 1991), 24–25.

11. Kate Aitken, *Kate Aitken's Canadian Cook Book* (Montreal: *The Standard*, 1945), foreword and 3.

12. Susan Goldenberg, "October 1930: Medical Breakthrough," *The Beaver* (October/November, 2005), 11.

13. Carol Ferguson and Margaret Fraser, *A Century of Canadian Home Cooking* (Scarborough, ON: Prentice Hall Canada, 1992).

14. Margaret Carr, "Cooking Chat," *Toronto Daily Star*, May 28, 1954, 38.

15. Tea Council of Canada press releases, Toronto, January 11, 1999, and April 22, 1999.

Chapter 17: Anything Baked by a Man

1. Mima Kapches, "Village Fairs/Foires de Villages," Ontario Archaeological Society, *Archaeological Notes*, Vol. 9, Issue 3 (May/June 2004), 14–15.

2. Marc Lafrance and Yvon Dessloges, *A Taste of History* (Ottawa: Environment Canada, 1989), 24 and 26.

3. "A Traveller's Impressions, 1792–93," in Gerald Craig, ed., *Early Travellers in the Canadas* (Toronto: Macmillan of Canada, 1955), 5.

4. *A Taste of History*, 24.

5. *Chasing the Dawn* (Halifax: City Markets of Halifax Cooperative Limited, 1998), various pages.

6. Howard Temperley, ed., *Gubbins' New Brunswick Journals, 1811 & 1813* (Fredericton, NB: Heritage Publications, 1980), 24.

7. David McGimpsey, "Canada's Oldest Marketplace," *Globe and Mail*, November 22, 2003.

8. *When the Work's All Done This Fall*, 21.

9. *Early Travellers in the Canadas*, 6.

10. Lucy Booth Martyn, *The Face of Early Toronto: An Archival Record 1797–1936* (Sutton West, ON: Paget Press, 1982), 16–17.

11. Jennifer Bain, "All the Flavours of the World," *Toronto Star*, September 28, 2003, B4.

12. *Record-News*, February 16, 1983, page 5, quoted in Glenn J Lockwood, *Smiths Falls: A Social History of the Men and Women in a Rideau Canal Community 1794–1994* (Smiths Falls, ON: Corporation of the Town of Smiths Falls, 1994), 363–64.

13. *Rideau Record*, February 9, 1888, page 4, quoted in Lockwood, *Smiths Falls*, 363–64.

14. *Rideau Record*, December 15, 1887, page 1, quoted in Lockwood, *Smiths Falls*, 364.

15. Isabel Champion, ed., *Markham, 1793–1900* (Markham, ON: Markham Historical Society, 1979), 266.

16. Cheryl MacDonald, ed., *School Days* (Nanticoke, ON: Heritage Enterprises, 1998), various pages.

17. *When the Work's All Done This Fall*, 277–78.

18. *A Taste of History*, 111.

19. Anne Hutten, *Valley Gold* (Baddeck, NS: Petheric Press, 1981), 135–36.

20. *Best of the Fairs* (Toronto: Canadian Association of Exhibitions and Robin Hood Multifoods Inc., 1986), various pages.

21. *Sharing Treasured Recipes* (Ladies Division, Norwood Agricultural Fair, 1978), 28.

22. Author's collection of prize lists.

23. Mark Kearny, "Everyone Can Win a Ribbon ... in the Right Category," *Globe and Mail*, September 28, 2005, A26.

Chapter 18: The Bountiful Harvest with Which Canada Has Been Blessed

1. Robert Barlow McCrea, *Lost Amid the Fogs: Sketches of Life in Newfoundland, England's Ancient Colony* (London: Sampson, Low, Son and Marston, 1869), 292–97.

2. Valerie Mah, "Chinese Food Traditions," in *From Cathay to Canada: Chinese Cuisine in Transition* (Willowdale, ON: Ontario Historical Society, 1998), 5.

3. Richard Hakluyt, *The Principall Navigations, Voiages, and Discoveries of the English Nation* (London: George Bishop and Ralph Newberie, 1589). Reprinted from the first edition of Hakluyt's *Voyages* by Rear Admiral Richard Collinson (New York: Hakluyt Society, 1987), 252.

4. Andrew Smith, "Talking Turkey: Thanksgiving in Canada and the U.S.," in *What's for Dinner: The Daily Meal Through History Colloquium* (Montreal: Unpublished Manuscript, November 2–4, 2005).

5. "A Victorian Thanksgiving," *The Woodside Chronicler* (Kitchener, ON: Woodside National Historic Site, Fall and Winter 1999), 2.

6. *Ibid.*, 2.

7. Katherine C. Lewis Flynn, *Mrs. Flynn's Cookbook* (Charlottetown: Ladies of St. Elizabeth's and Society in Aid of St. Vincent's Orphanage, 1931), 4. Reprinted by the Prince Edward Island Heritage Foundation in 1981.

8. Nellie Lyle Pattinson, *Canadian Cook Book* (Toronto: Ryerson Press, 1941), 22.

9. Alexandrine Gibb, "Queen and Guests Relaxed Despite Dinner Formality," *Toronto Daily Star*, October 15, 1957, 2.

10. *A Collage of Canadian Cooking* (Ottawa: Canadian Home Economics Association, 1979), 45.

11. *Oh, Canada!* 19.

12. *Toronto Star*, October 15, 2002, A3.

13. Captain J.E. Alexander, "Bytown and the Rideau Canal in the 1830s," in *Transatlantic Sketches, Comprising Visits to the Most Interesting Scenes in North and South America*, Vol. 2 (London, 1833), quoted in Gerald Craig, ed., *Early Travellers in the Canadas* (Toronto: Macmillan of Canada, 1955), 84.

14. Caroline Parry, *Let's Celebrate!* (Toronto: Kids Can Press, 1987). See various pages for detailed descriptions of thanksgiving celebrations, as well as celebrations around the year.

BIBLIOGRAPHY

Abrahamson, Hilary. *Victorians at Table: Dining Traditions in Nineteenth Century Ontario*. Toronto: Ontario Ministry of Culture and Recreation, 1981.

Agnew, Colin, Dorothy Duncan, and Jeanne Hughes, eds. *Celebrating One Thousand Years of Ontario's History*. Willowdale, ON: Ontario Historical Society, 2000.

Aitken, Julia, and Anita Stewart. *The Ontario Harvest Cookbook*. Toronto: Macmillan of Canada, 1996.

Aitken, Kate. *Kate Aitken's Canadian Cook Book*. Montreal: *The Standard*, 1945.

Alberta Pictorial Cookbook. Alberta: Nimbus Publishing. 1988.

Allen, G.P. (Glyn). *Days to Remember*. Toronto: Ontario Ministry of Culture and Recreation, 1979.

Ambrose, Linda M. *For Home and Country: The Centennial History of the Women's Institutes in Ontario*. Guelph, ON: Federated Women's Institutes of Ontario, 1996.

Asperne, James. *An Account of the Island of Prince Edward with Practical Advice to Those Intending to Emigrate*. London: James Asperne, 1883.

Balcom, B.A. *History of the Lunenburg Fishing Industry*. Lunenburg, NS: Lunenburg Marine Museum Society, 1977.

Barer-Stein, Thelma. *You Eat What You Are*. Willowdale, ON: Firefly Books 1999.

Barkey, Jean. *Stouffville 1877–1977*: Stouffville, ON: Stouffville Historical Committee, 1977.

Barss, Bunny. *Oh, Canada! A Celebration of Great Canadian Cooking*. Calgary: Deadwood Publishing, 1987.

Barss, Bunny, and Sheila Kerr. *Canadian Prairie Homesteaders*. Calgary: Barss and Kerr, 1985.

Beeson, Patricia. *Macdonald Was Late for Dinner: A Slice of Culinary Life in Early Canada*. Peterborough, ON: Broadview Press, 1993.

Benoit, Jehane. *Madame Benoit's Library of Cooking*. Vols. 1–12. Montreal: Les Messageries du St-Laurent Ltée., 1972.

Benoit, Jehane. *Traditional Home Cooking*. Saint-Lambert, QC: Les Editions Héritage, 1988.

Berton, Pierre, and Janet Berton. *Pierre and Janet Berton's Canadian Food Guide*. Toronto: McClelland & Stewart, 1974.

Best of the Fairs. Toronto: Canadian Association of Exhibitions and Robin Hood Multifoods Ltd., 1986.

Bidgood, Judy. *Tea-Time Victoria*. Victoria: Monk Publications, 1983.

Boegh, Beth, ed. "Homesteading at Pass Lake, 1924–1934: A Memoir by Karl (Charles) Hansen," *Papers and Records*. Thunder Bay, ON: Thunder Bay Historical Museum Society, 2002.

Brown, George W. *Building the Canadian Nation*. Toronto: J.M. Dent & Sons, 1958.

Brown, Ron. "At the (Railway) YMCA," *The Beaver*. Winnipeg: Canada's National History Society, 1999.

Burkhardt, Barbara Barrie, Angus McLean, and Doris Kochanek. *Sailors and Sauerkraut*. Sidney, BC: Gray's Publishing, 1978.

Burpee, L.J. "The Beaver Club," *Canadian History Association Report*. Ottawa: Canadian Historical Association, 1924.

Burritt, Mrs. "The Settlement of the County of Grenville," *Papers and Records*. Toronto: Ontario Historical Society, 1901.

Cambridge, John. *A Description of Prince Edward Island in the Gulph of Saint Laurence, North America*. Bristol, 1818.

Campbell, Marjorie Wilkins. *McGillivray, Lord of the Northwest.* Toronto: Clarke, 1962.

Canadian Encyclopedia, The. Second edition, Vol. 2. Edmonton: Hurtig Publishers, 1988.

Canadian Favourites: CCF Cook Book. Ottawa: CCF National Council, 1947.

Captain Kennedy Teahouse Cookbook. St. Andrews, MB: St. Andrews Anglican Church Women, 1987.

Champion, Isabel. ed. *Markham 1793–1900.* Markham, ON: Markham Historical Society, 1979.

Chiasson, Anne Marie. *Acadian Cuisine.* Paquetville, NB: A.M. Chiasson, 1981.

Clarke, Anne. *The Dominion Cook Book.* Toronto: McLeod & Allen, 1899.

Cole, Jean Murray. *David Fife and Red Fife Wheat.* Peterborough, ON: Lang Pioneer Village, County of Peterborough, 1992.

Collage of Canadian Cooking, A. Ottawa: Canadian Home Economics Association, 1979.

Collins, George, ed. *The Mousetrap Cookbook.* Calgary: Pleiades Theatre, 1989.

Concise Dictionary of Canadianisms, A. Victoria, BC: Gage, 1973.

Conlin, Joseph. "Old Boy, Did You Get Enough of Pie?" *Journal of Forest History.* Santa Cruz, CA: Forest History Society, 1979.

Cook Book 1980. Grand Falls, NF: Exploits Valley Senior Citizens' Club, 1980.

Cookee Book. International Falls, MN: Koochiching County Historical Society, 1985.

Coues, Elliott, ed. *New Light on the Early History of the Greater Northwest,* Vol. 1. New York: F.P. Harper, 1897.

Cox, Ross. *Adventures on the Columbia River.* London: H. Colburn and R. Bentley, 1831.

Craig, Gerald M., ed. *Early Travellers in the Canadas.* Toronto: Macmillan of Canada, 1955.

Dashwood, Richard Lewes. *Chiploquorgan or Life by the Camp Fire in Dominion of Canada and Newfoundland.* Dublin: R.T. White, 1871.

Davis, Richard C., ed. *Rupert's Land: A Cultural Tapestry.* Waterloo, ON: Wilfred Laurier University Press, 1988.

Day, David, ed. *Men of the Forest.* Victoria, BC: Aural History, 1977.

Densmore, Frances. *How Indians Use Wild Plants for Food, Medicine and Crafts.* Don Mills, ON: General Publishing, 1974.

Downie, Mary Alice, and Mary Hamilton. *and some brought flowers: Plants in a New World.* Toronto: University of Toronto Press, 1980.

Duncan, Dorothy, and Glenn J Lockwood, eds. *Consuming Passions: Eating and Drinking Traditions in Ontario.* Willowdale, ON: Ontario Historical Society. 1989.

Dutch Oven. Lunenburg, NS: Ladies' Auxiliary of the Lunenburg Hospital Society, 1953.

Engstrom, Emil. *The Vanishing Logger.* New York: Vantage Press, 1956.

Fagan, Brian M. *People of the Earth: An Introduction to World Prehistory.* New York: HarperCollins, 1995.

Ferguson, Carol, and Margaret Fraser. *A Century of Canadian Home Cooking.* Scarborough, ON: Prentice Hall Canada, 1992.

Flynn, Mrs. Katherine C. Lewis. *Mrs. Flynn's Cookbook.* Charlottetown, PEI: Prince Edward Island Heritage Foundation, 1981. Reprint of the original book published by the Ladies of St. Elizabeth's and Society in Aid of St. Vincent's Orphanage in 1931.

Fort William: Hinge of a Nation. Toronto: National Heritage Limited, 1970.

Foster, Nelson, and Linda S. Cordell, eds. *Chilies to Chocolate: Food the Americas Gave the World.* Tucson, AZ: University of Arizona Press, 1992.

Fowke, Edith. *Lumbering Songs from the Northern Woods.* Austin, TX: University of Texas Press, 1970.

Franchere, Gabriele. *A Voyage to the Northwest Coast of America.* Chicago, 1954.

Bibliography

From Saskatchewan Homemakers' Kitchens. Saskatoon: Saskatchewan Homemakers' Clubs, 1955.

From the Highlands and the Sea. Ingonish, NS: Ingonish Women's Hospital Auxiliary, 1984.

Glazebrook, G. de T., Katharine B. Brett, and Judith McErvel. *A Shopper's View of Canada's Past.* Toronto: University of Toronto Press, 1969.

Goldenberg, Susan. "October 30: Medical Breakthrough," *The Beaver.* Winnipeg: Canada's National History Society, 2005.

Hacquoil, Andrew. "Bunkhouses, Hauling Roads and Finnish Beer: The Logging Camps of Oscar Styffe Limited," *Papers and Records.* Thunder Bay: Thunder Bay Historical Museum Society, 1995.

Hannon, Leslie F. *Forts of Canada.* Toronto: Maclean-Hunter Limited and McClelland & Stewart, 1969.

Hassrick, Royal B. *The Colourful Story of North American Indians.* Secaucus, NJ: Derbibooks, 1975.

Heron, Craig. *BOOZE.* Toronto: Between the Lines, 2003.

Home Cookbook, The. North Vancouver, BC: Whitecap Books, 2002. Reprint of 1878 version published by Rose-Belford Publishing Company in Toronto.

Innis, Mary Quayle, ed. *Mrs. Simcoe's Diary.* Toronto: Macmillan of Canada, 1965.

Ingstad, Helge. *Westward to Vinland.* New York: St. Martin's Press, 1966.

_____. *Land Under the Pole Star.* New York: St. Martin's Press, 1966.

Jesperson, Ivan F., ed. *Fat-Back and Molasses: A Collection of Favourite Old Recipes from Newfoundland and Labrador.* St. John's, NF: Jesperson Press, 1980.

Kapches, Mima. "Village Fairs/Foires de Villages," *Archaeological Notes.* Toronto: Ontario Archaeological Society, 2004.

Knight, James, ed. *Canada 1812–1871: The Formative Years.* Toronto: Imperial Oil Limited. 1967.

Kowalchik, Claire, and William H. Hylton, eds. *Rodale's Illustrated Encyclopedia of Herbs.* Emmaus, PA: Rodale Press, 1987.

Kurelek, William. *They Sought a New World.* Montreal: Tundra Books, 1985.

Lacey, Laurie. *Micmac Medicines, Remedies and Recollections.* Halifax: Nimbus Publishing, 1993.

Lafrance, Marc, and Yvon Dessloges. *A Taste of History.* Ottawa: Environment Canada, 1989.

Langdon, Eustella. *Pioneer Gardens.* Toronto: Holt, Rinehart and Winston of Canada, 1972.

Lockwood, Glenn J. *Smiths Falls: A Social History of the Men and Women in a Rideau Canal Community 1794–1994.* Smiths Falls, ON: Corporation of the Town of Smiths Falls, 1994.

Long, J. *Voyages and Travels of an Indian Interpreter and Trader.* London: J. Long, 1791.

Lunn, Janet, and Christopher Moore. *The Story of Canada.* Toronto: Lester Publishing/Key Porter Books, 1992.

MacDonald, Cheryl, ed. *School Days.* Nanticoke, ON: Heritage Enterprises, 1998.

Macfie, John. *Now and Then: More Footnotes to Parry Sound History.* Parry Sound, ON: John Macfie, 1985.

MacKenzie, Susanne, and Maureen Freeman. *Welcome to Our House.* Sydney, NS: Sydney Bicentennial Commission, 1984.

Manitoba's Heritage Cookery. Winnipeg: Manitoba Historical Society, 1992.

McCabe, Shauna. *Destination Prince Edward Island.* Halifax: Nimbus, 2000.

McCrea, Robert Barlow. *Lost Amid the Fogs: Sketches of Life in Newfoundland, England's Ancient Colony.* London: Sampson, Low, Son and Marston, 1869.

McGraw, Bruce. *See You Next Summer: Postcard Memories of Sparrow Lake Resort.* Toronto: Natural Heritage/Natural History, 1998.

McIntosh, Dave. *When the Work's All Done This Fall.* Toronto: Stoddart Publishing, 1989.

McNaught, Frances, and Margaret Taylor. *Galt Cook Book.* Toronto: William Briggs, 1898.

Meinig, D.W. *The Shaping of America.* New Haven, CT: Yale University Press, 1986.

Mendelson, Susan. *The Official Cookbook of Expo 86.* North Vancouver, BC: Whitecap Books, 1986.

Merritt, Richard, Nancy Butler, and Michael Power, eds. *The Capital Years: Niagara-on-the-Lake 1792–1796.* Toronto: Dundurn Press, 1991.

Miller, Audrey Saunders, ed. *The Journals of Mary O'Brien 1828–1838.* Toronto: Macmillan of Canada, 1968.

Moore, Christopher. *The Loyalists.* Toronto: Macmillan of Canada, 1984.

New Brunswick Home Economics Association, ed. *New Brunswick Recipes.* Sackville, NB: Tribune Press Limited, 1978.

Newfoundlanders' Favourite Recipes. Mount Pearl, NF: Friendship Unit of the United Church Women of the First United Church, 1970.

Nightingale, Marie. *Out of Old Nova Scotia Kitchens.* New York: Charles Scribner's Sons, 1971, and Baddeck, NS: Petheric Press, 1978.

Nute, Grace Lee. *The Voyageur's Highway.* St. Paul, MN: Minnesota Historical Society, 1951.

Oliver, Carol J. *Newfoundland Recipes,* St. John's, NF: Robinson-Blackmore Limited, 1981.

"Oregon Territory, The," *The Builder,* Vol. 2, 1844.

Parry, Caroline. *Let's Celebrate!* Toronto: Kids Can Press, 1987.

Pattinson, Nellie Lyle. *Canadian Cook Book.* Toronto: Ryerson Press, 1923 and 1941.

Pelchat, André. "Ginseng Rush," *The Beaver.* Winnipeg: Canada's National History Society, 2004.

Petch, Carol. *Old Hemmingford Recipes.* Hemmingford, QC: Imprimie Cyan Printing, 1977.

Pioneer Recipes and Memories. Mindemoya, ON: Central Manitoulin Historical Society, 2004.

Powers, Jo Marie, ed. *Buon Appetito! Italian Foodways in Ontario.* Willowdale, ON: Ontario Historical Society, 2000.

Powers, Jo Marie, ed. *From Cathay to Canada: Chinese Cuisine in Transition.* Willowdale, ON: Ontario Historical Society, 1998.

Powers, Jo Marie, and Anita Stewart. *The Farmers' Market Cook Book.* Toronto: Stoddart Publishing, 1984.

Powers, Jo Marie, and Anita Stewart, eds. *Northern Bounty.* Toronto: Random House Canada, 1995.

Rich, E.E. "Pro Pelle Cutem," *The Beaver.* Winnipeg: Canada's National History Society, 1958.

Richar, Gustav A., ed. *Parry Sound 1887–1987 Historical Miniatures.* Nobel, ON: Morsel Press, 1987.

Robertson, J. Ross. *The Diary of Mrs. John Graves Simcoe.* Toronto: William Briggs, 1911.

Robertson Smith, Eleanor. *Loyalist Foods in Today's Recipes.* Hantsport, NS: Lancelot Press, 1983.

St. Luke's Cook Book. Winnipeg: St. Luke's Church, 1910.

Sansom, Joseph. *Travels in Lower Canada.* London: Sir Richard Phillips and Company, 1820.

Schlosser, Patricia, ed. *A Taste of the Arts.* Edmonton, AB: Edmonton Arts Cookbook Society, 1982.

Shalleck, Jamie. *Tea.* New York: Viking Press, 1972.

Sharp, James J. *Flavours of Newfoundland and Labrador.* St. John's, NF: Breakwater Books, 1981.

Spartan Cook Book, The. London: Sparta Women's Temperance Auxiliary, 1908.

Spicer, Ruth, and Marion Elliot. *Christmas Through the Years.* St. Stephen, NB: Print 'N Press Ltd., 1982.

Stefansson, Vilhjalmur. "Food and Food Habits in Alaska and Northern Canada," *Human Nutrition Historic and Scientific, Monograph III.* New York: International Universities Press, 1957.

Stewart, Anita. *The Flavours of Canada*. Vancouver: Raincoast Books, 2000.

_____. *The St. Lawrence Market Cook Book*. Toronto: Stoddart Publishing, 1988.

Storck, Peter L. *Journey to the Ice Age: Discovering an Ancient World*. Vancouver: University of British Columbia Press in association with the Royal Ontario Museum, 2004.

Stump, Sarain. *Two Forms of Art*. Saskatoon: Saskatchewan Indian Cultural College, 1973.

Tasker, L.H. "The United Empire Loyalist Settlement at Long Point, Lake Erie," *Papers and Records*. Toronto: Ontario Historical Society, 1900.

Thomas, Elinor. *A Loving Legacy: Recipes and Memories from Yesterday and Today, for Tomorrow*. Westport, ON: Butternut Press, 1987.

Tivy, Louis. *your loving Anna*. Toronto: University of Toronto Press, 1972.

Town, Florida. *The North West Company: Frontier Merchants*. Toronto: Umbrella Press, 1999.

Treasury of Newfoundland Dishes, The. St. John's, NF: Maple Leaf Mills, 1983.

Vennum, Jr., Thomas. *Wild Rice and the Ojibway People*. St. Paul, MN: Minnesota Historical Society Press, 1988.

Walker, Harlan. V., ed. *Feasting and Fasting: Oxford Symposium on Food and Cookery 1990*. London: Prospect Books, 1990.

Wallace, W.S. "Fort William of the Fur Trade," *The Beaver*. Winnipeg: Canada's National History Society, 1949.

Watson, Julie. *Favourite Recipes from Old Prince Edward Island Kitchens*. Willowdale, ON: Hounslow Press, 1989.

Weiner, Michael A. *Earth Medicine–Earth Foods*. New York: Collier Books, 1972.

White, Randall. *Ontario 1610–1985*. Toronto: Dundurn Press, 1985.

Whitehead, Ruth Holmes. *Elitekey: Micmac Material Culture from 1600 AD to the Present*. Halifax: Nova Scotia Museum, 1980.

Wright, J.V. *Ontario Prehistory*. Toronto: Van Nostrand Reinhold, 1972.

Young, A.H. "Letters from the Secretary of Upper Canada and Mrs. Jarvis to Her Father, the Reverend Samuel Peters, DD," *Annual Report and Transactions*. Toronto: Women's Canadian Historical Society of Toronto,1922–23.

Zinck, Hilda. *Green Shutters Cook Book*. Tantallon, NS: Four East Publications, 1983.

INDEX